Advance praise for

War of the Worlds to Social Media

"This fascinating volume traces the rich themes of new media, crisis and interactivity from the *War of the Worlds* broadcast to now, but even more importantly, these smart and engaged essays demonstrate strikingly just how well carefully researched media history can illuminate the present."
—David Goodman, University of Melbourne

"As a whole the book represents a thoughtful read for anyone who wants to dig a bit deeper, and a wonderful resource for those who want to stimulate debate in a class or reading group. The authors convincingly show that a historical grasp is essential to understand contemporary issues in the present, and that the narratives of the past can disguise just as much as they reveal."
—Tim Wall, Birmingham City University

"In this wonderful collection, the *War of the Worlds* broadcast represents, variously, the founding object of study in an emerging communication-industrial complex, a training tool for covering twenty-first century wars, and a template for understanding crisis communications ever since. A must-read for anyone interested in the symbiotic relationship between new communication technologies and the crises they mediate."
—Jason Loviglio, University of Maryland, Baltimore County

War of the Worlds to Social Media

David Copeland
General Editor

Vol. 12

The Mediating American History series
is part of the Peter Lang Media and Communication list.
Every volume is peer reviewed and meets
the highest quality standards for content and production.

PETER LANG
New York • Washington, D.C./Baltimore • Bern
Frankfurt • Berlin • Brussels • Vienna • Oxford

War of the Worlds to Social Media

MEDIATED COMMUNICATION IN TIMES OF CRISIS

EDITED BY Joy Elizabeth Hayes,
Kathleen Battles,
AND Wendy Hilton-Morrow

PETER LANG
New York • Washington, D.C./Baltimore • Bern
Frankfurt • Berlin • Brussels • Vienna • Oxford

Library of Congress Cataloging-in-Publication Data

War of the worlds to social media: mediated communication in times of crisis /
edited by Joy Elizabeth Hayes, Kathleen Battles, Wendy Hilton-Morrow.
pages cm. — (Mediating American history: vol. 12)
Includes bibliographical references and index.
1. War of the worlds (Radio program) 2. Radio broadcasting—United States—
History. 3. Radio broadcasting—United States—Social aspects.
4. Radio journalism. I. Hayes, Joy Elizabeth, editor of compilation.
II. Battles, Kathleen, editor of compilation.
III. Hilton-Morrow, Wendy, editor of compilation.
PN1991.77.W3.W37   791.44'72 —dc23   2013020018
ISBN 978-1-4331-1801-2 (hardcover)
ISBN 978-1-4331-1800-5 (paperback)
ISBN 978-1-4539-1180-8 (e-book)

Bibliographic information published by **Die Deutsche Nationalbibliothek.**
Die Deutsche Nationalbibliothek lists this publication in the "Deutsche
Nationalbibliografie"; detailed bibliographic data is available
on the Internet at http://dnb.d-nb.de/.

Editors' photo by Kyle Soyer. Left to right:
Wendy Hilton-Morrow, Joy Elizabeth Hayes, Kathleen Battles.

© 2013 Peter Lang Publishing, Inc., New York
29 Broadway, 18th floor, New York, NY 10006
www.peterlang.com

All rights reserved.
Reprint or reproduction, even partially, in all forms such as microfilm,
xerography, microfiche, microcard, and offset strictly prohibited.

Contents

Foreword: The Return of Radio vii
   Michele Hilmes

Acknowledgments ix

Introduction 1
   Kathleen Battles, Joy Elizabeth Hayes, Wendy Hilton-Morrow

Part 1: Looking Backward: War of the Worlds, Media Power, and Audiences "Talking Back"

Chapter 1: Exchange and Interconnection in US Network Radio: A Reinterpretation of the 1938 *War of the Worlds* Broadcast 19
   Joy Elizabeth Hayes and Kathleen Battles

Chapter 2: War of the Words: The *Invasion from Mars* and its Legacy for Mass Communication Scholarship 35
   Jefferson Pooley and Michael J. Socolow

Chapter 3: Assassination, Insurrection and Alien Invasion: Interwar Wireless Scares in Cross-National Comparison 57
   Kate Lacey

Chapter 4: Receiving the *War of the Worlds* "Panic" from Across the Atlantic: British Press and Public Responses in 1938 (and Since) ...83
   Neil Washbourne

Part 2: Backward and Forward: Media Forms, Conventions, and Crisis

Chapter 5: Network Radio's Greatest Test: CBS News' Coverage of the D-Day Invasion 109
Wendy Hilton-Morrow

Chapter 6: *War of the Worlds* as a Radio News Training Tool 125
Keith Somerville

Chapter 7: Body Contact: Interconnection and Embodiment in Howard Stern's 9/11 Radio Broadcast 143
Joy Elizabeth Hayes and Dana Gravesen

Chapter 8: Mediating Misinformation: Hoaxes and the Digital Turn 165
Zack Stiegler and Brandon Szuminsky

Part 3: Looking Forward: *War of the Worlds* and Social Media

Chapter 9: War of Worlds? Alternative and Mainstream Journalistic Practices in Coverage of the "Arab Spring" Protests 189
Diana Bossio and Saba Bebawi

Chapter 10: Social Media Curation and Journalistic Reporting on the "Arab Spring" 211
Vittoria Sacco, Marco Giardina and Katarina Stanoevska-Slabeva

Chapter 11: Microblogging and Crises: Information Needs and Online Narratives During Two "Bombing" Events in Nairobi, Kenya 237
Melissa Tully

Chapter 12: Risk, Crisis, and Mobilization in the Twitter Use of US Senatorial Candidates in 2010 257
Adam Rugg

Contributors 283
Index 289

FOREWORD

The Return of Radio

MICHELE HILMES

Radio is back! The genesis of this volume, marking the 75th anniversary of the broadcast of the *War of the Worlds* and linking it to current modes and moments of media communication, illustrates a phenomenon that has recently become apparent worldwide: After nearly fifty years of scholarly and critical neglect, radio has returned to center stage, as a mode of cultural expression, as a model for new media forms, and as a subject of scholarly inquiry. Certainly radio itself never went away; all through the decades of its surrender of the central spot in the living room to television, and its transformation into a marketing wing of the popular music industry, we have loved and depended on radio. Radio sets proliferated, no longer in the living room but virtually everywhere else in the house and outside as well, especially in our cars, workplaces, social spots, and commercial spaces. And during moments of crisis, as this volume demonstrates, its flexibility and portability as a medium took it into places and situations that no other technology could. It became our main emergency medium, our daily standby, a role it continues to this day.

Programs like *War of the Worlds* exemplify a particular kind of long-form radio "soundwork": a sonic text that employs the basic aural elements of speech, music, and noise to create dramatic fictional or factual experiences, often a combination of both. Typically speech is the dominant aspect of soundwork, with music and noise secondary but dramatically important, marking out a space between reality and affect. In the 1930s, Orson Welles and the Mercury Theater's self-reflexive use of radio broadcast conventions to tell a fictional story—that then became the genesis of real-life events—represents one type of creative soundwork mixing fact and fiction.

Norman Corwin's poetic mixtures of drama, song, and first-person address that mobilized a nation for war and celebrated its victories, in programs like *An American in England* and *On a Note of Triumph*, are another. Postwar, as *The March of Time*'s dramatized news stories gave way to a new documentary style of radio reporting and with television taking center stage, the long-form radio feature faded away in U.S. radio.

But recently that tide has turned, for reasons that this volume helps to explain and situate. Long-form radio has returned, in celebrated shows like *This American Life* and *Radiolab* along with many more, mostly in the thriving public and community radio sector. With them, an awareness of radio's long-suppressed history has come to the fore again as well. Partly this is due to the proliferation of online audio and of mobile digital devices over the last ten years, from the iPod to the smartphone to the tablet. Digital screens give soundwork a material presence it sorely lacked in the past, and connected portability allows sound to accompany us even more widely than ever before. New digital formats bring not only music but many new forms of sound expression into our everyday universe, from repurposed radio programs to specialized productions to the recycling of radio's past. Soundwork has an accessible archive now, to accompany its traditional stream.

And radio also continues to productively inform the use and deployment of digital media, from streaming music sites like Pandora to the constantly renewing stream of social media sites like Twitter. Radio was our first streaming medium: live, continuous, ephemeral, always supplying something new. During our first mediated worldwide social crisis, the Second World War, broadcast radio rose to new heights of creativity and of social impact due to precisely these qualities of immediacy and renewal, sparking panic, anxiety, criticism, academic study, and admiration. Social media sites like Facebook and Twitter, so key in today's media events and crises, use graphic speech instead of spoken word to convey the same kind of urgent, continuously updating stream of information and reaction to world events, far more accessibly and globally. The 75th anniversary of one of the world's best-known soundworks provides a timely demonstration of these continuities in our experience in times of crisis. It is the beauty of this volume to recognize and explore the connections between that time and ours, and the resonance between old media and new.

War of the Worlds to Social Media: Mediated Communication in Times of Crisis

Acknowledgements

Bringing any book to completion is always a team effort, but never more so than in the case of this project. As editors we would like to start by thanking all the contributors to this volume for their timeliness, patience, and collegiality in meeting deadlines, adapting pieces for this volume, and for inspiring us with their outstanding efforts. We have had the pleasure or working with scholars we long admired as well as meeting new researchers from the US, UK, Europe, and Australia. Along the way we are grateful for the support we have received from our home institutions, the University of Iowa, Oakland University, and Augustana College. We also would like to thank David Copeland for his insightful comments and guidance, along with Mary Savigar and everyone at Peter Lang for their help in bringing this book to publication. We also would like to thank Sherry Wynn Perdue for her copywriting expertise, Michael DeLuca for his patience and skill with formatting, and Alia Gant for indexing help. In addition, Joy and Kathy would like to acknowledge the early support we received from Tim Wall of *The Radio Journal*, and we thank the journal for permission to reprint a revised version of our article here.

Joy Elizabeth Hayes would like to thank the University of Iowa Department of Communication Studies for ongoing support and for the opportunity to work with so many outstanding graduate students over the years. Jiyeon Kang helped keep me on track, and Kathy and

Wendy were, and are, simply the best. Big-time support came from Ignacio González, and Alma and Jesús González-Hayes distracted me in every way possible, but especially with their big hearts, bottomless energy, and love. Barbara Fenton and Mya Hayes were always there when I needed them, and Miles Hayes and Jacqui Michel lent a helping hand. Thank you all so much!

Kathleen Battles would like to acknowledge Joy and Wendy, both whom have offered their support, friendship, and shared their intellectual passions for over a decade. I would also like to thank my always supportive colleagues at Oakland University, including our department chair, Jennifer Heisler for creating the time and space for completion of this project, and the "media ladies," Rebekah Farrugia and Erin Meyers for comments, conversation, and advice on anything from sources to formatting. Finally, thanks to my wonderful partner of 20 years, Rachel Andrews, who loves me enough to sometimes tell me what I don't want to hear, but in the process makes me a better person. To her I owe the most.

Wendy Hilton-Morrow would like to acknowledge the unfaltering support of her colleagues in the Department of Communication Studies at Augustana College. I also would like to thank the members of Augustana's Faculty Welfare Committee, Faculty Research Committee, and Presidential Fellowship Selection Committee for seeing the promise in this project and providing me the time and financial resources to complete it. I am indebted to my fellow lady editors, Joy and Kathy, who serve as my mentors, my colleagues, and my treasured friends. Finally, thank you to Jay, Matthew, Joshua, and Joseph for always helping me to maintain perspective.

INTRODUCTION

KATHLEEN BATTLES, JOY ELIZABETH HAYES AND WENDY HILTON-MORROW

On the night of October 29th, 2012, as "Superstorm" Sandy approached the New Jersey coast, Internet micro-bloggers from the Northeastern U.S. used Twitter to comment, in their droll way, on what many thought was an overhyped event. One author from New York tweeted a series of missives drawing on the October 30th, 1938 *War of the Worlds* broadcast. He quoted small bits of the radio play documenting the Martians' travels from New Jersey into Manhattan, and ended with the play's eerie "transmission": "2X2L calling CQ…. New York. Isn't there anyone on the air? Isn't there anyone on the air? Isn't there anyone…?" (Jake Womak, 2012).

On the surface it might seem strange for a Twitter user to invoke an event so far removed from contemporary concerns. After all, there was a vast difference between *War of the Worlds* and communication about Superstorm Sandy. One event was fake and one real; one was broadcast over the "old" medium of radio and the other over a "new" social media platform; one was seemingly unidirectional and the other part of a multi-directional barrage of data that no single person could possibly keep up with; and one carried the imprimatur of official speech while the other was a cacophony of decentralized voices. Yet, at the same time, an ode to the *War of the Worlds* broadcast perfectly suited storm-related Twitter traffic. In terms of context, both "attacks" were aimed at the New York City-New Jersey area, occurred right before Halloween, and raised questions about media misrepresentations and audience gullibility (Goodman, 2011; Gross, 2012). Both events also occurred in social environments marked by the dislocations of rapid technological change, economic and political instability, and a general sense of impending crisis. In terms of media, the play's brief, simulated radio news bulletins perfectly fit Twitter's technically clipped 140 character posts. Both broadcasting and Twitter were "new" media at the time of these events, and both provided instantaneous, real-time communication in a time of crisis.

Like radio during its "Golden Age," today's social media are shot-through and complexly intertwined with a sense of crisis. The 75th anniversary of the *War of the Worlds* broadcast encourages us to look both backward and forward: to re-examine the broadcast, and to consider how it continues to speak to our contemporary moment of media change and crisis. *War of the Worlds to Social Media: Mediated Communication in Times of Crisis* takes the notorious broadcast as a starting point to investigate continuities and discontinuities between old and new media and their use by citizens and institutions in times of crisis. The broadcast event deserves attention in its own right not only as a milestone in media history, but also because it highlights a number of issues that remain important in 21st century communication practices: the problem of misrepresentation in mediated communication; the importance of social context for interpreting communication; and the dynamic role of listeners, viewers and users in talking back to media producers and institutions. At the same time, the discourses swirling around our current media age allow us to rethink some of our central interpretations of the meaning of the broadcast in its own time. Through a re-examination of this iconic broadcast event, this collection brings an historical and theoretical perspective to bear on the question of media power and the ability of citizens to hear and be heard during times of crisis.

This volume explores how elements of the *War of the Worlds* broadcast resonate with our current media moment, marked by so many similar tensions. It largely focuses on two periods of "new media"—the radio era of the 1930s and the current era of digital media marked by the growing use of social media. Here we define newness not simply in terms of a new technological configuration of media, but in terms of a new discursive configuration of media. That is, media are "new" when popular, industrial, governmental, and academic discourses are focused on making sense of, defining, and setting the terms for our understanding of these media. Media can be made "new" again at various times when technology and discourses refocus their attention on a particular set of practices that are recognized as marking a departure from previous uses of the medium. The chapters in this volume also focus on various moments of crisis, but crisis broadly defined, including both the broader historical contexts of transformation and dislocation and the uneasy place of shifting media practices and technologies within those contexts. Finally, this collection seeks to explore the continuities and discontinuities between the new media moment of radio and our current new media moment marked by the rise of the internet, including social media, media curation platforms, and mobile networking. Simply put, the book asks: does *War of the Worlds* still matter?

Media and Crisis

While many of our most recent narratives of media transformation are undergirded by a progress narrative that relegates radio to a distant past and time of naïveté, we believe that taking radio more seriously can help us make sense of our current media moment. In particular, the authors in this volume explore a number of questions that allow us to interrogate dominant understandings of the meaning of the *War of the Worlds* event and gain insight into continuities and discontinuities in the media-crisis relationship between the era of broadcasting and the social media "revolution" of the first decades of the 21st century. First, what is the meaning of crisis in the age of electronic communication and how are media implicated in crises that they are presumably only reporting? Second, what factors shape the way that audiences and users respond to mediated crises and how should these responses be understood as modes of communication in their own right? That is, what kind of relationships do people build with media? Third, what roles do media conventions and forms play in crisis? How are conventions shaped by moments of crisis, and how do various conventional forms, in turn, shape our understandings of what a crisis is?

Since the first study of the *War of the Worlds* broadcast, scholars have emphasized the national scope of the "panic" inspired by the radio play, and expressed concern over the susceptibility of audiences to mass media messages (Cantril [with Gaudet & Herzog], 2008; Goodman, 2011). Further, the broadcast spawned anxiety over the ability of broadcasters to manipulate the conventions of the medium, and thus manipulate audiences. The *War of the Worlds* event marked a crisis concerning the development of the "new" medium of radio and its potential power to manipulate, deceive, misinform, and thus create chaos. As U.S. commercial radio matured in the crisis years of the Great Depression, its technological affordances, commercial control, and institutional arrangements all had the power to upend a whole host of social, cultural, industry, and technological norms in ways that linked radio to an ever present sense of immanent crisis.

Crisis has been conceptualized in several ways in relationship to media. Certainly the invocation of crisis communication is typically linked to the study of public relations impression management in the face of corporate or governmental accidents, mishaps, or tragedies. Crisis is also studied as a condition of rapidly proliferating forms of mass media and mobile communications. Crisis can be experienced both as a set of events in the world "out there" delivered to our consciousness by communication media, and as a series of technological, cultural, social, and economic changes seemingly "caused" by electronic media themselves (Doane, 1990). This volume examines crisis as something that is specifically linked to the emergence of "new" media and the disruptions they cause in the normative practices of media organizations and other social institutions. Crisis in this sense often appears as a conflict between historical actors trying to make sense of new communication tools, such as the tension between the press and radio in the 1930s, and the current tension between mainstream media outlets and users of social media.

A number of scholars have documented the association of new, emerging media with crisis and chaos (Heyer, 1995). Susan Douglas describes this process as a kind of "technological insurgency," in which people use new media to challenge social norms and explore new ways of being in the world (Douglas, 2004, p. 13). Brian Winston similarly identifies moments of "radical potential" in new media when users attempt to refigure existing social, political, and cultural relations. For both Douglas and Winston, these radical and insurgent moments are normally followed by a phase of cultural negotiation that involves suppressing this potential and re-domesticating the medium in a way that protects existing power relationships (Douglas, 2004; Winston, 1998). In the same vein, Tim Wu (2011) describes a recurrent "cycle" of cooptation of new media in which the "brave new technologies of the twentieth century"—which were initially explored freely and chaotically—came under the strict control of "privately controlled industrial behemoths, the 'old media' giants of the twenty-first" (p. 6).

New media also frequently emerge in historical moments of crisis, including times of rapid social change and economic dislocation. Radio was part and parcel of the broader historical changes captured by Raymond Williams (1974) in the concept of mobile privatization. Radio broadcasting developed in the aftermath of World War I, and for many became representative of the social upheavals of the Jazz Age and Great Depression (Doerksen, 2005). Similarly, internet-based social media also emerged in a time of crisis; a time of large-scale cultural, political, economic, social, and technological changes that remade life across many parts of the globe. Social media entered a global landscape marked by shifting global work patterns, the rise of forms of extremism, and the spread of democracy, along with increasingly threatening natural and man-made disasters (storms, epidemics, financial crises, and planet-threatening catastrophes).

The chapters in this volume are organized into three broad sections that take up different, yet interrelated aspects of "new" media and crisis and the broader questions of the volume. Section one, "Looking Backward: *War of the Worlds*, Media Power, and Audiences 'Talking Back,'" examines the ways that new media forms often create a sense of crisis regarding the susceptibility of audiences to new modes of communication. The chapters in this section work to call into question the very concept of "panic" associated with audience responses in times of crisis, and consider the question of audiences in a broader transnational context. Section two, "Backward and Forward: Media Forms, Conventions, and Crisis," specifically deals with the relationship between the forms and conventions of media—that is, both their communicative potential as well as the techniques developed to communicate through them—and crisis. Contributors consider the enduring legacy of *War of the Worlds* in developing conventions for covering crisis, the relationship between changing media forms and the ability to mediate crisis in very specific ways, and the relationship between media conventions and a longer history of media hoaxes. The final section, "Looking Forward: *War of the Worlds* and Social Media," examines how the themes surrounding media and crisis explored in the first two sections continue to resonate in our current era of social media. The contributors in this section consider both continuities and discontinuities with the *War of the Worlds* moment.

Looking Backward: *War of the Worlds*, Media Power, and Audiences "Talking Back"

The first four chapters explore the relationship between emerging media and crisis while specifically challenging dominant understandings of the *War of the Worlds* broadcast event. Both popular and scholarly examinations of the broadcast in the immediate aftermath and since have focused precisely on to what extent, and why, audiences were duped into believing the broadcast was true. Underlying this was an implicit fear of the power of centralized mass communication over trusting audiences whose critical abilities were often called into question. While scholars of social media focus on the ways that today's audiences both consume and produce media content, scholars of radio have begun to revisit the standing of the radio audience in order to consider the ways that the power dynamic between the radio industry and audiences was more complex than we usually consider.

For example, during the 1930s, as Elena Razlogova (2011) has argued, many in the radio industry regularly sought the input of audiences and were highly attuned to the desires of audiences, who despite the seeming one-way nature of commercial radio broadcasting, also saw themselves in a dialogic relationship with radio professionals. Further, the status of US radio as a "public interest" medium also allowed various groups to advocate for improved programming and standards. While not as robust as the kind of relationships enabled through forms of social media, there is nonetheless a great deal of continuity in the kind of relationships developed during the radio era and those of the social media era. Kathleen Battles (2010) has examined the ways the police forces and the producers of radio crime dramas specifically sought the participation of radio audiences as responsive citizen-combatants in the emerging "War on Crime." In the specific case of *War of the Worlds*, scholars have moved beyond the narrow characterization of audience responses as "panic," to look at the broader social discourses that shape the relationships between mass audiences and mass media. David Goodman (2011), for example, looks at the ways that debates about the broadcast were shaped by broader concerns over the rise of propaganda between the wars. These concerns focused on both the responsibility of institutions in marshaling the awesome persuasive power of modern communication technologies, and the responsibility of audiences in exercising their critical facilities in the face of these mass persuaders.

The first two chapters, in particular, consider the complex power dynamics in the relationship between the centralized institutions of broadcasting and radio audiences, placing *War of the Worlds* in a broader historical context in terms of media conventions, audience behaviors, and the developing field of Mass Communication. Joy Hayes and Kathleen Battles use a model of exchange and interconnection to identify continuities between the *War of the Worlds* broadcast event and contemporary media practices. Working against both a scholarly interpretation that reads the broadcast through the lens of an imposing national radio apparatus and the social psychological definition of "panic" used to interpret audience behavior, Hayes and Battles argue that listeners' primary response to the perceived crisis was communication: sharing information with family and friends and talking back to the media. The authors consider the ways that audiences attempted to "talk back" to broadcasters and officials during the broadcast in a way that points to interesting continuities with contemporary social media. In the second chapter, Jefferson Pooley and Michael Socolow re-examine the only slightly less infamous *Invasion from Mars* study and reveal the critical role that it played in helping Hadley Cantril and Paul Lazarsfeld obtain directorships of powerful academic institutes. Their chapter also shows how the exploitative, gendered conditions of early communication research helped produce a contradiction at the heart of the *Invasion from Mars* study between an emphasis on national "panic" and a more nuanced analysis of audience responses.

Two additional chapters place the *War of the Worlds* media crisis in its broader transnational context, examining the ways that questions about media conventions and audiences were taken up in different national contexts. Kate Lacey locates the *War of the Worlds* event within a larger trajectory of radio scares in Germany, the UK and the US during the 1920s and 1930s. Her chapter demonstrates how both the crisis of "new" media and the deepening global crisis exacerbated anxieties over the power of the radio medium and competence of the audience that led to divergent outcomes in different national contexts. Lacey argues that this pattern of radio scares indicates both the degree of trust and legitimacy that radio acquired in a relatively short time and the general belief that these broadcasts were unusual in misleading normally savvy media audiences. In the fourth chapter, Neil Washbourne analyzes four UK newspapers' coverage of the *War of the Worlds* "panic" and then looks more broadly at popular and scholarly discourse concerning the event. His chapter argues that initial UK press coverage expressed concern about an unreasoning mass public and implicitly suggested that Americans might be especially prone to such behavior. Washbourne also shows that the distinct history of mass communication study in the UK meant that scholars did not consider *War of the Worlds* to be a significant event in media history and theory until the rise of radio studies in the 1980s.

Taken together, these chapters call into question dominant interpretations of the *War of the Worlds* broadcast as telling a particularly dismal tale about both the power of broadcasting and the ability of listeners to make sense of the messages they hear. The authors reexamine the broadcast event through the lens of contemporary discussions about the relative activity of audiences, the politics of academic research, and the importance of placing media in their broader global context. In sum, these chapters allow us to consider the continued resonances of the *War of the Worlds* in our contemporary media environment and, at the same time, show how questions about audiences are always historically situated.

Backward and Forward:
Media Forms, Conventions, and Crisis

The chapters in this section examine the links between *War of the Worlds* and the forms and conventions of media, with a particular emphasis on how conventions can both engender crises and interpret them. As Hayes and Battles and Lacey argue, faith in conventions is key to understanding the power of media to shape audience responses. The crisis of "new" media also sits in a complex relationship with media conventions, which are themselves shaped by the technological affordances of particular media forms. One of the most stunning aspects of the *War of the Worlds* broadcast is the way it successfully mimed the forms and rhythms of broadcasting, playing on developing codes of radio to achieve a realistic effect. While the broadcast has been duly contextualized within the crisis of thirties America, it has not been adequately situated within the context of the emerging broadcast practices and conventions of the period. Conventions only make "sense" to audiences already familiar with certain cultural codes that make media content recognizable. Additionally, media conventions often play with, or off of, the specific technological and communicative capacities of particular media. In the case of radio, the key concern was how to produce dynamic and resonant images in the minds of listeners using only sound and silence (Verma, 2012).

As media become channels for crisis information, they create special conventions to cover crises, and thereby shape and even create a sense of crisis through the use of those conventions. Stuart Hall et al. (1978) argue that the conventional routines of government and media institutions could have the effect of producing the very "crisis" that they claimed to be attempting to solve, and that a crisis like an epidemic of muggings, was implicated in a broader series of structural and temporal transformation in terms of the market, political institutions and political and popular ideologies. Nimmo and Combs (1985) argue that while television news can report on an event occurring in the world as a crisis, it can also create a sense of crisis simply by drawing attention to some pattern of behavior. Daniel Berkowitz (1997) explores this in his study of how local reporters develop practices for determining what constitutes a crisis, when to devote resources to covering a crisis, and how to define events within a limited scope of what they believe will register with viewers as a "crisis."

Going beyond their ability to convey information or spark the imagination, we can also think of the ways that conventions link more broadly to forms of media that produce particular responses in audiences. For example, some media genres are designed to produce bodily responses, as Linda Williams (1991) argues in the case of horror, melodrama, and pornography. While some scholars contend that radio was experienced as ghostly and disembodied, studies done during the era indicate that audiences could build quite accurate visualizations of individuals based on their voice (Cantril and Allport, 1935/1971). The radio voice often was experienced as strongly embodied, and, thus, it is not surprising that it would evoke equally strong responses in audiences. As Verma (2012) contends, radio professionals expended a great deal of effort manipulating narrative, technology and sound to produce precise responses in radio audiences. Simply put, radio conventions played with both the disembodied presence of radio, its visceral and intimate mode of address, as well as the relationship between sound and space in order to develop conventions unique to its technological form.

Along with looking at conventions of thirties radio, chapters in this section also explore the impact of the "memory" of *War of the Worlds* on broadcasting practices during times of crisis at key moments from the 1940s through the early 2000s. In the fifth chapter, Wendy Hilton-Morrow examines CBS coverage of the 1944 D-Day Invasion of Normandy, France and shows the careful attention to potential audience responses that went into planning the broadcast. She argues that CBS used its D-Day coverage as a way to improve both its public image and its relations with federal regulators in the wake of the *War of the Worlds* broadcasting fiasco. A related chapter by Keith Somerville, a radio reporter and educator for the BBC, discusses the use of the *War of the Worlds* broadcast as a training tool for teaching reporters and editors how to cover unfolding crisis events. He argues that the broadcast provided a model of broadcast news that journalists could draw on to build crisis coverage that created a sense of constant contact with the listener. Both chapters place the question of conventions and crisis in broader historical relief, examining the ways that the *War of the Worlds* broadcast was both shaped by and ultimately shaped broadcasters' sense of responsibility to the public in developing conventions for covering crises that continue to this day.

Two additional chapters broaden the consideration of conventions to link them to media forms, examining the ways that conventions unique to specific media shape how crisis is covered and experienced by audiences. Joy Hayes and Dana Gravesen analyze shock jock Howard Stern's radio broadcast from New York City on the morning of 9/11. They argue that the broadcast extended conventions of crisis reporting highlighted in the *War of the Worlds* broadcast, at the same time that it prefigured the social media era by creating an interactive web of communication in a time of crisis. If listeners to the radio play *talked back* by calling the police, the press, and radio stations, callers to Stern's show used the more developed relationship between mobile telephony and radio to *talk through* the apparatus, so that Stern's radio body functioned itself as a mediator for the crisis. In the eighth chapter, Zack Stiegler and Brandon Szuminsky address the debated status of *War of the Worlds* as a media hoax, and explore the continuities and discontinuities of media hoaxes across mass and social media. They argue that the success of media hoaxes in both "old" and "new" media depends on some combination of faith and intimacy. With social media, however, the opportunities for hoaxes have increased due to the possibility of user-generated misinformation in an environment that often prioritizes speed over accuracy.

Looking Forward:
War of the Worlds and Social Media

The chapters in this section consider more fully the ways in which the relationship between media and crisis articulated in the *War of the Worlds* broadcast event—in terms of media newness, the power dynamics between audiences and media institutions, and the central place of media conventions in the construction of crisis—continue to resonate in our current era of new media. As Steigler and Szuminsky argue in their chapter on media hoaxes, there is a great deal of continuity across media in the potential for crisis caused by media's ability to fool audiences; however, each medium offers a different configuration for how that might occur. Our current era of social media is marked by a whole host of dramatic changes regarding institutions, traditional ideas about media audiences, and the very notion of what a medium is in an era of convergence. As many commentators note, we now live in the era of the media "user," who is often described as an active participant in contrast to the passive audience of yesterday. As Michael Mandiberg (2012) states, "At the end of this first decade of the twenty-first century, the line between media producers and consumers has blurred, and the unidirectional broadcast has partially fragmented into many different kinds of multidirectional conversations" (p. 1). He comments further on the blurring of new media audiences and producers in noting that, "from the audience's perspective, in order to experience the site you *have to become a media producer,* and from the organizations' perspective, without audience production their sites fail" (p. 2). From social networking sites such as Facebook, Twitter, Pinterest, Tumblr, YouTube, and Reddit, to easy-to-access and use blog hosting sites, to the ubiquitous comments sections on any number of amateur and commercial blog, entertainment, and news sites, today's user produces a fair amount of the media that many actually consume. In the process, questions about the power dynamics between audiences and institutions intertwine with questions about conventions in ways that both echo and break from the *War of the Worlds* moment.

These chapters examine the interplay between media institutions and a new generation of users who have the power to move beyond "talking back," yet continue to engage in a number of similar behaviors and raise similar sets of anxieties as the audience for *War of the Worlds*. As in the case of Hilton-Morrow's chapter on D-Day coverage and Somerville's chapter on training radio journalists in part two of the book, authors in this section demonstrate that media conventions and forms are still key to the way we grasp and make sense of crisis moments. However, media today are shot through with shifting relationships between users and official media producers. Two chapters consider the link between new media and conventions for reporting on crisis. Diana Bossio and Saba Bebawi study the interplay of traditional and alternative modes of online journalism. Examining online news coverage of pro-democracy demonstrations in Egypt and Libya on six separate days in early 2011, they argue that professional news organizations and audience-driven social media, while often characterized as oppositional forces, interacted and relied on each other during coverage of the crisis. In the tenth chapter, Vittoria Sacco, Marco Giardina and Katarina Stanoevska-Slabeva investigate the way that media professionals and amateurs used an emerging media content curation platform, Storify, to cover events of the so-called "Arab Spring." They argue that Storify both perpetuated and disrupted traditional news frames, or conventions, while raising concerns over the reliability of information sources. Both studies demonstrate the ways that "new" media forms threaten established institutional practices and disrupt conventional forms of conveying information in times of crisis. Just as *War of the Worlds* led the threatened newspaper industry to decry the recklessness of the radio industry, so "new" media platforms inspire fear and criticism on the part of traditional news institutions.

The final two chapters return to questions about the relationship between crisis and media audiences. Melissa Tully investigates social media communication surrounding a deadly bomb explosion and an unrelated bomb scare that occurred in Nairobi, Kenya within three days of each other in 2010. She identifies compelling similarities in public responses to both the Niarobi events and the *War of the Worlds* broadcast, including the effort to seek and share information on the part of users and audiences, and the importance of environment in shaping the response to media crises. In the final chapter, Adam Rugg analyzes the use of Twitter by U.S. Senatorial Candidates in 2010 and shows that Twitter was rarely used for two-way communication or user mobilization. Rather, Rugg observes that, much the same way that the *War of the Worlds* broadcast has been simplified into a metaphor for the emergent power of broadcasting, Twitter, and social media in general, have been simplified into a metaphor for spontaneous, democratic, two-way interaction. Both of these essays demonstrate interesting continuities between social media and the *War of the Worlds* event. As Tully details, the activities of social media users in the Nairobi bomb scares show a remarkable degree of similarity to the ways that *War of the Worlds* listeners used the available tools of communication, including their embodied social networks, to gather information and make sense of events. At the same time, Rugg demonstrates how our current hopes for the multi-directional, democratic potential of

Twitter are belied by the ways that those in power attempt to use social media in a way more akin to broadcasting.

Does War of the Worlds Still Matter?

In a word, yes. This collection shows the important continuities between the past and present: the continuity of questions of media power and the potential clash of "old" and "new" media in a changing media environment; the question of authority and access that determines who has the power to speak; and the question of how people process and make sense of information flows in fluid social situations that speak of danger. If *War of the Worlds* exposed the threat of the power of the few to overtake the airwaves and trick people into believing in global destruction, then social media represent the power of many and the fear that anyone might easily trick others. Just as the "crisis" of the radio was precisely linked to its perceived unidirectional power, then the "crisis" of social media is surely its decentralized power, and the fear that there are no filters or checks for information. Both national network radio and social media, equally, raise questions about who media audiences and users can trust, and how they can insert their own voices into vast communication systems that, while shifting over the past century, have been a continuous presence in the lives of everyday people.

In looking back, the contributors to this volume have commented upon the exceptional dynamism of radio broadcasting in modern life. The work of Douglas (2004), in particular, illuminates the long history of invention and reinvention that has marked American radio broadcasting from its early days as an amateur venture through to the rise of syndicated talk radio at the end of the 20th century. In the words of David Hendy (2008), "if there *is* an essential feature of the radio medium, it is this: its extraordinary *hybridity*. It is always and everywhere a vital, *involved* site of cultural exchange. It is always, of necessity, turning its face to the world" (p. 132). We argue that the history of heterogeneity and reinvention that has marked almost a century of radio broadcasting—one that has involved exchanges between various kinds of users, industries, technologies, and broader historical shifts—has a special affinity with forms of internet communication, and its history of invention and reinvention spurred on in large part by the activities of its users. As the *War of the Worlds* broadcast continues to stand as a testament to the dizzying nature of technological and cultural change that marked a historic moment of crisis, it continues to resonate in important ways with our current moment.

References

Berkowitz, D. A. (1997). Non-routine news and news work: Exploring what-a-story. In Berkowitz, D.A. (ed.). *Social meanings of news: A text-reader*. New York: Sage Publications.

Cantril, H., & Allport. G. W. (1971). *The psychology of radio*. New York: Ayer Company. (Original work published in 1935).

Cantril, H., Gaudet, H. & Herzog, H. (2008). *The invasion from Mars; A study in the psychology of panic*. New Brunswick, NJ and London: Transaction Publishers.

Douglas, S.J. (2004). *Listening in: Radio and the American imagination*. Minneapolis: University of Minnesota Press.

Goodman, D. (2011). *Radio's civic ambition: American broadcasting and democracy in the 1930s*. New York: Oxford University Press.

Gross, D. (2012, October 31). Man faces fallout for spreading false Sandy reports on Twitter. *CNN*. Retrieved from: www.cnn.com/2012/10/31/tech/social-media/sandy-twitter-hoax/index.html.

Hall, S., Critcher, C., Jefferson, T., Clarke, J. & Roberts, B. (1978). *Policing the crisis*. London, UK: Macmillan.

Hendy, D. (2008). Radio's cultural turns. *Cinema Journal, 48*(1). 130–138.

Heyer, P. (1995). *Titanic legacy: Disaster as media event and myth*. Westport, CT: Praeger.

Heyer, P. (2005). *The medium and the magician: Orson Welles, the radio years, 1934–1952*. New York, NY: Rowman & Littlefield.

Jake Womak. (2012, October 29). "2X2L calling CQ . . . New York. Isn't there anyone on the air? Isn't there anyone on the air? Isn't there anyone . . ." Retrieved from https://twitter.com/jwomack/status/263104361100623872

Nimmo, D. D., & Combs, J. E. (1985). *Nightly horrors: Crisis coverage by television network news*. Memphis, TN: University of Tennessee Press.

Popp, R. (2011). Machine-age communication: Media, transportation, and contact in the interwar United States. *Technology and Culture, 52*(3), 459–484.

Razlagova, E. (2011). *The Listener's voice: Early radio and the American public*. Philadelphia, PA: University of Pennsylvania Press.

Verma, N. (2012). *Theater of the mind: Imagination, aesthetics, and American radio drama*. Chicago, IL: University of Chicago Press.

Williams, L. (1991). Film bodies: Gender, genre, and excess. *Film Quarterly, 44*(4), 2–13.

Williams, R. (1974). *Television: Technology and cultural form*. New York, NY: Routledge.

Winston, B. (1998). *Media, technology, and society: a history: From the telegraph to the Internet*. New York, NY: Routledge.

Wu, T. (2011). *The master switch: the rise and fall of information empires*. New York, NY: Vintage Press.

PART ONE

Looking Backward: *War of the Worlds*, Media Power, and Audiences "Talking Back"

CHAPTER ONE

Exchange and Interconnection in US Network Radio: A Reinterpretation of the 1938 *War of the Worlds* Broadcast

JOY ELIZABETH HAYES AND KATHLEEN BATTLES

In this chapter, Hayes and Battles[1] explore the model of communication laid out in the sound-text of the *War of the Worlds* broadcast and the study of the event originally published in 1940 as the *Invasion from Mars: A Study in the Psychology of Panic*. In reinterpreting the radio play, the authors argue that it celebrated radio's ability to coordinate multiple communication media and create a "constant communicative presence" in which the listener was a central part. Although many audience members were frightened or disturbed by the broadcast, Hayes and Battles contend that the primary audience response was to communicate with others through social and technologically mediated networks.

Introduction

On the night of October 30, 1938, people across the United States tuned into a night of radio listening, by then the nation's most popular pastime. Listeners had several options for Sunday evening listening, including any number of local broadcasts, regional network shows, and programs offered by four national networks. Many chose to tune into NBC's enormously popular *Chase and Sanborn Hour*, featuring ventriloquist Edgar Bergen and his dummy, Charlie McCarthy, while some chose the more serious CBS program, *Mercury Theater of the Air*. While the corporate-sponsored *Chase and Sanborn Hour* offered big name stars in a variety format of music and comedy, the *Mercury Theater of the Air*, paid for by CBS, consisted of weekly plays dramatizing works of literature. For this particular evening, the Mercury Theater troupe had selected the H.G. Wells story, *War of the Worlds*. Up until moments before the broadcast, there was concern about whether the radio adaptation would be a success (Koch, 1970).

The program began with its usual opening: a version of Tchaikovsky's Piano Concerto #1 to signal the middlebrow cultural status of the show, the program header, and a bit of opening narration read by Welles to set the scene for the story. After this short setup, lasting two minutes, the program proceeded for approximately forty minutes as a series of dramatized radio broadcasts from various agencies that detailed the landing of Martians on a New Jersey Farm, their movement across the Hudson River into New York City, and finally, the destruction of that city, and presumably cities and towns around the globe. Indeed, the performance departed from commercial radio conventions of the era by holding off any break in the dramatic action for station, network, or program identification until the play's fictional radio network had been destroyed.

Newspapers immediately described the broadcast's impact as a national panic. Indeed, there were a number of listeners around the United States, and particularly in the New Jersey area, who did believe they were hearing actual news reports. People who believed the broadcast was real responded in a vast number of ways, from a woman cooking a final dinner for her family, to families gassing up their automobiles to drive out of New Jersey, to people sending out relatives to find further information, and calling radio stations, newspapers, and police stations to verify if this was indeed a real event (Cantril [with Gaudet & Herzog], 2008). In the days and weeks following the broadcast, thousands of newspaper articles were printed variously castigating Welles, the Mercury Theater players, and CBS for what many saw as an irresponsible hoax. Newspapers also carried strong indictments of radio listeners, taking them to task for their lack of critical ability and naïve acceptance of radio's authority (Goodman, 2011). As Campbell (2010) argues, newspapers greatly overstated the scope and ramifications of the *War of the Worlds* scare as a means of discrediting their upstart radio competitor.

In the wake of the widely reported panic, members of the Princeton Radio Research Project identified a unique research opportunity and began investigating listener responses to the broadcast. Hadley Cantril published the study in 1940 (with the assistance of Hazel Gaudet and Herta Herzog) as the *Invasion from Mars: A Study in the Psychology of Panic*. While the study argued that the public response to the broadcast needed to be situated in the context of social insecurity caused by the Depression and war scare, it carefully documented the power of radio over those listeners lacking the critical ability to distinguish between fact and fiction. In the aftermath, those in the radio industry were forbidden from simulating newscasts in fictional programs, CBS worked to rebuild its position as a trustee of the public interest, Welles parlayed the event into extended success in radio and film, and the nascent field of mass communication research gained momentum.

Exchange and Interconnection in 1930s Radio

No event has been used to symbolize the emergence of broadcasting as a mass medium as much as the *War of the Worlds* broadcast event. Both the radio "panic" and the study by Cantril, Gaudet and Herzog have provided rich fodder for a range of claims about the meaning of radio in 1930s America. Scholars have fetishized the event, in terms of the unique attributes of the broadcast itself, and the differential power of mass communication versus interpersonal communication, especially its power to influence a mass audience. While scholars have grown increasingly skeptical about the extent of the "panic" inspired by *War of the Worlds* (Socolow, 2008; Gosling, 2009; Campbell, 2010), they continue to interpret the event as a testament to the power of broadcast communication over audiences (Sterling, 2004; Douglas, 1999; Heyer, 2005; Sconce, 2000; Lenthall, 2007; Gosling, 2009). This interpretation of the event rests on the idea that, by the 1930s, radio broadcasting was a centralized, self-contained, one-way form of communication that enthralled listeners.

Yet, if one listens to the broadcast and reads closely the responses of listeners reported and interpreted by Cantril, Herzog, and Gaudet, it is clear that something else is happening. While scholars have taken the broadcast as a metaphor for the unidirectional nature of network radio, and the *Invasion from Mars* as evidence of the power of that relationship to blunt the critical facilities of an atomized audience, what this chapter focuses on, instead, is the remarkable amount of communicative activity surrounding the event. From the broadcast itself which deftly mimed the interactive nature of radio, to audience members who listened in groups, sought out information from their social networks, and generally reacted by communicating with those around them, what emerges is a series of interchanges that belie the ostensibly one-way model of communication that dominates interpretations of *War of the Worlds*.

This chapter proposes an exchange model of broadcasting that views two-way communication as a central part of radio's structure, technology, social setting, and discursive forms. This model views broadcast communication as an exchange between producers and listeners via the material relations of text and genre, industry and institution, technology and socio-cultural context. For example, in terms of radio's structure, the case of *War of the Worlds* highlights the fact that network-affiliate relationships of the Golden Age are best understood as examples of unequal exchange rather than domination. Although CBS had a strongly top-down approach to affiliate relationships, Boston's CBS affiliate simply decided not to air the *War of the Worlds* program, thus cutting off most New England listeners from the experience (Cantril [with Gaudet & Herzog], 2008). As Alex Russo's (2010) study of Golden Age radio contends, "Despite its image as uniform, consistent, and singular, the [network] system was limited, unstable, and hybrid" (p. 19). The influence of national networks was disrupted by local stations' efforts to bypass the networks and market their stations directly to national advertisers, and by their ability to get live and recorded programming from alternative sources such as regional networks (pp. 19, 76). Additionally, the mid-1930s saw several powerful independent stations come together to form the Mutual Network—a network model based on interactive program sharing rather than one-way distribution.

This exchange model of broadcasting also applies to program discourse, audience relations, and conditions of reception during the Golden Age. Throughout the 1920s and 30s, listeners were constantly asked to call, send letters, and interact in a variety of ways with broadcasters and their sponsors (Battles, 2010; Lenthall, 2007; Loviglio, 2005; Razlogova, 2006 and 2011; Vaillant, 2001). Broadcasters directly cultivated interaction with their audiences through these direct requests, as well as by adopting a chatty, conversational speaking style in order to simulate two-way communication (Marchand, 1985; Hayes, 2000; Loviglio, 2005). Finally, despite the continuing use of models of "atomized" audiences to understand the *War of the Worlds* broadcast, listeners were in fact embedded in highly interactive communicative environments. Listeners responded to what they heard over the radio by "talking back" to family, friends, authorities, and the media. In fact, many stations received so much feedback from listeners during the first section of the broadcast that they interrupted the network transmission to answer listener inquiries. In this way, audiences acted as participants in an increasingly interconnected world with multiple nodes of exchange and communication that, while highly centralized, still opened up spaces for public response and intervention.

This chapter argues that the *War of the Worlds* radio text did not express fear of network domination (Sconce, 2000; Miller, 2003), but anxiety about the loss of communicative interconnection, represented by the Martian's relentless destruction of communication and transportation. We reread the radio play in order to place it in its broader generic and technological contexts. We also reinterpret the findings of Cantril, Gaudet and Herzog (2008), highlighting what the interviewees said they were actually doing during the broadcast in order to consider the broad range of communicative activity taking place. Based on this reinterpretation of the *War of the Worlds* event, this chapter contends that radio communication should be understood as a process of interconnection and exchange between different nodes in a complex network of production, distribution and reception.

Constant Communicative Presence in the *War of the Worlds* Broadcast

The following analysis focuses on the first forty minutes of the broadcast—the portion that played with radio forms and conventions in order to mimic a breaking news report.[2] It traces the way the play represented radio by identifying its ability to shift between one-way and two-way modes of communication, and to connect listeners to other media via its "dispatch" function. We explore how the broadcast mimed, in condensed form, the routine rhythms of commercial network broadcasting through the use of announcers, updates, interruptions, music, and interviews. The play also drew on existing generic and aesthetic practices from broadcast news, crime thrillers, dramas, and military, police, and amateur radio. Rather than presenting radio as a dominating and invasive threat, we argue that *War of the Worlds* represented radio as a constant communicative presence made possible by a dizzying array of interchanges in which the listener played a central part.

That this was a radio play *about* radio was evident from the narrator's opening speech, delivered by Welles:

> It was near the end of October. Business was better. The war was over. More men were back at work. Sales were picking up. On this particular evening, October 30, the Crossley service estimated that thirty-two million people were listening in on radio. (*War of the Worlds*, 1938)

The specific mention of Crossley audience ratings provided the play's first reference to the exchange between broadcasters and audiences at the heart of U.S. network radio. It clued listeners into the fact that the story they were going to hear was about radio, but more than that: it was a story about radio audiences and how they responded to the medium. The play was about the connection between broadcasters and audiences that took place through a variety of communicative means, including the telephone surveys used by the Crossley ratings.

After the opening narration, the play positioned listeners at the center of a web of relations made possible by broadcast communication. In quick succession, the listener was given bulletins from the 'Intercontinental Radio News' in Chicago, brought 'live' to the Meridian Room of the Hotel Park Plaza in New York, and transported to the Princeton Observatory in New Jersey. From the Observatory, announcer Carl Phillips exhorted listeners to

> be patient, ladies and gentlemen, during any delay that may arise during our interview. Besides his ceaseless watch of the heavens, Professor Pierson may be interrupted by telephone or other communications. During this period he is in constant touch with the astronomical centers of the world . . . . (*War of the Worlds*, 1938)

As Battles (2010) argues, this atmosphere of constant connection was created through the linkage of radio as both a mass and two-way medium with other communication technologies (most importantly the telephone) to create the sense that one would never be out of touch with the wider world.

This sense of constant communicative presence was created throughout the broadcast by a series of dispatches from various locations. In fact, dispatch functioned as a central organizing principle of the *War of the Worlds* with broadcasting headquarters acting as the central site of coordination, using its communication technologies to both receive and send messages and resources. Beginning with the dispatched reporter, Carl Phillips, the play brought radio listeners an increasing array of voices, including the Brigadier General of the New Jersey State Militia and the Secretary of the Interior, all interconnected by the voice of the announcer. Information flowed into the network announcer from various media and sources, including a telephone operator who reported sighting the Martians "east of Middlesex within ten miles of Plainfield" (*War of the Worlds*, 1938). While the play was clearly designed to simulate radio news (Koch, 1970; Cantril [with Gaudet & Herzog], 2008; Douglas, 1999), little attention has been paid to the fact that *War of the Worlds* mimicked other conventions of network broadcasting. Simulation of radio was a key to radio crime dramas that sought to represent the growing use of shortwave radio by municipal and state police departments (Battles, 2010). Other programs specifically dramatized the use of radio in times of crisis. For example, *March of Time* included an episode about the Great Floods of 1937 that was dramatized as a series of ham radio broadcasts, and the acclaimed 1937 radio play, *The Fall of the City*, also used simulated radio broadcasts to dramatize the takeover of an unnamed city (Heyer, 2005; Verma, 2012).

The *War of the Worlds* interwove reports from different spatial locations to create what Neil Verma (2012) terms the "kaleidesonic" aesthetic common to 1930s radio dramas. He argues that the unique way that the broadcast played with this aesthetic contributed to its sense of impending doom. He notes that by the end of the first part of the play,

> it offers us *nowhere to be*. With no discernable proscenium, listeners assumed there was none. With a darkening stage and no seat before it, the edge of fiction dissolves. It is in the end a challenge to the very predictability that gives dramatic conventions their regularity, as well as to the sense of "scene" as a place that is not our own. The later abandons us right where we really are, huddled beside a radiophonic lifeforce dying before our very ears." (pp. 71–72)

For him, the radio play offered the listeners no point of audicposition, thus rendering them helpless before the apparatus.

Yet this seems to belie the evidence that listeners were, in fact, "positioned" as members of an interloping audience to a future radio broadcast. It also ignores the range of communication technologies represented in the broadcast through the centralized practice of dispatch. Dispatch as a trope became a key part of radio crime dramas like *Gang Busters* and *Calling All Cars* as the action that took place was often filtered through some sort of "headquarters," which managed a continual flow across space and time of incoming information from police radio and telephone calls, while at the same time dispatching information and resources to authorities and citizens. As Battles (2010) notes, crime dramas specifically encouraged citizens to listen to the radio and contact the authorities by telephone, identifying listeners as important components of the police "dragnet" made possible by new communication technologies. In this way, the trope of dispatch positioned listeners not simply as recipients of broadcast communication, but as active participants in a broader network of communicative exchanges.

While the play represented radio as creating a constant communicative presence, it is significant that the disabling of human communication emerges as a particular strategy of the Martian invasion. For example, as the announcer narrated the movement of Martians across New Jersey, he reported their deliberate efforts to, "uproot power lines, bridges, and railroad tracks" in an apparent effort to "crush resistance, paralyze communication, and disorganize human society" (*War of the Worlds*, 1938). The Martians wished to destroy what network radio made possible: integrated and coordinated communication.

It is also significant that the forms of exchange grew increasingly dialogic as the first part of the broadcast proceeded. After the Martians emerged from their ships at Wilmuth's farm, the play's representation of radio shifted progressively from a means of broadcasting to a national public, to a medium of two-way communication to coordinate military operations, to a mode of point-to-point communication via shortwave. For example, following an announcement that "special wires" had been run to "the battery of the 22nd Field Artillery, located in the Watchung Mountains," radio was used to facilitate conversation between an officer, gunner and observer. Once they were overcome by poisonous gas, the play made a jarring switch to a "commander" Voght of "army bombing plane, V-8-43, off Bayonne, New Jersey" who, accompanied by airplane sound effects, narrated the continued progress of the Martians until he himself was brought down in flames (*War of the Worlds*, 1938). By the final scene of the first half of the broadcast, *War of the Worlds* moved entirely to an interactive, amateur mode of radio address. An operator using amateur call letters 2X2L put out a general call to all available listeners: in amateur terms he called "CQ." He then attempted to make a more specific call to 8x3R, who responded, leaving 2X2L to ask where he was. The unidentified 2X2L ends the broadcast with the infamous refrain:

> 2X2L calling CQ ....
>
> 2X2L calling CQ ....
>
> 2X2L calling CQ .... New York
>
> Isn't there anyone on the air?
>
> Isn't there anyone...
>
> 2X2L—

The move to amateur radio happened after the network announcer essentially narrated his own death after continuing to relay dispatches up until the last minute (*War of the Worlds*, 1938). How, then, do we interpret the play's destruction of network broadcasting and its return to amateur radio?

Sconce (2000) views the destruction of the broadcast building as a deliverance from the power of the network (p. 125). Even Koch (1970) admits that, "Finally, after demolishing the Columbia Broadcasting Building, perhaps a subconscious wish fulfillment, I ended the holocaust with one lonely ham radio voice in the air, "Isn't there anyone on the air? Isn't there anyone?" (p. 15). As Koch (1970) indicates, however, the real end of the "holocaust" was not the destruction of CBS, but the void left by its destruction. What is scary about the end of the broadcast is not the loss of the network, but the loss of response. In contrast to Sconce's (2000) reading of *War of the Worlds* as a tale about network domination and the anxiety produced by an encroaching mass-mediated public sphere or Verma's (2012) reading of the play as a particularly chaotic and unanchored example of the kalediesonic aesthetic, the play is better understood as a story about the fear of communicative loss. The play ultimately becomes a play about the place of the listener in various forms of interlinked communication. Listeners at home were the reason for the play's existence; the imagined listeners of the fictional broadcast are also central in that they were the main "characters" of the drama. Ultimately the broadcast functioned to simulate the broadcast "network" not as a one-way relationship between an all powerful entity and the passive listener, but as a constant communicative presence in which the listener not only has an important stake, but also acts as a key player in the creation of such a presence.

Rethinking the "Panic"

Along with re-examining *War of the World's* representation of radio and its listeners, this chapter also revisits the initial characterization of the audience response as "panic." The authors of the *Invasion from Mars* study defined panic as "undirected" and "functionally useless" behavior undertaken when the Ego was fundamentally threatened and no remedy or escape seemed possible (Cantril [with Gaudet & Herzog], 2008, pp. 199–200). The "trauma" of panic might induce either "useless" action (like hysteria or wrapping ones children in blankets and driving at high speeds to escape the "heat ray" of the Martians), or inaction (resignation in the face of fear) (Cantril [with Gaudet & Herzog], 2008, pp. 96–97; Sconce, 2000, p. 113). A closer look at how the authors of the *Invasion from Mars* made sense of their findings, however, suggests that audience responses to the broadcast would better be characterized as efforts to communicate with a broad range of family, friends, authorities and institutions. The discussion below traces this process of communication from the point of reception, to the use of social networks to find out how to interpret the broadcast, to the process of communicating with media institutions such as newspapers and radio stations.

While the *Invasion from Mars* was subtitled, "A Study in the Psychology of Panic," the populations studied in both the national CBS survey and in the detailed interviews with 135 people in the Princeton, New Jersey area, are better described as follows: people who believed the broadcast to be a news report about real events and who responded in a variety of ways to that information. A closer look at the audience analysis indicates that most if not all of the listeners actively scrutinized the broadcast and interacted with other people about what they had heard. While many of those studied reported being "very frightened" by the broadcast, many others were not very frightened but only "disturbed," and still others reported that they remained calm despite believing that a real invasion was being reported.[3]

Interviews identified four types of listeners: People who made successful internal checks as to the truth of the broadcast, people who made successful external checks, people who made unsuccessful external checks, and people who made no effort to check the validity of the broadcast. People in the first three groups (about 68 percent) attempted to "check" the broadcast and determine that it was a play (Cantril [with Gaudet & Herzog], 2008, pp. 106–107). Those in the last group made no effort to do so. Although the last group did not attempt to check on the validity of the broadcast, most of the listeners in this group reached out to warn family and friends or cared for "hysterical co-listeners" (Cantril [with Gaudet & Herzog], 2008, p. 97). Indeed, many listeners were scared and even hysterical, but this does not mean that fear made them anti-social or non-communicative. On the contrary, social communication was the most common response to the broadcast.

Since most radio listening during the 1930s was done in families or other groups, the first communicative responses to *War of the Worlds* took place with fellow listeners. Responses were not just a product of the individual's encounter with the broadcast, but of the social relationships and interpersonal communication of those listening together. As one interviewee reported, "My sister, her husband, my mother and father-in-law were listening at home" when the broadcast started. Even as people narrated their reactions in the first person, their responses often indicated the group context of listening; for example: "I did not look for other stations because it said it was the only one not destroyed. We looked at the sky but could not see anything" (Cantril [with Gaudet & Herzog], 2008, pp. 94 and 100). From the beginning, then, interviewees indicated that their listening experience and response was a collaborative action undertaken with family, neighbors or friends.

The degree of social interaction produced by the broadcast is striking, both in the case of those who remained skeptical and those who failed to question the broadcast. While Cantril described this interaction as a "contagion of excitement" whereby one scared individual "infected" others with the same fear, it can also be read as a kind of social networking (Cantril [with Gaudet & Herzog], 2008, pp. 83, 140–142). There are a number of examples of people tapping into their social networks to get information, convey information, or seek support. One interviewee reported using her community resources in the following way: "My son came home during the excitement and I sent him out to find one of the elders in the church to see what it was all about." Another woman reported that as she was rushing with her son to the rooftop, "In passing I warned the neighbors on the higher floors. I was so terribly upset that they tried to calm me—they phoned the police and found out that it was all a play" (Cantril [with Gaudet & Herzog], 2008, pp. 94–95).

As the last example indicates, interviewees reported communicating not only with their peers, but with social authorities and mass media. Here we see the ways that listeners themselves used communication technologies to make contact with social authorities. As with the broadcast, interconnection and exchange are key to understanding the ways audiences both made sense of, and reacted to, the play. While Sconce (2000) emphasizes the event as one of noncommunication, reports following the broadcast demonstrate that people in fact actively worked to talk back to the network. Koch (1970) reports that the CBS switchboards were completely swamped and that "Some radio stations reported increases as much as five hundred percent over the usual Sunday night volume." In Seattle, it was reported that "calls poured into newspapers, press and radio bureaus by the thousands...police station switchboards were a blanket of white lights from incoming phone calls from listeners who thought they were hearing a bona fide news broadcast" (Koch, 1970, pp. 84–85, 95). Phone lines were tied up in New York and other areas. These examples indicate that audiences were not primarily passive or paralyzed, but rather acted to communicate with media outlets and social authorities.

Communication was the pervasive response of *War of the Worlds* listeners. By telephoning media and police stations, listeners responded to the broadcast as they did to many other radio calls, from serials to police dramas to comedy programs. Because of the extreme situation and the fear induced by the play, however, listeners' efforts to communicate were much more immediate and effective than in the case of other radio calls. First local stations, and then Welles and CBS, were forced to respond to listeners' calls and concerns.

Conclusion

Through an analysis of the sound-text of *War of the Worlds*, we show how the play explored the interactive, dialogical possibilities of radio through its interweaving of one-way transmission and two-way intercommunication throughout the play. We also argue for a reinterpretation of the *War of the Worlds* audience, claiming that the "panic" identified by Cantril, Gaudet and Herzog (2008) is better interpreted as the effort of listeners to "talk back" to broadcasters. In contrast to recent interpretations, we contend that the broadcast resonates with many other radio programs of the era in its effort to exploit the interactive excesses of broadcasting that centralized broadcast institutions could never fully contain.

The *War of the Worlds* event was certainly a significant moment in the development of broadcasting. It exposed and explored many things about the state of broadcasting after a busy decade that saw the seeming reification of radio as a technological, cultural and economic set of practices. It is clear that the historical actors involved in creating the event—from the play's producers to the millions of radio listeners to the scholars who sought to make sense out of the aftermath of the broadcast—understood that the broadcast said *something* about radio. Because of that, historians have likewise turned to the event, often treating it as a synecdoche for 1930s radio. Our reinterpretation here does not mean to displace the significance of the event, but instead to re-think the precise nature of that significance. Our goal is to consider the ways that radio was not simply a unidirectional broadcasting technology, but a technology, set of practices and even audience relations marked by a persistent tension between one-way and two-way communication. As a medium, radio was interconnected with a whole host of social and cultural practices related to communication and transportation. It is with these practices that the broadcast played.

Our reinterpretation of the *War of the Worlds* broadcast leads to several conclusions. First, it demonstrates the remarkable flexibility of radio even during the so-called "Golden Age" of network dominance. Networks were complex assemblages of exchange relations, not totalizing, dominating systems of control over the medium. Second, it suggests that radio was part and parcel of a broader system of exchange and interconnection between stations, between radio listeners, and between different communication technologies. Finally, it shows that radio was part of a broader process of transforming human relationships by enmeshing them in increasingly complex webs of communication and transportation. Similar to Raymond Williams' (1974, p. 26) concept of "mobile privatization," our model of exchange and interconnection attempts to describe a broad set of relationships between people and communication media, rather than focusing narrowly on audiences' abilities to make sense of specific media messages.

On the 75th anniversary of the *War of the Worlds* broadcast, we find ourselves in a moment that seems not so far removed from the one faced by our historical cousins: a de-stabilizing financial situation, war, and staggering social and technological change. If we continue to understand the broadcast as being about the dominant power of broadcasting, we miss the important continuities as well as breaks between past and present, and miss the opportunity to learn about how people made—and continue to make—sense of a changing world. Most importantly, we lose historical perspective on the experience of constant communicative interaction and exchange that we are so frequently told is a special condition of the digital age.

Notes

[1] An earlier version of this piece appeared in *The Radio Journal: International Studies in Broadcast and Audio Media* (2011). Thank you to Intellect Press for permission to use this here.

[2] We do not discuss the second half of the broadcast because it used a more conventional dramatic format, including a soliloquy/narration by Prof. Pierson and an extended dialogue between Pierson and a Stranger that could not be mistaken for a news report. The second half was clearly separated from the first half by two announcements that the program was a play and was not the part of the broadcast to which most listeners responded.

[3] Of the interview group, 39% reported being truly frightened, 37% were disturbed, and 24% were calm. The CBS survey, taken sooner after the broadcast, found that fewer people reported remaining calm: 60% frightened, 33% disturbed, 7% calm (Cantril [with Gaudet & Herzog], 2008, p. 106).

References

Battles, K. (2010). *Calling all cars: Radio dragnets and the technology of policing.* Minneapolis, MN: University of Minnesota Press.

Campbell, W. J. (2010). *Getting it wrong: Ten of the greatest misreported stories in American journalism*. Berkeley, LA and London: University of California Press.

Cantril, H. & Allport, G.W. (1986). *The psychology of radio*. Salem, NH: Ayer Co.

Cantril, H., Gaudet, H. & Herzog, H. (2008). *The invasion from Mars: A study in the psychology of panic*. New Brunswick and London: Transaction Publishers.

Douglas, S.J. (1999). *Listening in: Radio and the American imagination, from Amos 'n' Andy and Edward R. Murrow to Wolfman Jack and Howard Stern*. New York, NY: Times Books.

Goodman, D. (2011). *Radio's civic ambition: American broadcasting and democracy in the 1930s*. New York, NY: Oxford University Press.

Gosling, J. & Koch, H. (2009). *Waging the War of the Worlds: A history of the 1938 radio broadcast and resulting panic, including the original script*. Jefferson, NC: McFarland & Co.

Hayes, J.E. (2000). Did Herbert Hoover broadcast the first fireside chat? Rethinking the origins of Roosevelt's radio genius. *Journal of Radio Studies*, 7(1), 76–92.

Hayes, J. E., and Battles, K. (2011). Exchange and interconnection in US network radio: A reinterpretation of the 1938 *War of the Worlds* broadcast. *The Radio Journal: International Studies in Broadcast and Audio Media*, 9(3), 51–61

Heyer, P. (2005). *The medium and the magician: Orson Welles, the radio years, 1934–1952*. Lanham, MD: Rowman & Littlefield.

Koch, H. (1970). *The panic broadcast: Portrait of an event*. Boston, MA: Little, Brown.

Lenthall, B. (2007). *Radio's America: The Great Depression and the rise of modern mass culture*. Chicago, IL: University of Chicago Press.

Loviglio, J. (2005). *Radio's intimate public: Network broadcasting and mass-mediated democracy*. Minneapolis, MN: University of Minnesota Press.

Marchand, R. (1985). *Advertising the American dream*. Berkeley, CA: University of California Press.

Miller, E.D. (2003). *Emergency broadcasting and 1930s American radio*. Philadelphia, PA: Temple University Press.

Razlogova, E. (2006). True crime radio and listener disenchantment with network broadcasting, 1935–1946. *American Quarterly*, 58(1), 137–158.

Russo, A. (2010). *Points on the dial: Golden age radio beyond the networks*. Durham, NC: Duke University Press.

Sconce, J. (2000). *Haunted media: Electronic presence from telegraphy to television*. Durham, NC: Duke University Press.

Socolow, M.J. (2008). The hyped panic over 'War of the Worlds'. *Chronicle of Higher Education*, 55(9), B16–B17.

Sterling, C.H. (2004). War of the Worlds. *Museum of Broadcast Communications Encyclopedia of Radio*, 3, 1478–1481.

Vaillant, D. (2001). "Your voice came in last night ... but I thought ... it sounded a little scared": Rural radio listening and "talking back" during the Progressive era in Wisconsin, 1920–1932. In M. Hilmes and J. Loviglio, eds. *The radio reader: Essays in the cultural history of radio* (pp. 63-88). New York: Routledge.

Verma, Neil (2012). *Theater of the mind: Imagination, aesthetics, and American radio drama*. Chicago, IL: University of Chicago Press.

War of the Worlds (1938). CBS Radio Network, Sunday October 30th.

Williams, R. (1974). *Television: Technology and cultural form.* New York, NY: Schocken Books.

CHAPTER TWO

War of the Words: The *Invasion from Mars* and Its Legacy for Mass Communication Scholarship

JEFFERSON POOLEY AND MICHAEL J. SOCOLOW

In this chapter, Pooley and Socolow reevaluate the legacy of the *Invasion from Mars* study for the field of mass communication research based on new archival evidence about the authorship of the study. They show how the biased and exploitative conditions of early communication research helped produce a contradiction at the heart of the study. While Cantril's narrative emphasized the size and national scope of the panic, Herzog and Gaudet's research actually found weak media effects mitigated by intervening contextual and individual factors.

Introduction

Late in the evening of Sunday, October 30, 1938, Frank Stanton, CBS research director and future president, and his wife Ruth hurriedly drove down Madison Avenue towards CBS's headquarters at the corner of 52nd Street in New York City. On the car radio they caught the climax of *War of the Worlds*. Stanton realized earlier in the hour that the excitement and reports of panic that had begun to circulate represented one of the most fortuitous research opportunities in the history of radio. Upon arriving at the CBS building, he parked his car, took the elevator to his office, and composed a questionnaire—as quickly and accurately as possible—on the effects of the program. He telephoned Paul Lazarsfeld, head of the

Rockefeller-funded Princeton Radio Research Project, for a quick consultation,[1] and then phoned the Hooper Holmes Company in Atlanta, Georgia. Hooper Holmes specialized in personal interviews for the insurance industry, and, importantly, did not rely solely on telephones for their survey work.[2] Stanton carefully went over the samples he was interested in—by economic class, rural or urban residence, and other demographic considerations—and by the next morning fieldwork had commenced (Buxton & Acland, 2001, pp. 212–216; Stanton, 1991–1996, session 3 pp. 115–117).

Stanton recognized the unique research opportunity, but also "suspected that we [at CBS] were going to be charged with having stirred up the population" (Stanton, 1991–1996, session 3 p. 116). As it turned out, the FCC did not file an official complaint, and the "firehouse" data Stanton had culled was never published. But Stanton's study served as one of the main data sources for the most important scholarly study of the *War of the Worlds* "panic," the *Invasion from Mars*, cited throughout as *IFM* (Cantril [with Gaudet & Herzog], 1940). Stanton's study, as analyzed by Hazel Gaudet, supplied the bulk of the evidence for *IFM*'s important claim about "critical ability" and education as means of defense against powerful media messages.

Because of his crushing workload at CBS, however, Stanton would only play an advisory role in the project. Instead, the project fell under the purview of four key players: Paul Lazarsfeld, Hadley Cantril, Herta Herzog, and Hazel Gaudet. Lazarsfeld and Cantril parlayed the project into substantial research support from the Rockefeller Foundation's General Education Board, ensuring continuation of Lazarsfeld's Radio Research Project and startup of Cantril's Office of Public Opinion Research. Radio Project researchers Herzog and Gaudet, meanwhile, directed the bulk of the research and interpreted the findings. Herzog initiated the project by conducting a series of in-depth interviews with frightened listeners in the Princeton area almost immediately after the broadcast. Based on these interviews, she drafted a memo of preliminary analysis whose themes *IFM* later echoed with remarkable fidelity. Gaudet administered the research project and conducted the statistical analyses of both the CBS survey and the data from the final 135 interviews that supported Herzog's initial analysis. It is a telling irony, then, that while Lazarsfeld and Cantril engaged in a battle for authorship recognition, credit and oversight for over a year, much of the actual intellectual work was conducted, invisibly, by these two women. In the end, they were barely recognized in the published study. For some of the same reasons—the gendered division of labor and credit—the contributions of Herzog and Gaudet register only fleetingly in the surviving records. Still, it is possible to reconstruct their important roles with the fragmentary evidence that remains.

This chapter tracks the complex politics involved in the research and writing of the *Invasion from Mars* study—a book that stands alongside the broadcast itself as key to understanding the *War of the Worlds* phenomenon. It exposes the gender and class biases of academic culture that led to Cantril receiving authorship credit despite not having done the bulk of the work. Drawing on new archival evidence, the chapter illuminates the key contradiction at the heart of the *Invasion from Mars* study—namely its focus on the power of radio to create a national "panic," despite its findings of weak media effects mitigated by intervening contextual and individual factors (Hayes & Battles, 2011, pp. 54–55; Lowery & DeFleur, 1995, pp. 66–67; Socolow, 2008, ¶15). Cantril—who referred to the project as the "Mass Hysteria Study"—"sold" the research to the Rockefeller Foundation by emphasizing the size and national scope of the panic. As Stanton first realized, the fact that the broadcast appeared to have had such a strong impact was what made it worthy of study. Herzog and Gaudet, however, focused on the mediating factors that emerged in the survey and interview data. In line with her broader research focus on audience "gratifications," Herzog explored listeners' constraints and motivations, and proposed the study's central research question: why did some listeners "check up" on the validity of the broadcast while others did not?

Ultimately, this chapter reevaluates the legacy of the *Invasion from Mars* study for the field of mass communication research. First, it reveals that the study was key in garnering continued financial support for the Radio Research Project, which Lazarsfeld would soon move to Columbia University to become the Bureau of Applied Social Research. Second, it shows how the exploitative and biased conditions of early communication research helped produce a study that contributed to the notion of a broadcasting-induced mass hysteria despite its own more nuanced findings.

Contest and Conflict at the Radio Research Project

Lazarsfeld and Cantril welcomed the 1938 broadcast as an opportunity to secure the future of the badly managed Radio Research Project. Established in 1937, amidst a contested series of debates regarding the direction of radio broadcasting in the United States, the Rockefeller-funded Project was created by the ambitious psychologist Hadley Cantril, and formally housed at Princeton University. Cantril had come to the attention of the Rockefeller Foundation's John Marshall after Marshall read Cantril and Gordon Allport's 1935 collaborative book, *The Psychology of Radio*. While Cantril envisioned his role as providing "general direction," he invited Frank Stanton to act as the day-to-day executive director (Marshall, 1991–1996, session 3, p. 103). When Stanton decided to remain at CBS, Cantril and Marshall searched for a new director, and they settled on Paul Lazarsfeld just weeks before the project was to begin. However, Lazarsfeld and Cantril clashed almost from the start.

On one hand, both were similar in certain ways. They were charming, talented and ambitious. They shared a belief and interest in the newly emerging field of public opinion polling and its methods, and even had in common a commitment to the left that both men played down in the pursuit of academic distinction. But Cantril and Lazarsfeld were divided by circumstance and background, in ways that played out in a contentious relationship over resources, management style, and eventually authorial claim over the *IFM* study. Cantril was privileged, if not by birth, then by Ivy League pedigree. He was valedictorian at Dartmouth (Cantril, 2004, p. 387), which like other Ivy League schools remained in the interwar years a bastion of WASP exclusivity (Karabel, 2006). Cantril was debonair and polished, as Converse (1987, p. 144) concluded based on interviews with contemporaries. Lazarsfeld's place in the American academy, in contrast, was hard-fought and unstable. A Jewish Austrian émigré, escaping the rise of Nazism, Lazarsfeld used a growing network of social contacts to secure academic positions for himself at a number of schools.

Herta Herzog had been Lazarsfeld's student in Vienna (and later his wife), and was ambitious in her own right. She became a key player in the Project, developing what became the "uses and gratifications" approach to the study of media. She left the Project in 1943 to pursue a successful market research career at McCann Erickson (Herzog, 1994, pp. 6–8). While much is known about Cantril, Lazarsfeld, and Herzog, there is very little information about the fourth player in this drama, Hazel Gaudet. She was among the most active staff members at the Project, authoring or coauthoring two articles (Cantril & Gaudet, 1939; Gaudet, 1939) published in Lazarsfeld's *Journal of Applied Psychology* special issue. She was later credited as a co-author of *The People's Choice* (Lazarsfeld, Berelson & Gaudet, 1944), the landmark panel study, for her major role in the fieldwork and analysis. She remained with the Project through 1941, when she joined the Office of War Information (Simonson & Archer, 2008).

Initiating the Study

In the days following the *War of the Worlds* broadcast, scholarly effort was expended on two distinct fronts: while Herzog and Gaudet began collecting and analyzing data, Cantril and Lazarsfeld began jockeying for funding. Just three days after the broadcast, Herzog was in the field conducting in-depth interviews with listeners.[3] Over the next two months, she and four other female interviewers conducted interviews with 135 listeners, over 100 of whom had been chosen because they had claimed to be frightened by the broadcast (Cantril [with Gaudet & Herzog], 1940, pp. xiii–xiv).[4] The earliest interviews formed the basis of Herzog's November memo.[5] Lengthy excerpts from the full interview set would later dominate the published book's dramatic, scene-setting second chapter. (The book's first chapter was a reprint of the Welles transcript.)

Herzog's ([1938, November]) 14-page memo was based on the first 30 interviews—18 of which she conducted herself (Lazarsfeld, November 22, 1938). The memo's purpose, she wrote, was to bring out "those psychological categories which would seem useful for an analysis of the whole event" (p. 1). Her main conclusions, summarized on the last page, were strikingly similar to the core points elaborated in the published book. She concluded, for example, that one cause of the panic was listeners' "readiness to be afraid" (p. 2). Just two weeks before the broadcast, the Germans had annexed Czechoslovakia's Sudetenland, after the Munich acquiescence of British and French leaders. Recent natural catastrophes and Buck Rogers' Martian science fiction had all, she speculated, contributed to a "time out of joint" that primed listeners for "panic." The same point was elaborated in *IFM*'s seventh chapter ("The Historical Situation"), down to some of the specific language: "Are the times more out of joint now than they were in the golden 'nineties' or in 1925?" (p. 153).

Likewise, Herzog ([1938, November]) drew on the interviews to describe the broadcast's "realistic" features that, she argued, contributed to listeners' belief. She pointed to a technical virtuosity, as well as a series of devices used by Welles, including actual place names, the repeated interruption of a supposed music program, and the on-mic voices of scientists and government officials (pp. 5–8). *IFM*'s third chapter covered much the same "unusual realism" ground, including the "prestige of speakers" (pp. 70–71), the specific place names (pp. 72–73), and the music-program cross-cutting (pp. 68–69). Herzog (p. 5) discussed the importance of the "special confidence [listeners] have in radio as an institution," listing five interview snippets to support her claim; *IFM* concluded its nearly identical analysis by listing four of Herzog's five quotes (p. 70). Herzog (pp. 8–9) emphasized the importance of those who tuned in late (missing the disclaimer), a factor that *IFM* also stressed (pp. 76–84). Even Herzog's psychoanalytically informed speculation about the "thrill of disaster" (pp. 11–13) as a latent motive was written up in *IFM* with some of the same language and interview excerpts (pp. 161–164).

By far the most important probe in Herzog's memo was her extensive discussion of "checking up," a concept she apparently invented (pp. 9–11, 14). After all, the published book's most celebrated finding was its linkage of "critical ability" with listeners' tendency to seek out and confirm the broadcast's fantastic nature against other evidence. Although Herzog did not, in this early memo, tie "checking up" to education or critical ability—her colleague Hazel Gaudet performed the analysis of Stanton's CBS data that largely revealed the relationship—she did identify the immense significance of checking up to any further study. Referring to late tune-ins, she wrote, "The much more important psychological problem is to what extent people were able to check up on the authenticity of the broadcast ... probably one of the most important aspects of the event from a social point of view" (p. 9; emphasis in original). She continued, laying out what would become the animating question of the published book: "Here again a more elaborate study would try to compare the personality of those people who did not check up at all with those people who checked unsuccessfully and those people who really found out the truth by checking." The fourth, fifth, and sixth chapters, along with *IFM*'s conclusion, were largely concerned with making that comparison. Cantril's resistance to placing "checking up" at the center of the manuscript, until Lazarsfeld insisted just weeks before submission, may reflect his desire to underplay the central role of Herzog's ideas in the study.

Meanwhile, Lazarsfeld and Cantril were plotting to convince Rockefeller to release an emergency $3000 grant to support further research on the "Mass Hysteria Study." Lazarsfeld hoped that publications deriving from the *War of the Worlds* study would shore up the Princeton Radio Project's shaky case for renewal. In a mid-November memo to Cantril with the playful "From: Orson Welles, Director of Publications, Princeton Radio Research Project" heading, Lazarsfeld (November 18, 1938) admitted that he was "much worried about the fact that the prolongation of the project will come up with Marshall and the Foundation at a time when no major initiative of the project will be finished."

Although Lazarsfeld apparently deputized Cantril to direct the *War of the Worlds* study, archival records make abundantly clear that he never intended Cantril to take sole authorship credit for any eventual publication.[6] Cantril (November 21, 1938) did draft the Rockefeller proposal, which he submitted in late November. Perhaps at the suggestion of Rockefeller officials, Cantril submitted his proposal to the foundation's sister fund, the General Education Board (GEB). The "panic" over the *War of the Worlds* broadcast, he wrote (p. 1), provided an "almost unparalleled source of data" for both social psychologists and educators concerned about propaganda. He emphasized that Lazarsfeld, Stanton, and himself ("all trained psychologists interested in radio") had "already cooperated on a preliminary survey" (p. 3)—

thereby rendering invisible Herzog's crucial contribution. Cantril's proposal (p. 3) referred to a "written report by the [Project] directors." The clear implication that the study would be co-authored by Lazarsfeld and Cantril (and possibly Stanton) was confirmed at a meeting with a GEB official the next day. According to the GEB official's account (Havighurst, November 22, 1938), the write-up would be "published by the Princeton group." Lazarsfeld, the official recorded, "estimates that he could do a good job with $3,000," and has "already had members of his staff make thirty interviews." The focus on Lazarsfeld (and not just Cantril) is notable, as is the second erasure of Herzog's contribution. That contribution, moreover, is evoked in the suggestion—credited here to Lazarsfeld—to compare the "affected" group with listeners "not affected."

The *Invasion from Mars*

In late November—less than a month after the *War of the Worlds* broadcast—Rockefeller's GEB (November 28, 1938) awarded the $3000 grant. In the monthly bulletin to Trustees (December, 1938), Foundation officers highlighted the new grant. Except for some background on the Radio Project, the report to the Trustees was an edited down version of Herzog's November memo.

With the grant awarded, the study moved forward. At least for a time, Herzog remained heavily involved in planning the study's next phase. In a late November memo, Cantril (November 30, 1938) reported on a "conference" he and Herzog had the night before, to sketch "our general plans and purposes." The document laid out an elaborate plan for interviews in locations around the country, and designated Herzog as leader of over half the interview sites, including New York, New Jersey, Iowa, and New England.

The proposed budget, however, called into question Herzog's otherwise prominent role. Samuel Stouffer, for example, was slated to receive $400 for running the Chicago interviews. "The sum left for Herta," Cantril wrote, "is not much. She will, of course, be paid $3.00 for each interview and my thought was that there would be something left from the travel or special staff budget that could come to her at the end" (Cantril, November 30, 1938). Financial mismanagement was a hallmark of the Princeton Radio Research Project, and this example further demonstrates the casual devaluation of Herzog's labor by the Directors.

The national interviews were never conducted, or at least not incorporated into the published book. Herzog, however, continued to direct the New Jersey fieldwork, at least through December when the 135 interviews were completed (Gaudet, December 15–16, 1939). Her work on the study seems to have dropped away soon after, and by March Lazarsfeld (March 21, 1939) was writing to Cantril to pointedly "remind" him of "some private debts": "In a general way, [Cantril] owes Herta some money for her work in the first weeks of the Orson Welles Study." A detailed expenditure report (Princeton Radio Research Project, June 23, 1939) submitted to the GEB in June lists no compensation for Herzog among the 19 people receiving payment.

Around the same time—late 1938 and early 1939—Hazel Gaudet seems to have taken on a much more active role in the data collection and analysis. Gaudet, as Cantril (1940, p. xv) admitted in the *IFM* preface, directed the "actual administration" of the Welles study. "She not only made most of the tabulations based on the interviews," he wrote, "but many of the ideas reflected in the tabulations and the text were contained in her detailed memoranda to the writer" (p. xv). Unfortunately only two of those memos seem to have been preserved, one (Gaudet, August 17, 1939) with Gaudet's detailed comments on Cantril's "first draft" and another (Gaudet, January 26, 1940) with remarks on a chapter of the near-final manuscript. In both instances Gaudet used supportive page-by-page comments to suggest stylistic and substantive changes. In the earlier memo, for instance, she (August 17, 1939) wrote, "On the whole I feel that the psychoanalytic material detracts from your story a great deal and even sounds a little silly" (p. 6). Gaudet's suggestions were largely adapted. Her call to restrict the psychoanalytic analyses reminded Cantril that the study's significant quantitative results could be overshadowed. Her concerns were addressed, and, in this case, Gaudet's influential edits left their mark.

Cantril, however, expressed little confidence in Gaudet or her ideas. When asked by Marshall to suggest a researcher to review educational questionnaires related to another foundation project, Cantril

(May 11, 1939) recommended someone else, adding that Gaudet would make "an excellent assistant to the person in charge." Gaudet, he continued, "has a thorough grounding in psychology and statistics, but would not have the methodological or theoretical grasp needed to set up such a study." Cantril impassively disqualified Gaudet from a research opportunity at the same moment he had come to rely on her *IFM* analyses—which, by all evidence, were theoretically informed and methodologically sophisticated.

Meanwhile, in the months following the GEB grant award Cantril seems to have decided to assert control—and ultimately authorship credit—over the *War of the Worlds* study. Cantril's increasingly brazen efforts to publicize his role directing the study soon led to a stormy confrontation with Lazarsfeld. Since the first days after the broadcast, he fed stories about his role in the study to Princeton University press outlets. A November 2 story in the *Daily Princetonian* centered on the Project's planned study, with Cantril as the unmistakable source. The piece ("Welles' Broadcast Aids Psychologist") concludes with the time and room location of Cantril's social psychology course, directing readers to a "lecture today touching the Orson Welles broadcast and the aspects of mob behavior that were brought out by it." A follow-up piece the next day ("'Martian Invasion' Treated by Cantril," November 3, 1939) recounts his lecture. In December and January, these stories became more explicit about Cantril's leading role. A December 19 Associated Press story ("'Men from Mars' Not a Dead Issue Yet—Savants Enter Case," included in Cantril, 1938–1951) describes him as the study's director, as does a January 6 piece appearing in The *Daily Princetonian* ("Cantril Directing Hysteria Analysis").

Lazarsfeld had apparently not seen these stories, but did come across yet another article, running in The Princeton Alumni Weekly in mid-January ("Psychologists to Study Martian Hysteria," January 13, 1939). The story, referring to "Dr. Cantril's study," states that the project "will be greatly aided by work already performed at Princeton by Dr. Cantril in the Princeton Radio Project." Lazarsfeld was not mentioned, and he wrote Cantril about the oversight. Though Lazarsfeld's letter of complaint does not survive, it is clear from Cantril's (January 26, 1939) reply that Lazarsfeld had reacted angrily to the

Alumni Weekly article. Cantril took obvious umbrage at Lazarsfeld's accusation:

> I am glad you expressed yourself on the release, but I must say that the reaction seems a bit infantile. Perhaps we should have directors' uniforms with differential insignia. It is hard to imagine people like [Lawrence K.] Frank, [George] Gallup, [Gordon] Allport, [Daniel] Katz, [Samuel] Stouffer would maintain petty jealousies, and I should like to think that you, too, would have sufficient perspective not to let such trivia bother you.... In the official university release I clearly indicated that the whole project was under your direction.

Cantril wrote that, "I seldom see the sheet," and that the "report seemed quite harmless." He continued:

> If the project could go on completely without me I should honestly be much happier. But apparently I am a strategic link in the chain. I am willing to play the role only for two reasons: (1) [Princeton President] Dodds feels that we should not tell the Foundation outright that we do not want a renewal; (2) I am anxious to help you make a reputation and attain some sort of eventual security in these highly insecure days. Please believe me that these are my only motives.... If I have to become involved in many emotional reactions, I may reconsider my whole position.

That the professed concern for Lazarsfeld's "eventual security" is juxtaposed to the issue of the Project's renewal is ironic, since Cantril's letter carries the unmistakable implication that Princeton was no longer interested in serving as host. Lazarsfeld's security depended on the Project's renewal.

At stake here, too, was Lazarsfeld's sense of the prerogatives of the directorship: he, and he alone, should decide who directs a Project study. This extended to authorship as well: When the Project's first book was issued in 1940 as *Radio and the Printed Page*, it was solely credited to Lazarsfeld—despite the fact that many of its constituent chapters were written by Project subordinates (including Herzog). It is likely that the *IFM*, had Lazarsfeld succeeded in maintaining control over its destiny, would also have followed this director-as-author practice.

The Project's fate was hanging in the balance. Just days before the nasty exchange between Lazarsfeld and Cantril, the Foundation's John Marshall had secured a $750 internal grant to appoint a review committee to consider the Project's renewal (Rockefeller Foundation, January 25, 1939). Marshall's committee, a mix of academic and industry representatives, issued a report in March recommending renewal, but with a renewed focus on the "detailed analysis and interpretation of some of the material collected to date" (quoted in Morrison, 2005, p. 79). Rockefeller officials, however, opted to delay the renewal pending a more coherent write-up of the Project's research to date. Marshall cabled Lazarsfeld in mid-March: "DISCUSSIONS IN OFFICE INDICATE RELUCTANCE TO INVEST IN NEW RESEARCH PENDING FORMULATION OF PRESENT FINDINGS STOP FEELING HERE THAT NEED IS FOR BREATHING SPELL TO SAVE PROJECT FROM BEING VICTIM OF ITS OWN SUCCESS" (quoted in Morrison, 2005, p. 79).

Marshall gave Lazarsfeld until June 1 to assemble the Project's eclectic research portfolio into a summative manuscript. The Project staff threw themselves into the project—"day and night literally" (Lazarsfeld, 1969, pp. 328–329)—and submitted the draft on the morning of the deadline. Marshall was satisfied, and the manuscript was published the following year as *Radio and the Printed Page* (Lazarsfeld, 1940). The Foundation awarded the Project a temporary grant to prepare a proposal for a three-year renewal, which Lazarsfeld submitted sometime in the fall (Lazarsfeld, n.d. 1939).

Cantril (April 17, 1939) successfully used the Project's "breathing spell" sprint to press the Foundation to accept a delay in his delivery of the *IFM* write-up. He took at least some of the time, however, to chart out a new, solo project—involving the analysis of Gallup polling data—independent of Lazarsfeld and unconnected to radio. The two men were soon fighting over CBS and Gallup data and vying for new Rockefeller funds—all of it layered atop the ongoing *IFM* conflict.

Cantril (September 18, 1939) wrote to Marshall that he had just received a Lazarsfeld memo "regarding an extension of the Project to cover some of the radio problems arising out of the present European situation." He had also "gathered the impression that you and the others in the Foundation were interested in having some studies made very shortly on the ffects [sic] of war propaganda, changes in attitude, and the like." He was, he wrote, "very dissatisfied" with Lazarsfeld's memo, for "the new problems are far too important to become mere appendages of research already in progress." With considerable brio, Cantril proceeded to outline in great detail his Gallup proposal, reframed as a study of Americans' attitudes toward the war. He concluded:

> Please forgive me for butting into any plans you and Paul may have. Naturally, I have not written this to Paul and should prefer that you do not mention it to him. But I think one should definitely take a fresh start on so important a matter and, if possible, not be arbitrarily limited by a 'communications' category.

In his reply, Marshall (September 21, 1939) confirmed that he was, "still holding strictly to the position" that the Princeton Radio Project "undertake no fresh investigation until the present work of formulation is virtually complete." That could only change, Marshall added, with your "full concurrence and in all probability only on your initiative."

As for the Gallup proposal, Marshall continued, "I am of course particularly interested. . . . As a matter of fact, the whole question which underlies your letter is now being canvassed as rapidly as possible." Marshall, who remained supportive of the Project under Lazarsfeld's leadership, was now poised to take advantage of Cantril's new independence. In follow-up correspondence Marshall encouraged him to submit a revised proposal, which Cantril (November 13, 1939) delivered in mid-November.

Up until the publication of the *Invasion from Mars* in March 1940, Lazarsfeld and Cantril kept up their interlocked fight over Rockefeller money, the Project's future, and the *IFM* study itself. At the same time, both men needed the other's cooperation. Cantril discovered that, as a practical matter, he could not get the Welles manuscript published without Lazarsfeld's clearance. Lazarsfeld, likewise, came to realize that his plan to relocate the Project to Columbia could not move forward without Cantril's cooperation.

In a mid-October memo to Cantril, Lazarsfeld (October 12, 1939) pressed his case that *IFM* should center on "checking up," the theme that Herzog had highlighted almost a year earlier. Lazarsfeld wrote that he had, "a still stronger feeling that the emphasis of your study should be very strongly upon checking up." The fact that people panicked, Lazarsfeld continued, is not compelling. "However, what is so extremely interesting and deserves all generalization is the fact that after people were scared they were not able or not willing to check up to see whether it was true or not." Lazarsfeld, an especially savvy packager of concepts (Platt, 1996, ch. 7), urged Cantril to find a better phrase than "checking up," so that the idea "could be more easily merchandized."

Though collegial, Lazarsfeld's memo also served a tactical purpose: he was angling to bring Herzog back into the study, presumably to secure her co-authorship credit:[7]

> In case you have not enough time to do something about it, why don't you ask Herta to go over all the interviews and dig out everything she finds on check-ups and write to you an elaborate report on the check-up situation. Then you can take all the factual material she gives you and re-write it as the final chapter in your own interpretation. . . . I am sure that Herta would be willing to volunteer her help to make this improvement, if you agree with me that it is an improvement. I am stressing her possible help because I am quite sure that it would not do the situation justice if you just wrote a few pages about the check-up problem.

Cantril, previously eager to maneuver Herzog away, was suddenly receptive. In an undated reply to Lazarsfeld, he (1939, n.d.) wrote that he "simply MUST" submit the *IFM* manuscript by mid-November. Though he had only recently disparaged Lazarsfeld's war-related memo to Marshall, Cantril assumed a chummy tone. "So COULD Herta go at the job in the very near future?" he asked, estimating three days of "rather concentrated work." In the same jovial tone, he proceeds to nullify any future credit Herzog might claim: "God knows what her reward will be—except my continued admiration for her ability and a eulogistic footnote in the last chapter." There is no record suggesting that Herzog agreed to help under these conditions.

Lazarsfeld and Cantril continued to spar over the *IFM* manuscript. In a late November exchange, Cantril (November 25, 1939) flatly refused to make substantive changes suggested by Lazarsfeld, citing the impending deadline. "Since you and Frank [Stanton] have both read it carefully once, since I am satisfied that I have taken account of your suggestions, and since [Gordon] Allport—as a complete outsider—has caught no errors or misinterpretations . . . I have reached a stage where I must stop any major revisions." Lazarsfeld scribbled angry challenges to Cantril's deadline claims in the margin. Needless to say, Cantril's request, in the same letter, for Lazarsfeld's foreword was not granted—as the book was published without one. Lazarsfeld answered with an apparently bitter memo, judging from

Cantril's (November 29, 1939) curt reply: "I shall refrain from answering your classic letter. But it is hard to do so."

Just days later, however, the two men met face-to-face in a fascinating yet mysterious denouement to their long struggle. No account of the meeting survives, although Cantril (December 2, 1939), in coordinated letters to Lazarsfeld and Marshall, struck a surprisingly conciliatory tone. In the letter to Lazarsfeld, Cantril brought up what "I told you at the end of our discussion today—that I now for the first time honestly see what has been bothering you about the Invasion from Mars study." Lazarsfeld's methodological criticisms, Cantril continued, were finally clear. His failing was not the "common charge of 'mismanagement,'" but instead impossibly high standards. "So I can admit—since I now understand—that many of your troubles have been over genuine methodological procedures."

The letter comes off as a less-than-genuine statement, a suspicion confirmed, perhaps, by its transparent performativity. Indeed, the letter closed on a note of saccharine harmony that the two men's history rendered implausible: "Personally, I am enormously relieve [sic] that we at last know what has been the cause of our minor difficulties. In order that John Marshall should know how I feel, I am sending him a copy of this letter." That their difficulties were "minor" and mendable seems a message intended more for Marshall than for Lazarsfeld.

The accompanying letter to Marshall doubled down on the first letter's praise:

> Today, however, [Lazarsfeld] was able to verbalize for me in a really brilliant way his objections to my study and other studies of the project (including his own). I can see now for the first time the fundamental reasons for the delay we have been worried about with respect to the project. And in all fairness to Paul, I did want you to know at once that the delay now makes sense to me and would, I feel sure, make sense to anyone if Paul explained it to them the way he explained it to me.

Though impossible to prove, it is plausible to read Cantril's sudden camaraderie as evidence of a deal between the two men—a reconciliation of mutual expediency. After all, Cantril could hardly move forward with the *IFM* submission over Lazarsfeld's vociferous objections. Likewise, Lazarsfeld was days away from learning the fate of his proposal to relocate the Project to Columbia University—a move that Cantril could attempt to block. Both men, moreover, depended very much on Marshall's near-term favor: Lazarsfeld for the Columbia move, coupled with a three-year extension, and Cantril for the pending war-opinion grant. Cantril's closing paragraph, at any rate, strengthens this interpretation:

> In a conversation with [Princeton] President Dodds the other day, I gathered that he and [Rockefeller official] Mr. Stevens were quite worried about the slow rate of productiveness of the project. I can quite understand their point of view. But I should be very glad to discuss with Mr. Stevens, if you think it at all advisable, what I have finally learned about Paul's difficulties and the reasons for what has seemed a publication blocking.

Three days later, Cantril won the $15,000 grant (Rockefeller Foundation, December 5-6, 1939). Soon after he formally established a new Office of Public Opinion Research at Princeton to host his war-opinion polling and Gallup re-analysis. Just over a week later Lazarsfeld learned that his proposal to extend and move the Project was approved (Morrison, 2005, p. 75). It is likely that the pair of December grants were coordinated, enabling the two men to disentangle their long-fractious union.

The Publication and Its Legacy

The "Mass Hysteria Study" was finally published in March 1940 as the *Invasion from Mars*, with Cantril listed as sole author—though there was a "with the assistance of" credit for Herzog and Gaudet. The book's popular style, and its arresting topic, made for rapid sales, and *IFM* was later issued as a mass-market paperback. In the remembered history of media research, the book is exclusively associated with Cantril, and most bibliographic references drop the "with the assistance of" credit altogether. The book's ties to Herzog, Gaudet, Stanton and Lazarsfeld have long been forgotten.

Lazarsfeld was still bitter about Cantril's self-serving behavior years after the book's release. In a 1942 letter to a government official, he wrote that Cantril has "hardly done any original research," adding "I just want to be sure that in the field of research, moral and intellectual standards are not set by him" (quoted in Glander, 2000, p. 84). In a 1943 interview with a Rockefeller official, Lazarsfeld (March 29, 1943) called Cantril "pathologically ambitious" and dismissed his work on the *IFM* project as "laughable."

Lazarsfeld had tried, in the run-up to the book's publication, to get Herzog recognized as co-author. Still-incensed, he published Herzog's key memo in a 1955 collection, with an editorial introduction that asserted the clear priority and originality of this Herzog memo over the published report under Cantril's name (Herzog, 1955, p. 420). As late as 1975 he was still writing of his "justified complaint" against Cantril, that he "forced me to make him co-author of the Invasion from Mars while he had practically nothing to do with it" (quoted in Pasanella, 1994, p. 30). Of course Cantril had not settled for co-author. Stanton (March 29, 1943), too, savaged Cantril to a Rockefeller official. He claimed that Cantril had refused to revise a "completely unsatisfactory" draft, and insisted on sole authorship even after Stanton and Lazarsfeld had rewritten the manuscript.

Stanton and Lazarsfeld left a record of complaints, mainly because they were asked. In the end neither man's career suffered as a result of Cantril's recognition grab. We cannot know if Herzog and Gaudet harbored similar grievances, since their accounts of the *War of the Worlds* project were never solicited. Both women left academic life for other pursuits, but it is impossible to judge whether a just share of IFM authorship would have made a difference in their life courses. Lazarsfeld (February 17, 1938), in an early memo addressing Stanton's apprehension over credit, made an offhand comment that applied well to the Project's largely forgotten female staff: "I think it will be the destiny of all of us directors to sink a lot of ideas into other people's studies." Lazarsfeld's indifferent attitude towards the exploitative aspects of research collaboration under his direction is indicative of academic practice between the wars. That he could confidently voice such an attitude to Stanton shows his belief that claiming credit for the work of others was a standard practice at the Radio Research Project.

In sum, this chapter reveals important blind spots concerning the history and legacy of the *Invasion from Mars* study. While two ambitious men jockeyed for credit and control over the study, two women made extensive research contributions that today remain unrecognized. Archival documents indicate the extent to which both Cantril and Lazarsfeld simultaneously undervalued and exploited Herzog and Gaudet's work for their own academic achievement (although

Lazarsfeld made some efforts to gain co-authorship credit for Herzog). Completion of the study helped to ensure continued Rockefeller Foundation support for mass communication research along the model of the Princeton Radio Research Project. Indeed, the *IFM* study played a central role in helping Cantril and Lazarsfeld obtain directorships of powerful academic institutes that would shape the future of research into mass communication and public opinion.

This chapter also reveals the extent to which the gender- and class-biased conditions of early communication research helped produce the conflict at the heart of the *Invasion from Mars* study. The case of Herta Herzog is instructive in this respect. The *IFM* is etched in memory as a chronicle of unbridled panic. But the text itself, especially the core chapters, tells a different story about critical ability as an effective defense against media-induced psychosis. One reason that the book's freshest insight gets so routinely misremembered is that Cantril himself insisted on a dramatic prose-style and chapter structure, and exaggerated the extent of the panic (Socolow, 2008). In part, we suggest, this was a product of Cantril and Lazarsfeld's need to "merchandise" the study in order to attract funding from the Rockefeller Foundation. To draw attention and resources, the study mimicked the theatricality of the *War of the Worlds* broadcast. Herzog's original analysis is an especially good place to recover the *Invasion from Mars*'s most important finding: some listeners checked up on the validity of the broadcast, for discernible reasons. With Herzog's guidance, we might recover that crucial, and still relevant, point in *IFM* itself.

Notes

[1] Lazarsfeld (1969, p. 313) later claimed that he called Stanton, not the other way around. Stanton's accounts, however, are far more detailed and correspond with other particulars, including the arrangements for the CBS study.

[2] Telephone surveys excluded a large percentage of Americans who did not have telephones in the 1930s.

[3] Herzog (1994, p. 6), states that her interviews began the day after the broadcast: "I still recall with pleasure the interviewing the day after the CBS broadcast of 'The Invasion from Mars' to find out why some listeners had been scared." A later document (Rockefeller Foundation, December 1938) refers to the "Wednesday following the broadcast"—November 2.

4   One index of female researchers' virtual anonymity is that *IFM* (p. xiv) names these four as "Mrs. Paul Trilling, Frances Ginevsky, Mrs. Richard Robinson, and Mrs. David Green."

5   Though the memo is undated, Lazarsfeld (November 18, 1938) makes a pointed reference to it, which would place its composition in the first half of the month.

6   Pasanella (1994, p. 15), in her guide to Lazarsfeld's papers, refers to a "November memo," which she quotes: "Had will be in charge of the study and will draw a compensation of $400 for it.' The memo could not be located in the Lazarsfeld papers.

7   In his memoir, Lazarsfeld (1969, p. 313) documents his effort to secure Herzog recognition: "at that time I had hoped Dr. Herzog would receive a major share of the credit for her imaginative work on that study."

References

Buxton, W. J., & Acland, C. R. (2001). Interview with Dr. Frank N. Stanton: Radio research pioneer. *Journal of Radio Studies, 8*(1), 191–229.

Cantril directing hysteria analysis. (1939, January 6), *Daily Princetonian*.

Cantril, A. H. (2004). Cantril, Hadley. In J. G. Geer (Ed.), *Public opinion and polling around the world: A historical encyclopedia* (Vol. 1, pp. 387–391). Santa Barbara, CA: ABC-CLIO.

Cantril, H. (1938–1951). [Faculty and professional staff files]. Princeton University Archives, Department of Rare Books and Special Collections, Princeton University Library.

Cantril, H. (1939, December 2). [Letter to John Marshall, including letter to Paul Lazarsfeld]. General Education Board Archives (Series 1, Box 361, Folder 3723). Rockefeller Archive Center, Sleepy Hollow, NY.

Cantril, H. (1939, November 29). [Letter to Paul Lazarsfeld]. Paul Felix Lazarsfeld Papers (Box 26, Folder "PRRP 6"). Columbia University Rare Books and Manuscript Library, New York, NY.

Cantril, H. (1939, November 25). [Letter to Paul Lazarsfeld]. Paul Felix Lazarsfeld Papers (Box 26, Folder "PRRP 6"). Columbia University Rare Books and Manuscript Library, New York, NY.

Cantril, H. (1939, November 13). [Letter to John Marshall, including "A Proposed Study of the Effect of the War on Public Opinion"]. Rockefeller Foundation Archives (RG 1.1., Series 200, Box 270, Folder 3216). Rockefeller Archive Center, Sleepy Hollow, NY.

Cantril, H. (1939, n.d.). [Letter to Paul F. Lazarsfeld]. Paul Felix Lazarsfeld Papers (Box 26, Folder "PRRP 6"). Columbia University Rare Books and Manuscript Library, New York, NY.

Cantril, H. (1939, September 18). [Letter to John Marshall]. Rockefeller Foundation Archives (RG 1.1., Series 200, Box 270, Folder 3216). Rockefeller Archive Center, Sleepy Hollow, NY.

Cantril, H. (1939, May 11). [Letter to John Marshall]. General Education Board Archives (Series 1, Box 361, Folder 3723). Rockefeller Archive Center, Sleepy Hollow, NY.

Cantril, H. (1939, April 17). [Letter to Robert Havighurst]. General Education Board Archives (Series 1, Box 361, Folder 3723). Rockefeller Archives Center, Sleepy Hollow, NY.

Cantril, H. (1938, November 30). "Outline for Welles Study." Paul Felix Lazarsfeld Papers (Box 26, Folder "PRRP 6"). Columbia University Rare Books and Manuscript Library, New York, NY.

Cantril, H. (1938, November 21). "Proposed Study of 'Mass Hysteria.'" General Education Board Archives (Series 1, Box 361, Folder 3723). Rockefeller Archives Center, Sleepy Hollow, NY.

Cantril, H., & Gaudet, H. (1939). Familiarity as a factor in determining the selection and enjoyment of radio programs. *Journal of Applied Psychology, 23*(1), 85–94.

Cantril, H., & Allport, G. (1935). *The psychology of radio.* New York, NY: Harper & Bros.

Cantril, H. [with Gaudet, H. & Herzog, H.] (1940). *The invasion from Mars: A study in the psychology of panic.* Princeton, NJ: Princeton University Press.

Converse, J. (1987). *Survey research in the United States: Roots and emergence 1890–1960.* Berkeley: University of California Press.

Gaudet, H. (1940, January 26). [Memo to Hadley Cantril, "Chapter VI-Orson Welles"]. Paul Felix Lazarsfeld Papers (Box 26, Folder "PRRP 6"). Columbia University Rare Books and Manuscript Library, New York, NY.

Gaudet, H. (1939, August 17). [Memo to Hadley Cantril, "OW first draft"]. Paul Felix Lazarsfeld Papers (Box 26, Folder "PRRP 6"). Columbia University Rare Books and Manuscript Library, New York, NY.

Gaudet, H. (1939). The favorite radio program. *Journal of Applied Psychology, 23*(1), 115–126.

Gaudet, H. (1938, December 15–16). [Two memos to Herta Herzog]. Paul Felix Lazarsfeld Papers (Box 26, Folder "PRRP 6"). Columbia University Rare Books and Manuscript Library, New York, NY.

General Education Board. (November 28, 1938). [Grant-in-aid for the Welles study]. General Education Board Archives (Series 1, Box 361, Folder 3723). Rockefeller Archives Center, Sleepy Hollow, NY.

Glander, T. (2000). *Origins of mass communications research during the American Cold War.* Mahwah, NJ: Lawrence Erlbaum.

Havighurst, R. J. (1938, November 22). [Summary of interview with Paul F. Lazarsfeld and Hadley Cantril]. General Education Board Archives (Series 1, Box 361, Folder 3723). Rockefeller Archives Center, Sleepy Hollow, NY.

Hayes, J. E., & Battles, K. (2011). Exchange and interconnection in US network radio: A reinterpretation of the 1938 *War of the Worlds* broadcast. *Radio Journal, 9*(1), 51–62.

Herzog, H. (1994, September 12). [Letter to Elisabeth Perse]. Available at Simonson, P., & Archer, L. (2008). Pioneering women in media research. http://outofthequestion.org/userfiles/file/Herta%20Herzog%20%28Sept%2012

%201994%20to%20Elisabeth%20Perse%29.pdf

Herzog, H. (1955). Why did people believe in the 'Invasion from Mars'? In P. F. Lazarsfeld & M. Rosenberg (Eds.), *The language of social research* (pp. 420–428). Glencoe, IL: Free Press.

Herzog, H. ([1938], [November]). Inter-office memorandum (Orson Welles broadcast). General Education Board Archives (Series 1, Box 361, Folder 3723). Rockefeller Archives Center, Sleepy Hollow, NY.

Karabel, J. (2006). *The chosen: The hidden history of admission and exclusion at Harvard, Yale, and Princeton.* New York, NY: Mariner Books.

Lazarsfeld, P. F. (1969). An episode in the history of social research: A memoir. In B. Bailyn & D. Fleming (Eds.), *The intellectual migration: Europe and America 1930–1960* (pp. 270–337). Cambridge, MA: Belknap Press.

Lazarsfeld, P. F., Berelson, B., & Gaudet, H. (1944). *The people's choice: How the voter makes up his mind in a presidential campaign.* New York, NY: Duell, Sloan and Pearce.

Lazarsfeld, P. F. (1943, March 29) [Summary of interview of Paul Lazarsfeld]. Rockefeller Foundation Archives (RG 1.1, Series 200, Box 270, Folder 3224). Rockefeller Archive Center, Sleepy Hollow, NY.

Lazarsfeld, P. F. (1940). *Radio and the printed page.* New York, NY: Duell, Sloan & Pearce.

Lazarsfeld, P. F. (1939, October 12). [Memo to Hadley Cantril, "Analysis of Check-ups in Orson Welles Study"]. Paul Felix Lazarsfeld Papers (Box 26, Folder "PRRP 6"). Columbia University Rare Books and Manuscript Library, New York, NY.

Lazarsfeld, P. F. (1939, n.d.). Proposal for continuation of Radio Research project for a final three years at Columbia University. Paul Felix Lazarsfeld Papers (Box 26, Folder "Radio Research Project - Proposals"). Columbia University Rare Books and Manuscript Library, New York, NY.

Lazarsfeld, P. F. (1939, March 21). [Memo to Hadley Cantril and Frank Stanton]. Paul Felix Lazarsfeld Papers (Box 3A, Folder "Frank Stanton & Hadley Cantril"). Columbia University Rare Books and Manuscript Library, New York, NY.

Lazarsfeld, P. F. (Ed.). (1939). Special issue on radio research and applied psychology. *Journal of Applied Psychology, 23*(1).

Lazarsfeld, P. F. (1938, November 22). [Memo to Frank Stanton]. Paul Felix Lazarsfeld Papers (Box 3A, Folder "Frank Stanton II"). Columbia University Rare Books and Manuscript Library, New York, NY.

Lazarsfeld, P. F. (1938, November 18). [Memo to Hadley Cantril]. Paul Felix Lazarsfeld Papers (Box 3A, Folder "Frank Stanton & Hadley Cantril"). Columbia University Rare Books and Manuscript Library, New York, NY.

Lazarsfeld, P. F. (1938, February 17). [Letter to Frank Stanton]. Paul Felix Lazarsfeld Papers (Box 3A, Folder "Frank Stanton II"). Columbia University Rare Books and Manuscript Library, New York, NY.

Lowery, S. and DeFleur, M. L. (1995). *Milestones in mass communication research: Media effects.* White Plains, NY: Longman Publishers.

Marshall, J. (1939, September 21). [Letter to Hadley Cantril]. Rockefeller Foundation Archives (RG 1.1., Series 200, Box 270, Folder 3216). Rockefeller Archive Center,

Sleepy Hollow, NY.

"Martian Invasion" treated by Cantril (1938, November 3), *Daily Princetonian*.

Morrison, D. E. (2005). *The search for a method: Focus groups and the development of mass communication research*. New Barnet, UK: John Libbey Publishing.

Pasanella, A. K. (1994). *The mind traveller: A guide to Paul F. Lazarsfeld's communication research papers*. New York: Freedom Forum Media Studies Center.

Princeton Radio Research Project (1939, June 23). Study of public reactions to the Orson Welles broadcast [budget]. General Education Board Archives (Series 1, Box 361, Folder 3723). Rockefeller Archive Center, Sleepy Hollow, NY.

Psychologists to study Martian hysteria (1939, January 19), *The Princeton Alumni Weekly*.

Rockefeller Foundation (1939, December 5–6). [Grant for studies of public opinion]. Rockefeller Foundation Archives (RG 1.1., Series 200, Box 270, Folder 3216). Rockefeller Archive Center, Sleepy Hollow, NY.

Rockefeller Foundation (1939, January 25). [Internal grant for PRRP review]. Rockefeller Foundation Archives (RG 1.1., Series 200, Box 271, Folder 3233). Rockefeller Archive Center, Sleepy Hollow, NY.

Rockefeller Foundation (1938, December). [Excerpt from confidential monthly bulletin to Trustees]. Rockefeller Foundation Archives (RG 1.1., Series 200, Box 271, Folder 3236). Rockefeller Archive Center, Sleepy Hollow, NY.

Simonson, P., & Archer, L. (2008). Pioneering women in media research. http.www.outofthequestion.org/Women-in-Media-Researsh.aspx

Socolow, M. (2008). The hyped panic over 'War of the Worlds.' *The Chronicle Review*, 55(9), B16.

Stanton, F. (1991–1996). [Oral history interview of Frank Stanton, by Mary Marshall Clark]. Columbia Center for Oral History, New York, NY. http://www.columbia.edu/cu/lweb/digital/collections/nny/stantonf/

Stanton, F. (1943, March 29) [Summary of interview with Frank Stanton]. Rockefeller Foundation Archives (RG 1.1., Series 200, Box 270, Folder 3224). Rockefeller Archive Center, Sleepy Hollow, NY.

Welles' broadcast aids psychologists (1938, November 2), *Daily Princetonian*.

CHAPTER THREE

Assassination, Insurrection and Alien Invasion: Interwar Wireless Scares in Cross-National Comparison

KATE LACEY

In this chapter, Lacey argues that the *War of the Worlds* broadcast was not the first "radio scare" of its kind, but followed in the footsteps of a 1926 British production, *Broadcasting from the Barricades*, and a 1930 German radio broadcast, *Der Minister ist ermordet!* (*The Minister's Been Murdered!*). Drawing on newspaper reports from Germany, as well as the UK and US, Lacey shows how public discourse surrounding these fictional broadcasts referred back to the ones before, even across national borders. She contends that some audience members perceived the dramas as real because a) they played convincingly with the developing conventions of live news reporting; and b) they drew on a prevailing climate of fear (social, economic, and political) to enhance the believability of their fictional crisis reports.

Introduction

The Berlin audience tuning into the radio one late September evening in 1930 heard the station break into an orchestral recital with the following announcement:

Achtung! Achtung! This is Berlin and Königs Wusterhausen. The

German Foreign Minister returning from the Geneva Conference has been murdered on his arrival at the Friedrichstrasse railway station in Berlin. There will now therefore be a change to this evening's programs. (*Reichsrundfunkgesellschaft* (RRG), *Berliner Börsen-Zeitung*, Sept. 26, 1930)[1]

The Weimar Republic was at the time riven by political extremism and uncertainty and the assassination of a leading member of the Government promised to hurl the infant democracy into still deeper crisis.

Except it never happened. This was simply the controversial twist to a radio play broadcast by the Berlin radio station on September 25, 1930. But with its make-believe newsflash and as-live reporting of a subsequent putsch, the broadcast unleashed fear among listeners that they were witnessing the unfolding of a right-wing coup in the streets of the capital. This was no idle threat against the backdrop of increasing militancy in the country, and countless listeners bombarded the station, the authorities and the press with requests for more information. There were even reports of some disquiet abroad ("'Contretemps,'" 1930, p. 9).

As a wireless scare, Erich Ebermayer's *Der Minister ist ermordet!* (*The Minister's Been Murdered!*) had some obvious similarities to the *War of the Worlds* broadcast some eight years later, as did an even earlier example of a broadcast in the UK that also used the nascent codes of news reporting to describe an escalating riot and the lynching of a government minister. *Broadcasting from the Barricades* was a twenty-minute satirical skit broadcast in January 1926 by the British Broadcasting Company, the precursor of the British Broadcasting Corporation.[2] Against the background of rising tensions that were to lead to the General Strike, this obviously fictional report nevertheless similarly caused a degree of fear and consternation among some of its listeners. Neither of these two earlier wireless scares resonates in the popular memory in the same way as the *War of the Worlds*, nor have they attracted anything like the same degree of scholarly attention.[3] This chapter examines the reasons for the different trajectories of these broadcast events, as well as what they have in common as media events in times of crisis. The story of these earlier wireless scares draws attention to the way in which these media events—all inspired by fictional news reporting and in some way tapping into an already existing climate of fear—exhibit many common traits while at the same time highlighting how such events played out in different ways in specific national and political contexts. Moreover, within that story, there emerges a degree of cross-reference in the international press coverage of these successive events that says something about their gradual mythologization, not to mention the caricaturing of gullible foreign audiences according to national stereotypes.

Drawing primarily on archival and newspaper sources, this chapter explores the controversy surrounding the broadcast of a play in the fractious political climate of Weimar Germany and how the fallout from that broadcast then fed into the increasingly polarized approaches to radio policy. The chapter also sets the broadcast in the context of experimentalism in German radio drama and the interplay with other forms of newly invented broadcast genres that exploited radio's liveness. It shows how the right-wing nationalists exploited the scandal to rein in the more progressive elements of Weimar radio, while future propagandists learned an important lesson about the power of the radio to influence and deceive the listening public. The earlier British play, meanwhile, was a self-referential parody of the emerging genre of broadcast news that highlighted the extent to which both broadcasters and listeners were still honing their craft just a couple of short years after public broadcasting began.

In examining the public reaction to these plays, this chapter reveals how debates about the (ir)responsibility of broadcasters and the (in)vulnerability of audiences—so familiar to scholars of the *War of the Worlds* event—were inflected in a European context of public service broadcasting and against a background of class division and street politics. In so doing, it highlights the parallels and differences between these earlier broadcasts and the more famous American radio scare of 1938, and so contributes a cross-national perspective that is so often missing in broadcasting histories.

Radio in the Weimar Republic

The Weimar Republic (1918–1933) was established in the aftermath of Germany's defeat in the First World War, a defeat that had plunged the country into a period of economic, political and social turmoil. The liberal Weimar Constitution was set against a background of political fragmentation and burgeoning extremism on left and right, fuelled by post-war recriminations and mistrust. The economy, already in crisis due to the War and demobilization, was further stung by the punitive reparations imposed by the victors at Versailles. When Germany failed to keep up its payments, the French occupied the Ruhr region, exacerbating the sense of crisis. The government's response of printing money only fed a spiralling inflation that reached its height in the autumn of 1923, producing iconic images of people wheeling barrows of worthless paper money through the streets. The general atmosphere of chaos and abandon was reflected in new social and cultural practices that gave rise in almost equal measure either to declarations of moral panic or celebrations of the potential for radical renewal. Following the hyperinflation, currency reform, the injection of American money, and a program of rationalization ushered in a period of relative stability—only to come to an abrupt end with the Wall St. Crash of 1929. The privations of the Depression in Germany were harsh, and provided a fertile context for the political extremism that, by the start of 1933, led the National Socialists to power. In short, the Weimar Republic reeled from one catastrophe to another, and on many different levels was marked by a general sense of instability, transience and crisis.

It was into this febrile mix that public radio entered in November 1923—at the height of the Great Inflation, and against a background of separatist extremism, such as Hitler's failed Beerhall Putsch earlier that month in Munich. Thousands of men returning from the war had been trained in radio technology, and the spectre of radio as an interactive communications technology in the hands of either the extreme left or right haunted the mainstream political imagination. Although the 1918 Constitution explicitly guaranteed freedom of speech and prohibited censorship, radio was never considered for such freedoms: its potential as a medium for political influence and agitation was all too evident to the authorities.

In this context, German radio came to be established as a closely regulated network of regional state-owned stations broadcasting pre-approved programs produced by companies funded in part by private capital, but closely controlled by local and national government, and aimed at licensed listeners (Lerg, 1970, p. 373). The key programming policy developed under the head of German radio, Hans Bredow, was to keep politics off the air altogether. To this end, broadcasts were screened ahead of transmission by politically appointed censorship bodies and local cultural advisory boards. As a result, most output tended to be rather bland, running scared of both controversy and innovation, and reducing this brand new medium of communication to a channel for recycling established cultural forms.

There were, however, notable exceptions to this "defensive modernization" (Führer, 1996, p. 777), particularly where there were visionary directors who wanted to develop new "radiogenic" art forms, and who were tuned in to the broader culture of experimentation and daring characterizing so much of Weimar film, theatre, literature, music, cabaret and criticism. One such visionary was Hans Flesch (1896–1945), the first artistic director of the radio station in Frankfurt. Flesch quickly built up a reputation for sponsoring avant garde artists on the air—during his career he commissioned, among others, Paul Hindemith, Arnold Schönberg, Bertolt Brecht, Kurt Weill, Walter Benjamin, Walter Ruttmann and Alfred Döblin. By 1929, he had been poached by Hans Bredow to head the Berliner Funk-Stunde in order to rescue the waning artistic reputation of the country's largest and most important station (Leonhard, 1997, pp. 81–85; Weil, 1996). The broadcast of *Der Minister ist ermordet!* just a few months into his tenure was to prove a great test for Flesch's commitment to innovative and provocative broadcasting.

On October 24 1924, just seven months after the very first broadcast in Frankfurt, Flesch had produced his now famous "study for a broadcast grotesque," *Zauberei auf dem Sender* (*Magic on the Radio*). This was the first bespoke radio play ever broadcast in Germany. *Magic on the Radio* was set in the radio station itself and, rather like *War of the Worlds* some fourteen years later, offered a critical self-reflection on the world of broadcasting and the conventions it was beginning to establish (Gilfillan, 2009, p. xxi). Flesch wanted to exploit the new technical and artistic potential that the radio offered, not least its liveness, its distant and dispersed audience, and its disembodied voice. An extraordinarily imaginative production, it had its characters—a magician and a fairy-tale teller—interrupting the apparently bona fide announcer, and incorporated as sound effects the kind of white noise and other interference that was so common a part of the listener experience in the early 1920s. In this way it was an early demonstration of radio art as acoustic montage, as the art of the machine, as construction and not just reproduction. It was also a satirical and playful exploration of radio as illusion, magic, simulation, deception (Hagen, 1999). In so doing it put center stage the question of radio's trustworthiness; the same question that would be at the heart of the wireless scares to come. The placelessness, the invisibility, the transitoriness of radio, all raised questions about how the audience was expected to listen in good faith, trusting in radio's illusion of the real, its construction of authority.

If it was the job of the new radio art to question and probe the realist and reproductive aesthetic that was already dominating the schedules, it was, for Flesch, the job of radio more generally to bring news of public life instantaneously, directly and vividly to the ears of the listening public—a job that was foiled by both technical and political constraints. Flesch realized that if the Grunewald went up in flames, or civil war broke out—or if a Minster was assassinated in the street—the radio could not report it live (Hagen, 1999). In fact, just a month before his arrival in Berlin, there had been several days of violent confrontation between Communist protesters and the Prussian police following the banned May Day demonstrations, that had left some thirty civilians dead and over a thousand taken into custody. The radio had been so reticent to cover the events—the press relished reporting—that a young man who had been listening to his radio walked, unsuspecting, into the street and was hit by a bullet (Weil, 1996, p. 240). The events of *Blutmai* (Bloody May) certainly heightened the divisions not only between left and right, but between the Communist Party and the governing Social Democrats. Indeed there was a marked rise in support for the National Socialists as a radical alternative after *Blutmai*—exacerbated by the onset of the Depression—even in staunchly Marxist areas of the capital, like "Red" Wedding (Bowlby, 1986).

There was general acclamation for Flesch's appointment in the liberal and leftwing press, which hoped he might be able to make some progress in refreshing the stale and unadventurous schedules of the Funk-Stunde. The right-wing *Deutsche Zeitung* however, warned its readers to expect him to undertake the same "bolshevist dictatorship" as he had practiced in Frankfurt where listeners had been "pained by the horrors of the so-called "new art" (RRG, *Deutsche Zeitung*, Apr. 30, 1929). In one interview, Flesch explained that his central watchword would be "tolerance." His aim was to bring "contradictory and antithetical opinions to the microphone," and hoped it would be reciprocated by "the same degree of tolerance among our listeners." The radio could be a salve for the political intolerance disfiguring German public life, if it could teach people to listen to one another again (*Funk*, Mar., 1930, cited in Jelavich, 2009, p. 60). It was to prove a vain hope, and the wireless scare of 1930 was just one indication of how the radio simply became another battlefield on which the opposing forces faced each other down.

On his arrival in Berlin in June 1929, Flesch was charged with renewing the "dilettantish" phase of radio with a new professionalism. One of his priorities was to encourage live journalism, by charging journalists to "sniff out" stories for immediate transmission. He had already been responsible for other journalistic innovations at Frankfurt, for example the live radio reporting pioneered in a series called *Disorientated Microphone* by Paul Hindemith (to whom he was related by marriage) and the celebrated reporter, Paul Laven. For the first time, listeners heard live soundscapes of the city and interviews with "ordinary" people talking about their everyday lives and problems (Laven, 1975, p.17; Schivelbusch, 1982, p. 65). And it had been under Flesch's direction in 1927 that Germany's first series of explicitly politicized talks was aired. *Gedanken zur Zeit* (*Thoughts on the Times*) allowed speakers with different points of view to take to the microphone in turns, "unhindered and unscripted" (Heitger, 1998, pp. 218–219). In Berlin he wanted to bring microphones into parliament, the courts, and connect public halls by cable to the studios to bring the radio right into the heart of public life; but he was foiled by the prevailing strictures on political content (Flesch, 1930). However, he got around the restrictions to a certain extent with a monthly *Retrospective* made up of recorded speeches and public events ("Die akustische," 1930, pp. 7–8; Heitger, 1998, pp. 409–410).

Flesch's reforms were not restricted to journalistic coverage. He declared that the radio's content was life in all its guises (Weil, 1996, p. 226). One of his most celebrated commissions was Walter Ruttman's now iconic imageless "sound film" of Berlin, *Weekend*. He also set up the world's first studio dedicated to "new music" and radio experimentation. Another innovation was a new department for the "artistic word," with Edlef Köppen as its head. It was here where the decision to broadcast Ebermayer's play was taken, with Max Bing, one of the in-house directors, appointed to direct under the watchful eye of Alfred Braun, then head of drama and radio plays (Leonhard, 1997, p. 292). Braun was a familiar voice to listeners as he'd been the station announcer in Berlin from the beginning (his famous "Achtung! Achtung! Hier ist Berlin!" was the blueprint for the play's own newsflash), as well as reporter, scriptwriter and director. He was also another leading light of experimental radio, and advocate of the "acoustic film," works that garnered both extravagant praise and virulent criticism from different quarters of the polarized press.

At first, the press had largely been behind Flesch's reforms, but by mid-1930 there was again talk of a "storm of dissatisfaction" swirling around the Berlin wavelength (RRG, *Berliner Lokalanzeiger*, Apr. 13, 1930), and more frequent attacks by the right-wing about the "class-war propaganda" and "radio monopoly" propagated by the Funk-Stunde (RRG, *Berliner Westen*, Mar. 27, 1930). It was in opposition to the perceived "red domain" of the Berlin radio that a new listeners' organization was established, the Reichsverband Deutscher Rundfunkhörer (National Union of German Radio Listeners), with the aim of mobilizing a "resistance" made up of "bourgeois, Christian and nationalist" listeners (Koch & Glaser, 2007, pp. 101–102; Ortsgruppen, 1931, p. 5).[4] The Union quickly grew and, in time, would provide many of the leading figures of the Nazi radio system. Indeed, the organization of listeners was increasingly politicized on both sides (Lacey, 2005). The worker's radio movement was well established in Germany and, earlier in the month in Prague, delegates from across Europe had agreed to establish a Workers' Radio International (RRG, *Leipziger Volkszeitung*, Oct.10, 1930).

Dramatic License and Dramatic Censorship

By 1930, Erich Ebermayer (1900–1970) was becoming an established writer of expressionist novellas and dramas, and was moving in the artistic and bohemian circles in Munich, counting Klaus Mann and

Ernst Toller among his friends. He had already had one play broadcast, the story of *Kaspar Hauser,* an adaptation of his first theatrical success in Hamburg (which had starred the young Gustav Gründgens). He was also appearing regularly on the airwaves throughout Germany, reading from his novellas and poems ("Schriftsteller," 1924–32).

Yet despite Ebermayer's growing reputation, *The Minister's Been Murdered!* did not get on to the air without a struggle—indeed, there was almost as much controversy in advance of its airing as in its wake. The two-hour drama was loosely based on events eight years previously, when the then Foreign Minister, Walter Rathenau, had been assassinated by right-wing extremists, shortly after signing the Treaty of Rapallo with the Soviet Union. Ebermayer's father had been a lawyer for the prosecution in the trial of Rathenau's assassins, and Ebermayer had written the play hoping it might draw attention to the senselessness of the extreme right-wing's political murders. In January 1930, Ebermayer sent the script to the regional radio station *Mirag* (Mitteldeutscher Rundfunk AG), based in Leipzig, where the new station director, Ludwig Neubeck, had ambitions to refresh the literary output of the station (Leonhard, 1997, p. 293). At first it seems it was warmly received, but by mid-February 1930, the *Mirag* management, recognizing the potential sensitivity of the plot, had got cold feet and called Ebermayer before the censors (Direktion Mirag, 1930, p. 17). The play was rejected on both cultural and political grounds, to be neither broadcast from Leipzig, nor relayed from any other station that might accept it. One of the arguments that swung the decision was that Ebermayer had published "unfounded" claims about political interference at the station in the *8 Uhr-Abendblatt* three days earlier on March 14, namely that the scheduled broadcast had been stalled by objections raised by Dr. Ziegler, a Nazi party member on the board of censorship. Although the meeting rejected Ebermayer's version of events, it decided not to demand a retraction (Miraghaus, 1930).

Ebermayer's article had been published under the unambiguous headline, "Radio Censorship at Mirag: Thuringian Nazi prevents the broadcast of a play." It argued that the treatment of his play was politically partisan and marked a new low in the intellectual bullying of the broadcasters and the responsible authorities (RRG, *8 Uhr Tageblatt,* Mar. 14, 1930; *8 Uhr-Abendblatt,* Oct. 3, 1930). Ebermayer maintained that within two days of his submitting the manuscript, the head of the literary department, Dr. Eugen Kurt Fischer, had expressed his delight at receiving such a well-achieved piece of work and that he would press for it to be broadcast, subject to only minor changes. In a second meeting, according to Ebermayer, the details of the direction, the casting and the contract had all been settled for a first broadcast to go ahead on March 28 at 8pm, jointly with the station at Breslau. Happy that all was settled, the playwright went on a foreign trip, only to hear through the grapevine some four weeks later that his play had been rejected for political reasons. Ebermayer's letter to the newspaper was a protest at the "grotesque" way in which a play—which had won the plaudits and support of the literary department for its educational and radiogenic merits and that was supportive of the constitutional state—should be foiled by a lone National Socialist voice on the *political* board of review.

The machinations behind the broadcasting of this play, whatever the truth of them, were caught up in the increasingly bitter battles playing out between the parties and in the press about the merits or otherwise of an increasing politicization of the airwaves, which was itself an echo of the increasingly bitter politics playing out between an increasingly confident nationalist right wing and a reinvigorated left. Parties at both extremes were still banished from the airwaves, despite a gradual reinterpretation of the "non-political" guidelines that allowed political opinions into the schedules, if tempered by the watchwords of "parity" and "balance" (Lacey, 1996, pp. 49–53).

The script was eventually picked up by the newly adventurous Funk-Stunde in Berlin, although even there it was not unanimously welcomed (Jelavich, 2009, p. 118), and was duly broadcast at 8pm on September 25. The furor caused by the broadcast was immediate and widespread. The decision to present the events of the drama as if in real time played a large part in the scare, unleashing a wave of rumours about the assassination of the current Foreign Minister, Julius Curtius, and the imminence of a right-wing coup. Curtius, a member of the rightist German People's Party (DVP) had, co-incidentally, recently been attending a European conference in Geneva which, together with the memory of Rathenau's assassination still fresh in the collective memory, made the scenario all the more credible.

The broader political context also played its part in convincing the audience that what they were listening to was actuality rather than drama. Political militancy was intensifying as the economic Depression deepened. Indeed, just two weeks before the broadcast, a third of the electorate had voted for anti-establishment parties, with the Nazi Party—until recently a marginal group easily dismissed—having made significant gains. There had been growing tension in the streets of Berlin and elsewhere, and rumors of a fascist putsch were already rife.[5]

The play was broadcast on the same day that Hitler made a widely reported, inflammatory speech when he appeared as a witness for the defence in Germany's Supreme Court in Leipzig during a high-profile case where three army officers were accused of treason for plotting a Nazi coup. While trying to make the case that theirs was an ideological, not a militaristic movement, and that they respected the rule of law, Hitler nevertheless declared that, "when our movement wins its legal struggle [...] November 1918 will find its retribution, and heads will also roll" (Hitler cited in Hett, 2008, p. 73). Some listeners to the play that night apparently thought that the head of the Foreign Minister was the first such head to roll.

Responses to the broadcast should also be situated within a broader controversy over the responsibilities and censorship of drama on the radio, the direction of the Berlin station in particular, and the on-going politicization of the radio system that Hans Bredow had been determined to keep strictly above the fractious politics of the period. Various papers reported that the government had managed to delay the broadcast of the play until after the elections, but that it had not been able to prevent it altogether (RRG, *Deutsche Tageszeitung*, *Börsen-Zeitung* and the *Berliner Illustrierte Nachtausgabe*, Sept. 27; *Germania* and *Der Reichsbote* Sept. 30, 1930). Indeed, it seems that the regional board of censorship had overturned the advice of the Minister of the Interior, Joseph Wirth, to reject the play outright (RRG, *Frankfurter Oder Zeitung*, Sept. 28, 1930), who later expressed regret that the play had been broadcast in such a way (*Mitteldeutsche Zeitung* and *Essener Volkszeitung*, Sept. 28, 1930; RRG, *Rheinische Zeitung*, Sept. 27).

The right-wing press was variously astonished, dismayed and outraged that the Berlin station had managed to put on a play that portrayed right-wingers as lawless assassins. They called for the government to take action to root out and remove those "mindless" men responsible for such "scandalous," "tasteless," and "incomprehensible" programming, programming that was in danger of sparking not only internal rumor-mongering and unrest but international consternation, too. The story about the alarm in Berlin and the provinces was carried in the international press, including the *New York Times* ("Murder Play," 1930, p. 22), the *Manchester Guardian* ("Wireless Causes a Scare," 1930, p. 13), and European papers (RRG, *Die Reichspost*, Vienna; *National Bruxellois*, Sept. 27, 1930; *Petit Journal*, Paris; *Prager Tageblatt*, Prague). *The Times* of London reported, for example, that newspaper offices and the Foreign Office had been "overwhelmed with telephonic inquiries, some of them from outside Germany's frontiers" ("'Contretemps,'" 1930, p. 9).

Most of the regional press in the country at large simply reported the play as "a bad joke" or a "grotesque misunderstanding" (*Allensteiner Zeitung*, Sept. 27, 1930RRG; *Rhein-Main Volkszeitung, Hannoverscher Curier*), although some played on the tastelessness and lack of tact in the capital (RRG, *Münchener Neueste Nachrichten*, Sept. 27, 1930). The left-wing press in Berlin meanwhile generally applauded the contemporary relevance of the play's subject matter, but some quarters still questioned whether the director had "lost his senses" in choosing to start the play by mimicking an emergency announcement, and that care had to be taken by those in charge of such a powerful medium (RRG, *Berliner Tageblatt*, Sept. 27, 1930). The *Welt am Montag* (RRG, Sept. 27, 1930), a socialist paper, made the telling point that there had not been anything like as much outcry in the right-wing press when Rathenau had been assassinated for real.

Other press coverage concentrated on the artistic ambition of the play and admired the way the director had experimented with unconventional methods. The *Berliner Börsencourier* welcomed the way the play brought radio drama closer to the present and rejected conventional techniques, and appreciated the director's attempts to underscore the drama of the situation with acoustic innovations. *Tempo* thought that the elegance of its direction, the surefootedness of the storyline and the passion of its argument, made it simply the best contemporary piece that had been heard on the radio in recent years.

Vorwärts was impressed by the way the responsible figure of the Minister was contrasted with the "shadowy figures of the uninhibited, immature but politicized youth" (RRG, *Berliner Börsencourier, Tempo, and Vorwärts*, Sept. 26, 1930).

Several papers commented on the play's realism. The *BZ am Mittag* praised the play for having demonstrated a new standard for modern, topical radio art, and suggested that in blurring the distinction between life and art, it took the venerable traditions of realist theatre to new heights. *Der Kleine Journal* blamed the furor on the fact that the usual output of the drama department was so dull that most listeners just turned off when they heard the word, *Hörspiel* (radio-play). In fact, most of those who had been taken in by the announcement of the assassination, it suggested, would have been tuning in to wait for the news bulletin. That view was not shared by the *Berliner Morgen-Zeitung*, which said that with the sensationalist direction of this play the Funk-Stunde had taken realism too far (*Berliner Morgen-Zeitung*, Sept. 27, 1930; *Der Kleine Journal*, Oct 3; RRG, *BZ am Mittag*, Sept. 26 and 29).

Finally, other papers reflected on what the broadcast had to say about the power of radio and the vulnerability of audiences. The *Magdeburger Generalanzeiger* thought the play had performed an invaluable service in demonstrating the extraordinary power of the radio news service, and the woeful gullibility of some sections of the listening public (RRG, *Magdeburger Generalanzeiger*, Sept. 27, 1930). The *Chemnitzer Neueste Nachrichten* meanwhile playfully wondered if the sensation-hungry public would believe an announcement relayed from London that "Lloyd George has vanished without trace" (RRG, *Chemnitzer Neueste Nachrichten*, Sept. 27, 1930). The *12 Uhr Blatt*, however, ran a headline, "Much ado about nothing," suggesting it was only the "weaker" members of the audience who had been affected and that this was a small price to pay for "lively, topical and activist radio." The reason for all the hoohah, it claimed, was simply to whip up a political frenzy against Flesch (RRG, *12 Uhr Blatt*, Sept. 26, 1930).

Indeeed, one of the immediate consequences of the broadcast and the Interior Ministry's intervention was to sharpen the sense of crisis that had been brewing around the direction of the capital's radio station over the last year. Although the appointment of Flesch as director of the Berliner Funk-Stunde a year before had been widely welcomed by radio insiders and the liberal and leftist press (Leonhard, 1997, p. 82), his appointment, and his policy of sponsoring avant-garde art and increasing the coverage of current affairs, had also sharpened the view of the right-wing that the Funk-Stunde was a hotbed of bolshevists putting out Marxist propaganda.

The *Berliner Morgenpost* echoed a view that had long been dominant in Weimar radio, namely that politics did not belong on the air, especially at such a time of political tension (RRG, *Berliner Morgenpost*, Sept. 28, 1930). The *Deutsche Tageszeitung* went much further, arguing that the Berliner Funk-Stunde had for a long time been slowly "killing itself" with its taste for politics, but that this was the ultimate suicide attempt, inviting the "tendentious" playwright Ebermayer to strike the final blow. Its headline ran, "Die Funkstunde ist ermordet!" In the most bitter attack on the "red station," the paper speculated that the supply of decent plays must be "devilishly thin." They congratulated the Funk-Stunde on the awe-inspiring success of the directors in playing with public opinion, challenging the nation and attacking the people. It was called a "radio putsch" in which the station had relentlessly exploited the turbulent times for its leftist propaganda (*Deutsche Zeitung*, Sept. 27, 1930; RRG, *Deutsche Tageszeitung*, Sept. 26).

In more extreme quarters, the modernist radio experiments were decried as a Jewish pestilence. Ebermayer was described as both a "Systemdichter" (a System Poet) and a "Judenfreund" (Friend of the Jews). *Der Minister ist ermordet!* and the surrounding uproar was seized on by his critics as evidence that Flesch was not up to the job of "cleansing" the Berlin station of its worst excesses although it was Edlef Köppen who came closest to being relieved of his post (RRG, *Frankfurter Oder Zeitung* and *Neue Mannheimer Zeitung*, Oct. 1, 1930).[6] With a particularly chilling turn of phrase, one paper looked forward to the time when the Nazis would be powerful enough for the Funk-Stunde to be finally "mucked out" [*ausgemistet*] (cited in Jelavich, 2009, p. 119).

Despite talk of their likely dismissal following the broadcast, Flesch, Köppen and Braun all survived at the Funk-Stunde until 1932, albeit weakened by the scandal, and increasingly compromised by the worsening political situation. Their much-heralded radio adaptation of Döblin's *Berlin Alexanderplatz* due for broadcast later that month, for example, was never aired, caught up in the post-election anxieties as well as the *Minister* affair (Jelavich, 2009, p. 119; Ryder, 2012, p. 36). Flesch eventually became the most prominent victim of the nationalist re-organization of German radio under the new Radio-Commissar of the Ministry of the Interior, Erich Scholz, dismissed because of "cultural-political considerations." Flesch and Braun were later among a group of leading radio pioneers who were incarcerated and subjected to a show trial once the Nazis came to power (Leonhard, 1997, pp. 333–334). Most of the new appointments made during the closing months of the Weimar Republic were chosen for their politics rather than their talents or experience in broadcasting. Flesch's successor as station director, Richard Kolb, was at least a radio theorist—but also an enthusiastic propagandist for the Nazis. When the Nazis came to power in 1933 and were able to take complete control of the airwaves, Kolb and his colleagues, under the rubric of Goebbels' new Ministry of Propaganda, were certainly all too aware of the potential of dramatic, emotional broadcasts to mobilize and intimidate the radio audience.

London's Wireless Scare of 1926

When *The Times* reported on *Der Minister ist ermordet!*, it reminded its readers that, "the incident recalls a similar *contretemps* in London some time ago, when listeners were alarmed by a vivid description of a revolution said to have broken out in London." ("'Contretemps,'" 1930, p. 9). The scare had occurred in the wake of a short BBC production, *Broadcasting from the Barricades,* aired on January 15, 1926 from Edinburgh which, tongue-in-cheek, feigned a breaking news report about a violent uprising in central London. The "burlesque" begins with its author and presenter, Father Ronald Knox (1888–1957), in the guise of a donnish broadcaster with a pronounced lisp, concluding a lecture on eighteenth century literature. He then segues into a parody of the ponderous BBC announcing style, relaying news of an angry crowd (led by a Mr. Poppleberry of the "National Association for the Abolition of Theatre Queues") apparently assembling in the capital:

> The crowd in Trafalgar Square is now assuming threatening dimensions. Threatening dimensions are now being assumed by the crowd which has collected in Trafalgar Square to voice the grievances of the unemployed. . . . ("Father Knox's Saturday," 1926, p. 5)

The broadcast then returns to apparently normal service, with a musical number, weather and cricket results, before returning to the now threatening mob which, over the course of the deadpan comic drama, replete with sound effects—still a rarity on the air in those days—destroys the Savoy Hotel, attacks the wildfowl in St. James' Park, and lynches a fictional government Minister called Mr. Wutherspoon, before marching on Parliament and bringing Big Ben crashing to the ground.

Just three years since public broadcasting debuted in the UK there were not yet any standardised conventions for relaying catastrophes as they unfolded; yet despite the sense of realism achieved by moving back and forth between regular programming and the increasingly urgent news bulletins, it still seems unlikely in retrospect—and indeed to many at the time—that anyone could have been taken in by such comic reporting:

> The Clock Tower, 320ft in height, has just fallen to the ground, together with the famous clock Big Ben, which used to strike the hours on a bell weighing nine tons. Greenwich time will be given this evening, not by Big Ben, but will be given from Edinburgh on Uncle Leslie's repeating watch. Uncle Leslie's repeating watch will be used for Greenwich time this evening instead of Big Ben, which has just fallen to the ground under the influence of trench mortars. ("Father Knox's Saturday," 1926, p. 5)[7]

The rioters finally march on the BBC studios in Savoy Hill but, unlike the Martians who would later destroy the CBS building in *War of the Worlds*, they end up in the waiting room, reading copies of *Radio Times*.

Despite all the textual clues that this was a fictional representation—not to mention the pre-broadcast warning—there were plentiful reports of listeners confused, concerned or outraged by the "irresponsible" broadcast. The story was widely repeated of a woman who had fainted and of city officials from Nottingham to Newcastle who were apparently ready to call in the troops ("That BBC Scare," 1926, p. 2). The Dublin correspondent of *The Times* reported that, "stories spread through the city like wildfire" and that "many timid folk were genuinely startled by the news" ("Father Knox's Wireless Talk," 1926, p.

6). There were even reports of celebrations in Ireland as people believed that the House of Commons had been blown up, and the Irish government made diplomatic enquiries to establish the truth (Walker, 2011 as cited in Wilkes, 2011). Back in London, the phone lines at Savoy Hill had started ringing within 20 minutes of the broadcast, and so the news bulletin later that night tried to reassure its listeners, albeit in a somewhat exasperated tone:

> Some listeners who apparently only heard part of Father Knox's talk at 7.40 this evening did not realize the humorous innuendoes underlying his imaginary news items and have felt uneasy as to the fate of London, Big Ben, and other places mentioned in the talk. As a matter of fact, the preliminary announcement stated that the talk was a skit on broadcasting and the whole talk was, of course, a burlesque, and we hope that any listeners who did not realise it will accept our sincere apologies for any uneasiness caused. London is safe. Big Ben is still chiming, and all is well. ("Wild Tales ... " 1926, p. 10)

The Edinburgh producers were apparently rather buoyed by the proof of how realistic their sound effects had been, and one was quoted as saying, "I think that we are entitled to regard the whole thing as a compliment to ourselves" ("London Is Safe," 1926, p. 2). However, when the scale of the scare became evident, the BBC issued a more formal apology, expressing regret that any listeners had been "perturbed by this purely fantastic picture" ("Britain Is Alarmed . . . " Jan 18, 1926). In the end, despite the press excitement, the 249 complaints received by the BBC were far outnumbered by the number of positive letters received, and applications for receiver licenses showed a marked increase in the wake of the broadcast (Snoddy, 2005). Although there were rumours that Knox had been blacklisted by Reith, his friend, Evelyn Waugh, maintained this was not the case, and that in fact within a few months Knox was on the air again, parodying a scientific talk, "illustrating the sounds, now made audible to the learned, of vegetables in pain" (Waugh, 2005, p. 290).

Part of the explanation for the scale of the reaction has been attributed to the fact that there was heavy snow in the country on the day of the broadcast, meaning that there was a delay in the morning papers, and that this kept rural listeners believing the capital was in flames. It might also explain why, by the time the press was ready to respond, the story was largely about the irresponsibility of the BBC (a reaction motivated by the prevailing poor relations between the press and the radio), than about the putative panic itself. The Catholic paper, *The Tablet,* was just one that took Father Knox to task for treating such a serious topic as a "Red Revolution" so facetiously, writing that, "There are in England groups of hireling Communists who must have been enormously encouraged by the fact that many Britons were badly scared last Saturday" (cited in Waugh, 2005, p. 290). Indeed, the Russian Revolution was still fresh in the memory, as were reports of unrest in Germany and elsewhere. Moreover, it was broadcast only a few months before the crisis of the General Strike, at a time when class relations in the country were as strained as they'd ever been. It is worth noting that the vast majority of "listeners-in" during this early period would have been the middle classes who had most to fear about news of a proletarian—almost alien—insurrection (Crook, 1999, p. 124).

Evelyn Waugh (2005, p. 290), reflecting on the broadcast, maintained that it had had serious repercussions for revealing to politicians "the gullibility of simple people by this new apparatus," and was one of many to suggest that Welles had known of *Barricades*, and had set out to imitate the effect. Certainly, the event had received fairly prominent coverage in the United States. The day after the broadcast, the *New York Times*, for example, reported that: "Great excitement and fear were caused here [London] and in all parts of Great Britain and Ireland ... " ("Britain Is Alarmed," 1926, p. 3).

Just as with the *War of the Worlds* episode twelve years later, listeners were said to have been fooled by having tuned in after the warning that the news items were not to be taken seriously, together with a combination of rumor and newspaper coverage that heightened the effect. And, just as in the coverage of *War of the Worlds*, wonder was expressed that anyone could have been so naïve as to have been taken in by it, or so dainty as to have been physically affected.[8] A week later, another article described how the skit saw:

> harrowed ladies in remote country districts, who [...] in great consternation barricaded themselves behind their bedroom doors. One impressionable Sheriff in a northern county telephoned to the Mayoress of Newcastle to ask what the Lord Mayor and constabulary were doing to stave off the Red ruin.

The report went on to reflect that, "It was a good story, and the newspapers were full of it." In a final flourish, it summed up the event in a way that manages to be patronizing not only about gullible listeners in general, but about women in particular and indeed the British altogether: "It was thoroughly representative of this stodgy old country and the dear old ladies who have abandoned knitting needles for wireless sets" (Marshall, 1926, p. E1).

The scare had fewer repercussions for broadcasting policy than in the German case, although a few weeks later the *Daily Mirror* reported that, "another storm has arisen on the wireless waves." Chastened by the recent experience, the BBC was apparently now standing firm on their right of censorship having discovered that, "the ear is evidently even more sensitive than eye and ear combined. What can't be seen may easily be believed. The imagination supplies what the eye does not behold." The *Mirror* commented sardonically, that the BBC should then avoid all but "unexceptional" items, in order to avoid shocking or confusing "the evidently numerous people who have tender wireless nerves." It suggested, however, that "bold sensation-lovers" would "object to having the mild pace set for them by invalids," and took the opportunity to underline the need for an alternative broadcaster to the BBC, whose monopoly contract was up for renewal later that year ("Broadcast Nerves," 1926, p. 7).

The *Barricades* incident was also reported in the German press. Where the *New York Times* had thought the English particularly gullible, *Der deutsche Rundfunk*, rather presciently asked, "Would not many people in Germany, where we actually have experienced such events, have been duped by such a 'burlesque'?" (Bußmann, 1926, cited in Jelavich, 2009, p. 522). By the time of the *War of the Worlds* panic, Hitler was in power at the head of a regime that believed unreservedly in the power of radio propaganda; nevertheless he used news of the American panic to claim the immunity of the German people to such scaremongering, saying the *Volk*, "shall not succumb to a fear of bombs, falling—let us say—from either Mars or the moon" (Hitler speech of Nov. 8, 1938 as cited in Goodman, 2011, p. 267).

Conclusion

Neither *Broadcasting from the Barricades* nor *The Minister's Been Murdered!* have acquired the iconic status of the *War of the Worlds* scare. Any number of reasons might be mooted for that—the context and timing of the broadcast, the size of the available audience and the scale and public dimension of the reactions, the celebrity of its authors, the influence of the subsequent scholarly attention absorbed by a radio play about radio that seemed to reveal so much about broadcasting and its audiences. Indeed, the reaction to the *War of the Worlds* broadcast is very often told as a media-centric story. It was, of course, a drama that played self-reflexively on the broadcast construction of reality and to that extent it shared something with both of the earlier examples that had also appropriated the representation of breaking news. It also caused fear among those listeners who were not tuned in or attuned to the framing devices both in print and on air that announced these "news bulletins" as part of a drama.

All the examples demonstrate something about the degree of authority and trust that had remarkably quickly been established by the broadcasters, not least evidenced in the subsequent public debates about whether these dramas had taken the trust of their audiences in vain—or whether they had done the public a service in puncturing people's blind faith in the broadcast word. Certainly, too, the extent of the press coverage and commentary is notable in all three cases, and no doubt served to magnify the meaningfulness of these events at the time and in retrospect; although it is also the case that the impact of all three broadcasts was heightened, circulated and tested by word of mouth either in the home, on the streets, or on the telephone.[9] Moreover, inasmuch as these are media-centric events, they are also very much about press-radio relations at a time when the new medium of radio was threatening to usurp the newspaper as the primary source of topical and authoritative information.

The debates surrounding the more extreme reactions reported in the wake of these broadcasts in all three cases are also incarnations, of course, of on-going debates about the gullibility, nervousness and inattention of mass audiences. Primarily, these judgments about the audience were used as markers of distinction, revealing at least as much about the critics as about the listeners. But it is interesting to note how the transnational coverage of these "panicked" audiences reveal national as well as gendered and class stereotypes in this regard. Indeed, the international coverage of all three broadcasts is interesting in its own right, reinforcing the sense that these were highly unusual events and that the prevailing assumption was actually that listeners of whatever nationality, political persuasion or educational status very rarely "misunderstood" broadcast address. Moreover, the way in which public discourse surrounding each new event referred back at some point to the one before, even across national borders, indicates how these events took on a mythical status that outlived and exceeded any immediate effect they might have had. While coverage and commentary at the time was briefly intense in all cases, their lasting effect was to have become touchstones in the on-going debates about the relative power and responsibilities of the media and their publics.

All three broadcasts also play with the complex interchange between fact and fiction, artifice and reality, reporting and imagination, crisis and composure. They resonated because they all, in their different ways, dealt with disasters that were not only reported in the contemporary broadcasting vernacular of unfolding catastrophes, but seemed plausible within the listeners' wider experience of events and discourses unfolding in the public sphere, be they insurrections, assassinations or threats of invasion.

The differences between the three incidents, however, are also instructive. They are, in part, to be explained by the different status that radio itself had acquired over the twelve years between 1926, when broadcasting genres were still in flux, through 1930 when in Germany, as elsewhere, there was a new focus on using the radio for live coverage of unfolding events, to 1938 by which time radio news in America had achieved a degree of familiarity and authority for large sections of the population. The *Barricades* skit, never intended as a serious critique of the broadcast form, seems not to have caused any great national soul-searching about the intelligence or otherwise of the British people; nor did it inspire any great internal policy discussions within the BBC. Reith was famously ill disposed to audience research, and it seems as if he was just as unimpressed with demands to change company policy in the wake of this untoward and unexpected audience reaction. While opinions differ on whether the Mercury Theater production deliberately set out to cause a stir, there was clearly some anticipation of controversy in advance of the Berlin broadcast, but the risk was taken deliberately by a station management committed to artistic experimentation and faith, against the odds, in the tolerance of the listening public. In this respect, it is noteworthy that the European examples were broadcast on public service stations that had a near monopoly of listeners unlike the Mercury Theater of the Air, which was only ever intended as minority radio—generally achieving less than 4% of the available audience in 1938 (the comedy on rival network NBC, being ten times as popular) (Goodman, 2011, p. 258).

The *War of the Worlds* shared a sense of the fantastical with the *Barricades* broadcast, but shared the aspiration to "quality" drama with Ebermayer's play. The latter is distinguished by its being based on recent historical events with its intention more to provide a critical dramatization and commentary on the prevailing political situation than a parody or reflection on the medium of communication. The commentaries on the response to the German broadcast were also defined at least as much by the stark political divisions as by the cultural divide. Where the prolific debate in America in 1938 centred, broadly speaking, on the varieties of self-government required of listeners to mitigate against media manipulation as a way of off-setting the prospect of more restrictive regulation of the airwaves or constraints on the constitutional freedoms of speech, the debate in Germany centered much more on the shortcomings of the broadcasters, and the wireless scare of 1930 became another small stepping stone on the path to the centralization and political control of the airwaves.

Notes

[1] The article was entitled, "Great Mischief and Grotesque Tastelessness at the Berlin Radio Station." The German newspaper references throughout are taken primarily from the *Reichsrundfunkgesellschaft* (RRG) clipping file, held at the Bundesarchiv (BArch), file R78/836, pp. 157-166.

[2] The BBC has a short soundclip of the broadcast available as part of its 90 X 90 series; a collection of ninety 90-second clips from spanning 90 years of BBC history. *The Riot that Never Was* is available at http://www.bbc.co.uk/programmes/p0103xc0.

[3] There are only the scantest references to *Der Minister* in the standard histories of German radio (Bausch, 1956; Dussell, 2004; Leonhard, 1997; Lerg, 1970), or even, with the exception of Jelavich (2009, pp. 117–119), in the more specialized literature on German radio plays (Bösch and Borutta, 2005, p. 25; Hagelüken, 2008, p. 38, n. 13; Hörburger, 1977, p. 393; Leonhard, 2001, p. 1473; Schätzlein, 2001, p. 184; Schwitzke, 1963, pp. 41 and 107). For discussions of the BBC play, see Crook (1999, pp. 123–124) and Walker (2011, p. 55).

[4] See also, RRG, *Berliner Illustrierte Nachtausgabe*, Jun. 6, *Deutsche Tageszeitung*, Aug. 9, and *Ulmer Tageblatt*, Aug. 11, 1931.

[5] The Communist paper, *Die Welt am Abend*, for example, published a story about how the Americans were implicated in a conspiracy with Chancellor Brüning and the German bankers to institute a Nazi coup d'état. Though there was plenty of violence on the streets, by this time Hitler was clear that he did not want a coup, but was confident he could manipulate the existing system to come to power (Burke, 1994, pp. 81–3).

[6] It was in 1930, incidentally, that Köppen's celebrated autobiographical anti-war novel, *Heeresbericht*, was published, written in the style of an acoustic montage (Schafnitzel, 2003).

[7] Uncle Leslie was one of the *Children's Hour* presenters in Edinburgh.

[8] This play is cited as a previous example of a panic broadcast in Cantril's study, ([1940]2009), p. xxvii.

[9] See Hayes and Battles (2011) for a detailed of discussion of the role of social and technological networks in the *War of the Worlds* response, even during a period of centralized media.

References

Bösch, F., & Borutta, M. (2006). Medien und Emotionen in der Moderne: Historische Perspektiven. In F. Bösch & M. Borutta (Eds.), *Die Massen bewegen: Medien und Emotionen in der Moderne* (pp. 13–41). Frankfurt a.M.: Campus Verlag.

Bausch, H. (1956). *Der Rundfunk im politischen Kräftespiel der Weimarer Republik 1923–1933*. Tübingen: Mohr.

Bowlby, C. (1986). Blutmai 1929. Police, parties and proletarians in a Berlin confrontation. *The Historical Journal, 29*(1), 137–58.

Britain is alarmed by burlesque radio "news" of revolt in London and bombing of commons. (1926, Jan. 17). *New York Times*, p. 3.

Broadcast nerves. (1926, Feb. 9). *Daily Mirror*, p. 7.

Burke, B.V. (1994). *Ambassador Frederic Sackett and the collapse of the Weimar Republic, 1930–1933*. Cambridge, UK: Cambridge University Press.

Bußmann, E. (1926, Feb. 21). "Revolution im Rundfunk: Eine mißglückte Funkburleske in England." *Der Deutsche Rundfunk, 4(8)*.

Cantril, H., Gaudet, H. & Herzog, H. (2008). *The invasion from Mars: A study in the psychology of panic*. London, UK: Transaction Publishers.

Carter Hett, B. (2008). *Crossing Hitler: The man who put the Nazis on the witness stand*. Oxford: Oxford University Press.

"Contretemps" of a Berlin broadcast. (1930, Sept. 27). *The Times*, p. 9.

Crook, T. (1999). *Radio drama: Theory and practice*. New York, NY: Routledge.

Die akustische Monatsschau des Rundfunks. (1930). *Funk, 7(2)*, 7–8.

Direktion Mirag. (1930). Letter to the Finanzgerichtspräsident Dr. Gerlach (Feb. 14). BArch R78/602, p.17.

Dussell, K. (2004). *Deutsche Rundfunkgeschichte*. Konstanz: UVK.

Father Knox's Saturday night: "The revolution of 1926." Had listeners-in excuse for alarm? The skit reproduced. (1926, Jan. 19). *The Manchester Guardian*, p. 5.

Father Knox's wireless talk: An imaginary revolution explained. (1926, Jan. 18). *The Times*, p. 6.

Flesch, H. (1930). Report to the Prussian justice minister, September 13. BArch R78/602, pp.79–80.

Führer, K. C. (1997). A medium of modernity? Broadcasting in Weimar Germany 1923–1932. *The Journal of Modern History, 69(2)*, 722–53.

Gilfillan, D. (2009). *Pieces of sound: German experimental radio*. Minneapolis, MN: University of Minnesota Press.

Goodman, D. (2011). *Radio's civic ambition: American broadcasting and democracy in the 1930s*. New York, NY: Oxford University Press.

Hagelüken, A. (2008). Eine originäre Kunst für das Radio. In H. Schulze (Ed.). *Sound studies: Traditionen-methoden-desiderate: eine Einführung* (pp. 29–56). Bielefeld: transcript Verlag.

Hagen, W. (1999) Der neue Mensch und die Störung: Anmerkungen zum frühen Hörspiel in Deutschland. Retrieved from http://www.whagen.de/Habilitation/NeueMenschStoerung.

Hayes, J. & Battles, K. (2011). Exchange and interconnection in US network radio: A reinterpretation of the 1938 *War of the Worlds* broadcast. *The Radio Journal: International Studies in Broadcast and Audio Media, 9(1)*, 51–62.

Heitger, U. (1998). *Vom Zeitzeichen zum politischen Führungsmittel: Entwicklungstendenzen und strukturen der Nachrichtenprogramme des Rundfunks in der Weimarer Republik, 1923–1932*. Münster: Lit Verlag.

Hörburger, C. (1977). Zum Problem der literarischen und rundfunkpolitischen Anpassung der Hörspielautoren der 20er Jahre an das Medium Rundfunk. In H. Kreuzer & V.Canaris (Eds.), *Literaturwissenschaft—Medienwissenschaft* (pp. 44–60). Heidelberg: Quelle and Meyer.

Jelavich, P. (2009). *Berlin Alexanderplatz: Radio, film, and the death of Weimar Culture*. Berkeley: University of California Press.

Koch, H.J. & Glaser, H. (2007). *Ganz Ohr: Eine Kulturgeschichte des Radios in Deutschland*. Cologne: Böhlau Verlag.

Köppen, E. (1930/2004). *Heeresbericht.* Munich: Deutsche Verlags-Anstalt.
Knox, R.A. (1928). A forgotten interlude. In *Essays in satire.* London: Sheed and Ward.
Lacey, K. (1996). *Feminine frequencies: Gender, German radio, and the public sphere, 1923–1945.* Ann Arbor: University of Michigan Press.
Lacey, K. (2005) Öffentliches Zuhören: Eine alternative Geschichte des Radiohörens. In D. Gethmann & M. Stauff (Eds.), *Politiken der Medien* (pp.195–210). Zurich-Berlin: Diaphanes
Laven, P. (1975). Aus dem Erinnerungsbrevier eines Rundfunkpioniers. In G. Hay (Ed.). *Literatur und Rundfunk. 1923–1933* (pp. 5–33). Hildesheim: Gerstenberg.
Lerg, W.B. (1970). *Die Entstehung des Rundfunks in Deutschland: Herkunft und Entwicklung eines publizistischen Mittels.* Landau: Knecht Verlag.
Leonhard, J. F. (Ed.). (1997). *Programmgeschichte des Hörfunks in der Weimarer Republik.* Munich: Deutscher Taschenbuch Verlag.
Leonhard, J. F., Ludwig, H. W., & Schwarze, D. (Eds.). (2001). *Medienwissenschaft: Ein Handbuch zur Entwicklung der Medien und Kommunikationsformen.* Berlin: de Gruyter.
London is safe: BBC's "news" of revolution scares Britain: Big Ben blown up! (1926, Jan. 18). *The Daily Mirror,* p. 2.
Marshall, E. (1926, Jan. 24). Hoaxes and politics fail to win Britain: Father Knox's radio revolution and Lloyd George's shifts fall flat with public." *New York Times,* p. E1.
Miraghaus, Leipzig, minutes. (1930). (Mar. 17). BArch R78/602, p. 23.
"Murder play on Berlin radio starts assassination rumors." (1930, Sept. 26). *New York Times,* p. 22.
Ortsgruppen funksobleute minutes. (1931). (Dec. 3). BArch NS2/1178, p. 5.
RRG, *Reichsrundfunkgesellschaft* (National Radio Company) Press Clipping File. (1930–1932). Bundesarchiv (Federal German Archive) R78/386, 157–166). Berlin-Lichterfelde, Germany.
Ryder, R.G. (2012). When only the ears are awake: Günther Eich and the acoustical unconscious. In F. Feiereisen & A. Merley Hill (Eds.), *Germany in the loud twentieth century: An introduction* (pp. 35–50). Oxford. UK: Oxford University Press.
Schätzlein, F. (2001). Mobile Klangkunst. In A. Stuhlmann (Ed.). *Radio-kultur und Hörkunst: Zwischen Avantgarde und Popularkultur, 1923–2001* (pp. 176–195). Würzburg: Verlag Königshausen & Neumann.
Schafnitzel, R. (2003). Die vergessene collage des ersten weltkrieges edlef koppen: Heeresbericht (1930). *Amsterdamer Beiträge zur neueren Germanistik, 53*(1), 319–341.
Schivelbusch, W. (1982). *Intellektuellendämmerung. Zur Lage der Frankfurter Intelligenz in den zwanziger Jahren.* Frankfurt a.M.: Insel-Verlag.
Schöning, K. (1991). The contours of acoustic art. *Theatre Journal, 43*(3), 307–324.
Schriftsteller im Rundfunk: Autorenauftritte im Rundfunk der Weimarer Republik 1924–32. [German Radio Archives register of authors on the air.] Retrieved from http://www.dra.de/rundfunkgeschichte/schriftsteller/index.php

Schwitzke, H. (1963). *Das Hörspiel: Dramaturgie und Geschichte*. Köln/Berlin. Retrieved from http://www.mediaculture-online.de/Geschichte-desHoerfunksHoers.123+M5e79b9133cf.0.html.

Snoddy, R. (2005). Show that sparked a riot. *BBC Newswatch* (June 13). Retrieved from http://www.bbc.co.uk/newswatch/.

"That BBC scare: A lord mayor's view." (1926, Jan. 19). *Daily Mirror*, p. 2.

Walker, D. (2011). *BBC Scotland: The first 50 years*. Edinburgh, UK: Luath Press.

Waugh, E. (2005). *Two lives: Edumund Campion and Ronald Knox*. London, UK: Continuum.

Weil, M. (1996). Hans Flesch: Rundfunkintendant in Berlin. *Rundfunk und Geschichte*, 4, 223–43.

Wild tales: Wireless listeners' alarm: Father Ronald Knox causes a stir. (1926, Jan. 18). *The Glasgow Herald*, p. 10.

Wilkes, D. (2011). "Bolsheviks are attacking the palace and Big Ben has been destroyed: The fake BBC radio bulletin that terrified listeners in 1926." *Mail Online* (Oct. 12). Retrieved from http://dailymail.co.uk.

Wireless causes a scare: Rumour of minister's "assassination." (1930, Sept. 27). *The Manchester Guardian*, p. 13.

CHAPTER FOUR

Receiving the *War of the Worlds* "Panic" from Across the Atlantic: British Press and Public Responses in 1938 (and Since)

Neil Washbourne

In this chapter, Washbourne offers new evidence about the popular and scholarly reception of the *War of the Worlds* broadcast event in the UK. His finding that the UK press provided scant coverage of the "panic" underlines the importance of contextualizing the event as part of the struggle between "old" and "new" media in the US. That is, the US press was highly motivated to probe and criticize the *War of the Worlds* broadcast as evidence of the irresponsibility of its upstart radio competitor (Campbell, 2010). In general, the UK press coverage articulated the same concerns expressed in the US press that the "panic" evidenced the general public's inability to exercise critical faculties in the new media environment. In terms of scholarly reception, Washbourne finds that the focus of early UK media studies on television led to a lack of attention to the *War of the Worlds* until the rise of UK radio studies in the 1980s.

Introduction

This chapter explores the transatlantic, British, immediate and subsequent response to reports coming from America regarding the 1938 *War of the Worlds* broadcast event. The initial UK reception of the broadcast focused on sensational accounts of the "panic," including some implicit claims that Americans were more prone to such responses, but mostly universalized concerns about all listeners in a massively extended and intensified modern media environment. After this initial response, the broadcast received scant attention until the mid-1970s and after when the event became the subject of both popular and scholarly attention. Finally, the chapter considers British responses to the broadcast in the light of accounts (Camporessi, 1994; Hilmes, 2003, 2011) of the important and on-going links between US and British broadcasting in the twentieth century and since (cf. Washbourne, 2010, pp. 51–77).

This chapter examines British responses to the event by analyzing four national newspapers' coverage of the "panic." Two are elite 'broadsheet' newspapers; *The Times* (cf. 1938a, 1938b; 1938c) and *The Manchester Guardian* (1938a, 1938b, 1938c), and two are popular "tabloid" papers; the *Daily Mirror* (1938a, 1938c) and the *Daily Express* (1938a, 1938c). In the following sections of the chapter I trace public awareness of the broadcast event after the immediate period of reception, using all references to the broadcast in national newspapers of record (largely *The (Manchester) Guardian*; *The Observer*; and *The Times*) as a proxy for public awareness. I argue that it was not until the 1970s and 1980s that the *War of the Worlds* broadcast became a taken-for-granted item of "cultural literacy" in the UK due to television and press coverage of the event and publication of the memoirs and obituaries of participants. I further argue that overwhelming concern with contemporary (UK) television ensured that UK media studies—emerging from the later 1960s—barely mention the broadcast and then only in the later 1970s. Rather, the quasi-canonic status of the *War of the Worlds* as a media text was tied to the rise of radio studies as a discipline in the UK beginning in the 1980s.

Analysing the UK Press Coverage: November 1938

Although the broadcast led to some newspaper coverage, it was mentioned on the front page only once and there was no sustained and continuing engagement with the event after early November 1938. For example, it is not mentioned in the *The Times'* obituary of H. G. Wells, even in passing or by implication (*The Times*, 1946) and hardly mentioned again until the Quito, Ecuador radio panic of 1949 (*The Times*, 1949; *The Manchester Guardian*, 1949a, 1949b). Much of the coverage in 1938 in all four newspapers (*Daily Express*, 1938a, 1938b; *Daily Mirror*, 1938a, 1938b; *The Manchester Guardian*, 1938a, 1938b; *The Times*, 1938a, 1938b) focused on the "panic" aspect of response to the broadcast. For instance, the story headline in the *Daily Mirror* on November 1st sought to express how extreme the reaction was—"'War' Scare Victims flock to doctors with radio shell shock"—packing into the headline danger ("War"), anxious reactions (scare), animal behaviour (flock), and a new communications phenomenon (radio shell shock) itself drawing on the experience of the First World War and a medical model of listener impairment and intensity of the effects signalled through repetition (*Daily Mirror*, 1938a).

The predominant content in headlines on days one and two of the newspaper response was to link "war" and "panic" even if some papers played down the reactions supposedly involved. For example, one tabloid offered this tempered observation: "Official inquiry to follow 'war' panic broadcast" (*Daily Express*, 1938a). *The Times* was also quite measured in announcing, "Panic caused by Broadcast . . . " (*The Times*, 1938a), and *The Manchester Guardian*, like *The Times*, opted for understatement in its headline suggesting the audiences for the radio play were "Upset." Follow up stories also characterised the emotional reaction of audiences in America in their headlines, using words like "scared" (*Daily Express*, 1938c) and "'War' Panic" (*The Manchester Guardian*, 1938c).

The deep concern with panic was played out in the content of the articles, in particular in the tabloid newspapers. The *Daily Express* reported on "mass hysteria and panic throughout the United States" (1938a). The *Daily Mirror* discussed the "nervous prostration" of the audience that was "crying hysterically", that the broadcast led to "stampede" and "panic" and that some listeners believed an invasion was occurring of "German troops in powerful 'planes and Zeppelins.'" The paper further asserted that the reaction among the Black population of Harlem was the worst manifestation of this hysteria and that (unnamed) Columbia (and other) University "psychologists" dubbed "last night's madness as the greatest example of mass panic in world history" (*Daily Mirror*, 1938a). *The Manchester Guardian* (1938a) reported on "a remarkable wave of panic"—a Le Bon type image of individuals acting as a "psychological crowd" even when not constituting a physical one (Carey, 1992, p. 27; Le Bon, 2005, p. 16; Freud, 2001, pp. 72–3), and asserted that "[a] wireless audience of the entire nation was fooled to a considerable extent." *The Times* (1938a) used the "panic" more as the pre-text for a leader article criticising the United States' unpreparedness for the bomber war seen to be certain to break out soon in Europe.

Since the broadcast was hardly heard in the UK and because of its distinctive nature and its acclaimed effects, the press—with the exception of the *Daily Mirror*—gave significant attention to the *realism* of the broadcast.[1] The *Daily Mirror* (1938a) merely asserted that the listeners mistook the "fantasy" for "news" without suggesting that anything distinctive in the broadcast itself made that likely. The *Daily Express* (1938a) states that the broadcast inserted US locales for the original English ones in Wells' story, was "super-realistic," and "was produced with such vividness that some listeners believed it was fact, not fiction." The use of American locales, faithfully reproduced news bulletins and newsflashes, and the breathless tone of the broadcast (as reproduced in *The Times* by the use of hyphens) were explored in the two other papers. *The Manchester Guardian* (1938a) explained its distinctive form and content thus:

> a vivid account . . . [t]he programme began with music by a New York City hotel dance band, which was interrupted suddenly by a Columbia news announcer who reported that violent flashes on Mars had been observed by Princeton University astronomers. The music was resumed, but was soon interrupted again for a report that a meteor had struck New Jersey. Then there was an account of how the meteor opened and Martian warriors emerged and began killing local citizens with death-rays. Martians were also observed moving towards New York with the intention of destroying the city. Many people tuning in to the middle of the broadcast jumped to the

conclusion that there was a real invasion [. . .] in spite of repeated announcements during the broadcast that the drama was purely fictional.

In spite of the fact that *The Times* (1938a) used some of its news report to criticise America's lack of preparation for real-world air attacks, it explored, in the fullest mode of all four papers, what distinguished the broadcast:

> The story . . . [had an American locale substituted for the English [of Wells' novel] The programme opened with the usual announcements . . . then a setting was built up, first a weather report, then a programme of dance music from a fictitious hotel. In the middle of a number came a "flash" about an astronomer having observed a gas explosion on Mars. News bulletins and descriptive broadcasts followed rapidly—just as in the recent European crisis. A "meteor" had landed near Princeton, New Jersey, killing 1,500 persons. No it was not a meteor, it was a "metal cylinder"—and the top unscrewed—and monsters crawled out armed with death rays—and they were impervious to bullets—and they were marching on New York—and martial law had been declared and State Militia were out. And so on, all told in a voice of doom.

The Times pointed out that the play mimicked emerging broadcast news conventions, such as the newsflash, that had become common features of radio news "in the recent European crisis." These broadcast news practices were being intensively developed by US broadcast networks (CBS, NBC and Mutual) and, to a lesser extent, by broadcasters in the UK and Europe (Vaughan, 2008, pp. 61, 83, 103–4).

The broadsheet newspapers, therefore, give us more of a sense of what was distinctive about the broadcasts, whereas the tabloids—in particular the *Daily Mirror*—make it difficult for us to see how such responses to the broadcast were possible. By giving few details of the very distinctive nature of a broadcast described by experts (psychologists) as, "the greatest example of mass panic in World History" (*Daily Mirror*, 1938a), tabloid coverage implies that something about American listeners made them liable to panic. But such claims are not made openly in any of the newspapers nor even reported upon by any informants cited by the papers. Whether racist ideas as well as anti-American chauvinism may be "silently" at play would need further research to clarify in the papers' coverage of related issues. However, racism might be implied by the *Daily Mirror's* (1938a) focus on the panic lingering longest in Harlem, "where hundreds prayed nearly all night in the street. Hundreds fought their way into Father Divine's famous temple 'to see the end of the world come.'"

Certainly we can easily find in the British press of the time distinctive and sometimes negative characterisation of American audiences (Brown, 1938). However, the details of the coverage and the interest taken in the story also suggest and foreground universal concerns about the reasoning abilities of modern citizens. It should be noted that it was extremely common for intellectuals of both left and right in the UK at the time to be deeply concerned that their fellow Britons were almost hopelessly irrational and apathetic (Williams, 1996, pp. 64–5, 107) and even congenitally deficient (Carey, 1992; Childs, 2001). The pessimistic H.G. Wells certainly took the latter view (Carey, 1992, pp. 123, 128, 135). Such apathy, however, usually was talked of in terms of the passivity of the populace (closer to the *Daily Mirror's* "shell shock") not their frenzied panic (the *Daily Express's* "mass hysteria"). The poet, Louis MacNeice, cut through these self-serving claims with his observation that, "the crowd are always *other* people [my italics]" (Williams, 1996, p. 81).

Those universal concerns were raised in *The Manchester Guardian's* (1938c) coverage, on November 2nd, of a speech by Professor J. Graham Kerr, a member of the House of Commons (M.P.). Here Kerr was reported as responding to "the 'war' scare in the United States on Sunday." Kerr argued that modern citizens needed protection from "an intensive bombardment [his words]" which the journalist summarized as, "by means of the press, the wireless and the cinema." Such bombardment was seen as an infection requiring "immunisation" through proper (i.e., scientific) training. In a community with such training, Kerr asserted, "such nonsense would have no effect whatever. Everyone would have known there were no such things as Martians, no more than there was any such thing as a Loch Ness Monster."

Further evidence for the universality of such media concerns can be gleaned from Tom Harrison, a Mass Observation organizer and popular anthropologist, who reviewed Hadley Cantril's *The Invasion from Mars* study. Written for the magazine, *The Listener*, Harrison's review foregrounds conditions in common in developed societies, arguing that Cantril's study is "a handbook both to the nervous tension which underlies so much of modern life (even in peacetime) and to the immense power of radio . . . " (Harrison, 1941).

Orson Welles, mentioned in five stories, was the only individual directly associated with the broadcast identified in the immediate UK press coverage (*Daily Express*, 1938a; *Daily Mirror*, 1938a; *The Manchester Guardian*, 1938a, 1938b; *The Times*, 1938a). In the *Daily Express* he was referred to as making, "the imaginary details more interesting to American listeners" as the 23 year old "adapter . . . [who] substituted the names of American towns and cities for the English ones mentioned in the . . . [original] story." He was also referred to as "the producer" and cited as expressing regret that the broadcast "caused some apprehension." In the *Daily Mirror* (1938a) Welles was also referred to as "the producer" and the story implied that Welles was not entirely innocent of the likely effects of broadcast:

> . . . one man who knew the truth was as nearly on the verge of a breakdown as the misled millions. He was Orson Welles, the twenty-three-year-old theatre-radio prodigy who produced the radio version. "Too bad, too bad, terrible, terrible," he moaned today, "many people got excited but didn't we keep reminding them it wasn't really true?"

The Times (1938a) gave a little more detail on Welles' background: "[He] is known as an innovator on the New York stage. He dramatizes a book or a play every Sunday night on the wireless. . . ." *The Times*, however, made no claims concerning Welles' complicity in the "panic." *The Manchester Guardian* (1938a), likewise, gave a short account of who Welles was and his "responsibility" for the broadcast.

Presumably because of assessments of the interest of UK readers, the press gave more attention to H. G. Wells; the source of the story broadcast and of other stories exploring the complexities and perils of modern mediated life (Williams, 2007). Wells was mentioned in nine stories (*Daily Express*, 1938a, 1938c; *Daily Mirror*, 1938a; 1938c; *The Manchester Guardian*, 1938a; 1938b; *The Times*, 1938a, 1938b, 1938c), of which only three focused in any detail on his involvement in the aftermath of the broadcast. All three of these stories featured Wells' name in the headline (*Daily Mirror*, 1938c; *Manchester Guardian*, 1938b; *The Times*, 1938a). Though the other six stories merely confirmed H. G. Wells as the originator of the novel dramatized for radio, several of them gave Wells such prominence in the first paragraph as might confuse a reader into thinking Wells' role was greater (*Daily Express*, 1938a, 1938c; *Daily Mirror*, 1938a; *Manchester Guardian*, 1938a).

Two of the three stories that focus on H.G. Wells' role in the aftermath concern the use that Orson Welles and CBS made of the copyright permission they had to adapt and dramatize Wells' story (*The Manchester Guardian*, 1938b; *The Times*, 1938a). Their likely joint source is a Reuters news release to which *The Manchester Guardian* (1938b) gives credit. The story cited Wells' New York representative, Mr. Jacques Chambrun, as the source of Wells' views—and the latter was "deeply concerned." He further suggested that Orson Welles and CBS had overstepped their rights in adapting and dramatizing his story "with a liberty that amounts to complete rewriting and made the novel an entirely different story." H.G. Wells' concern appeared to be to make sure that he was not associated with the broadcast in particular to maintain his book sales in America and ensure that he did not get caught up in the litigation reported to be on the minds of "listeners who plan to sue the radio company and *everyone* responsible for the broadcast [my italics]" (*Daily Mirror*, 1938a). Negative outcomes did not, however, transpire for H. G. Wells. A *Daily Mirror* (1938c) report on the 14th November asserted that the "hysteria" associated with the *War of the Worlds* broadcast gave promotional attention to Wells, and led to the re-release, on Broadway, of the British film made of his novel *Things to Come*.

For all the interest shown in the *War of the Worlds* "panic" story, it only made the front page once and that was a story of less than 125 words (*Daily Express*, 1938c). The front pages of the tabloid newspapers for November 1st, 1938, when the "panic" story entered the British press, were made up of three kinds of stories in order of prominence: an impending European war and preparations being made for it; crime, murder and mysterious deaths; and celebrities. War preparations were dominant in the press because the broadcast occurred in the immediate post-Munich crisis period in which British diplomacy, of which the *Daily Express* was a devoted, even deluded supporter, seemed not to have achieved it aims and war became increasingly likely.[2] Only in the tabloid *Daily Mirror* (1938b) did the prominence of such war preparations have to compete equally with crime stories, in this case an American bank raid by "a pretty blond gun-girl, aged eighteen, and her boy friend," who held up a bank in Brookings, South Dakota. Such stories of (especially, American) "glamorous crime" were a pretty regular feature of the *Mirror's* coverage from the mid-1930s as it sought to increase its market (Wickham Stead, 1938; Smith, 1975; Conboy, 2002).³ In this context, human-interest stories of crime, capers and celebrity clearly outweigh a "panic" in America around a phenomenon—the radio drama—that, unlike an American film, was not directly experienced in the UK.

In contrast to U.S. newspapers, the UK press abandoned the "panic" story after a couple of days. The story had little sustained impact, as it was only mentioned in the press and magazines a handful of times between November 1938 and the Quito, Ecuador, *War of the Worlds* panic of 1949 (*Daily Mirror*, 1939a; Silvey, 1939; Harrison, 1941; *The Manchester Guardian*, 1940, 1949a, 1949b). This is despite the fact that there were many occasions on which a mention of the broadcast might be expected, including other radio hoaxes and panics that were experienced between those dates (*Daily Express*, 1940, 1949; *Daily Mirror*, 1939b), and the death of H. G. Wells (no mention in *The Times*, 1946, obituary).

War of the Worlds in the UK in the Post-War Period 1949–1970

Welles and the *World of the Worlds* panic did not become a taken-for-granted piece of common knowledge during this period. UK press references to the broadcast during this period were few, and made largely in relation to the Ecuadorian "panic" of 1949 and Welles' growing fame.⁴ For example, the "Panic in Ecuador: Broadcast of a Martian invasion" headline of a small story on p. 5 of *The Manchester Guardian* (1949a) leads to a story of about 200 words that details the deaths and injuries caused by the panic over the realistically staged broadcast and the subsequent riot by listeners. H. G. Wells has billing as the author of the original story and the only mention of the original broadcast follows thus: "It was 'The War of the Worlds' which inspired Mr. Orson Welles's famous broadcast in New York in 1938." The following day *The Manchester Guardian* (1949b) used its "Miscellany" column (views not news) to explore what we should learn from such a radio panic: "It really begins to look as though it would be better to forbid all broadcasts about Martian invasions [. . . .] With the world in its present jumpy state it would obviously be safer to have no dealings with radio representations of that risk." In this second article about the "Ecuador panic" the original is also mentioned rather briefly: "The Orson Welles [broadcast] from New York just before the recent war stirred up one of the most remarkable examples of mass panic and hysteria ever known."

Mention of the broadcast also appears in press coverage of Orson Welles as a director, producer, actor and dominating personality. For example, a substantial and appreciative profile mostly of Welles' film career (*The Observer*, 1955b) fitted the broadcast neatly into a broader account of the creativity of "an incomparable bravura personality." In addition, Welles' appearances on television garnered some interest (*The Manchester Guardian*, 1955a, 1955b; *The Observer*, 1955a, 1955b, 1955c) and he became so familiar through these appearances that he even became the subject of a throw away gag by Dickie Valentine, a British entertainer, who did impressions of the famous including one "of Mario Lanza (contriving at the same time to look like a small-sized Orson Welles)" (*The Observer*, 1955a). There was no further mention of the *War of the Worlds* broadcast in coverage of Welles' television career, despite the fact that an episode of the BBC's 'Orson Welles' Sketchbook' television series (one of six fifteen minutes episodes), broadcast on June 6th, 1955 and mentioned in *The Observer* profile, was devoted to interplanetary invasion in which Welles reported: "I was rather closely involved with what purported to be an invasion from Mars . . . we once sent some of them [Martians] to America, via the radio" (Orson Welles' Sketchbook, 1955). No mention in the press occurred even in passing, although Welles spoke directly to the audience through a single camera for fifteen minutes concerning the form and effects of the broadcast, the Cantril (1940) study, and the "fact we weren't as innocent as we meant to be, when we did the Martian broadcast."

The last press mention of the *War of the Worlds* broadcast before the 1970s concerns a documentary-style broadcast hoax about the reunification of an East German village into West Germany. The mention of the broadcast is ritualistic and vague: "[t]he effect was like that of Orson Welles's notorious radio version of 'The War of the Worlds' in the United States 30 years ago" (*The Observer*, 1969).

UK Media Studies, Television Audiences and the Bypassing of *War of the Worlds*

UK media studies scholarship almost completely bypasses reference to Welles and the broadcast due to an overwhelming focus on television (Hall and Whannell, 1964, pp. 20, 23, 259–61, 292–3; Tucker, 1966, p. 186).[5] Other classic works of UK media studies do not mention the broadcast either (Briggs, 1961, 1965; Donovan, 1991; Scannell and Cardiff, 1991; Scannell, 1991; Crisell, 1997, 2009; Curran and Seaton, 1997; Street, 2006). Further, there is only a single mention in any review or article, and then only in passing, in the most important UK media studies academic journal, *Media, Culture & Society*, published since 1979 (Glevarec, 2005).

UK Media Studies took off just as television became the dominant domestic medium. Consequently, both scholars and funding agencies, including the state, took primary interest in television (Halloran, 1968, p. 7). Simplifying greatly, we can divide UK media studies of this period into two strands. First, some scholars took a communication approach, which was very much influenced in theory and method by the range of US communication studies produced from the 1940s on. This group, especially associated with the University of Leicester, explored media effects as a complex phenomenon beyond any notion of stimulus-response models of behavior (Halloran, 1968, pp. 12–13; Halloran, 1970, p. 22), paying particular attention to "problem viewers" and the ways they use media, such as "juvenile delinquents" who sought out exciting rather than educational or cultural television (Halloran, Brown and Chaney, 1970, pp. 170, 172). A second scholarly group that emerged in association with the Centre for Contemporary Cultural Studies took a more self-consciously "critical" stance. Their concerns focussed around problematizing the "media text" in terms of the range of meanings associated with its reading and use, and the degree to which powerful agents could dominate these readings (encoding), constraining, if not determining, the meanings made from them (decoding) (Morley, 1980, pp. 9–15; Ruddock, 2001, pp. 116–27; Washbourne, 2010, pp. 102–8). For both groups, television became the dominant medium for analysis, occasionally supplemented by attention to the popular press (Smith, 1975; Ruddock, 2001: p. 121).

The attention of both UK media studies camps to media audiences might have led to considerable interest in the *War of the Worlds* broadcast, and might especially have encouraged engagement with Cantril's (1940) "hybrid" research (Ruddock, 2001, pp. 44–47; Hayes and Battles, 2011, esp. p. 55). However, the focus on contemporary UK media and culture left little room for interest in radio history. Some references to the broadcast did occur in UK media studies mostly after the 1970s, when it became an object of (educated) everyday knowledge (see the next section). For example McQuail (1977, p. 86) in a critical review of effects research, mentioned both the broadcast and the Cantril study in a sentence in which he expressed suspicion of claims about "collective panic," and suggested that precisely because of Cantril's research this "is the case most often cited." In the same year, Tunstall, in an influential book about the power of US media and Americanization provocatively titled *The Media Are American* (1977, p. 205), explored the financing of the Cantril study and implied that the "rather pedestrian findings and asides of liberal concern" aided CBS radio in disarming "more sweeping criticisms."

Popular Appreciation of Welles and Knowledge of the War of the Worlds

Even if Frances Gray's 2004 claim that "[e]veryone knows the story of Orson Welles's radio production of H. G. Wells's the *War of the Worlds*" (Gray, 2004, pp. 256–7) is hyperbolic, it became plausible in the UK due to the role of television and press coverage of the broadcast beginning in the 1970s. As we saw earlier, Orson Welles's television performances in the UK in the 1950s enhanced his profile as a personality, but it was his appearances, most importantly in 1974, on Michael Parkinson's BBC One popular Saturday night chat television show that played the largest role in circulating the story of the broadcast (Crook, 1999, p. 109; Crook, 2012).

The *War of the Worlds* broadcast became more widely known, too, through memoirs of Welles' radio company. John Houseman, the formal producer of The Mercury Theater broadcasts, was particularly prolific. He wrote three volumes of published autobiography available in the UK (cf. Houseman, 1972), which were excerpted, cited or reviewed in the British press (*The Times*, 1962, 1973a, 1973b, 1975; *The Observer*, 1973). Furthermore, Houseman's death warranted an obituary (*The Times*, 1988c), as did others members of Welles' radio company; the character actor Paul Stewart (*The Times*, 1986); and the radio and screenwriter Howard Koch (*The Times*, 1995, cf. Koch, 1975, 1979). Such on-going and sometimes very substantial referencing of the broadcast (*The Times*, 1973a) added to many other general references (*The Observer*, 1978; *Daily Express*, 1988, 1990; *The Times*, 1992, 1994a) greatly extended and intensified potential knowledge of the broadcast and "panic" in the UK making it an object of educated cultural literacy.

These references, however, were in some tension with perceptions of Welles' predominant role, in Europe, as a great filmmaker (and personality). Interest in the broadcast often followed from interest in Welles' cinematic career. That notion of the residing creative genius of film was a product of French intellectual cinephiles as they revelled in a backlog of American cinema denied them by wartime occupation (*The Observer*, 1991). *Citizen Kane*, made with unprecedented creative control and visionary cinematic devices, became the model film for auteur theory; it was voted the best film of all time every decade between 1962 and 1992 (*The Observer*, 1991; *The Times*, 1999). Interest in "cinematic" Welles specifically is present across an array of press stories beginning in 1980 (*Guardian*, 1982, 1985, 1986. 1990, 1997; *The Observer*, 1985; 1991; *The Times*, 1980, 1985a, 1985b, 1997, 2000a). It was also the focus of the BBC TV programme in 1982, *The Orson Welles Story*, a three hour long interview illustrated with film clips (*Guardian*, 1982; *The Times*, 1999).

Such rich and abiding interest in Welles' film output, however, did not completely overwhelm interest in the "panic" broadcast. For example, it was noted every time another "fictional documentary" created anxious audiences (*Daily Express*, 1977; *The Observer*, 1987; *The Times*, 1994b, 2001). It was often referred to when the distinctive virtues or possibilities of radio were explored (*Guardian*, 1995; *The Times*, 1982, 1988b, 1989), and the on-going interest in the dramatic which it highlighted led to the creation, in the UK, of plays concerning Welles' radio and cinema career (*The Times*, 2000a, 2000b, 2006).

Such knowledge was also encouraged through Welles biographies—published during the year of his death (and 70th birthday)—some of which especially keenly excavated the radio years (Leaming 1985; *Guardian* 1990). The distinctiveness of the *War of the Worlds* broadcast was illustrated through the US documentary "The Night that Panicked America" (*The Observer*, 1975), which, however, does not seem to have garnered a great deal of attention. A later BBC programme in the *Timewatch* documentary strand did garner attention in part because each newspaper made the programme a highlight for the evening's viewing and because that television documentary strand had a regular and substantial audience (*Guardian*, 1988a, 1988b; *The Observer*, 1988; *The Times*, 1988a). It was likely the first sustained coverage of the Welles broadcast—with excerpts and use of American newspaper headlines—which a large scale UK audience had seen.

Hearing the broadcast for oneself and assessing the radio drama became possible in 1995 as it was released in the UK as a popular audiotape with "the bits of hiss and crackle that give it a nice period feel" (*The Guardian*, 1995). Further, it was possible to assert that the *War of the Worlds* as Welles' masterpiece was; "as good as the very best of his filmmaking and better than most of it" (*The Guardian*, 1995). The BBC also broadcast the original drama the following year on Radio 2, a station with an audience in excess of 10 million listeners, on the anniversary date of the original broadcast (*The Times*, 1996). Now familiarity with the broadcast did exist even if it had limits. In spite of the fact that Cantril's (1940) *Invasion from Mars* study was published and reviewed in the UK in 1941 (Harrison, 1941), even educated newspaper cultural critics such as Bernard Levin, (also widely known in the UK as a cultural critic appearing on television), could assert unfamiliarity with the study prior to 1984. He was given a copy of the 1966 edition by a visiting American friend in that year (*The Times*, 1984). In reading the study he argues that such media "panic" could happen again and in the UK.

UK Radio Studies and Canonization of the *War of the Worlds*

During the period in which Welles' broadcast became an everyday item of knowledge in the UK, there also arose a movement of academics and practitioners specializing in radio. This began in the 1980s, in particular in response to the expansion in the number of local BBC and commercial radio stations—and thus the need to educate, practically and critically, their present and future personnel. Radio studies scholars at this time would have been aware of the broadcast as a result of the popular media coverage analysed above. However, such popular everyday knowledge can be difficult to pin down. Two of those radio scholars report that they are not sure when they heard of it first:

> . . . as a child. It feels like one of those bits of history and popular culture that's somehow always been there. . . . It's possible my first awareness of it was only when I had just joined the BBC in 1987. (Hendy, 2012)

> I can't remember. It was probably in a history programme about 1938, or a documentary, or when Orson Welles was interviewed by Michael Parkinson. (Crook, 2012b)

The breadth of radio studies research can be given illustration through reference to specialist UK radio studies publications each of which at least discusses Welles' broadcast—that it has become quasi-canonic (Crisell, 1986; Lewis and Booth, 1989; Scannell, 1991; Shingler and Wieringa, 1998; Crook, 1998, 1999, 2012a; Barnard, 2000; Hendy, 2000; Street, 2002; Gray, 2004; Chignell, 2009; Starkey and Crisell, 2009).

Canonization did not imply that the *War of the World* broadcast "panic" had achieved a settled meaning; rather, it meant that UK radio scholars perceived the *War of the Worlds* media text and listener reactions to be productive sites for thinking through texts, audiences and contexts. Crisell's work (1986, pp. 206–7, 217) drawing on Cantril's study began the UK canonization and forms a key reference for the later work of Hendy and Crook. Hendy recalls that he first read about the Welles broadcast as part of his BBC journalism training in 1987, and in a more sustained way in the following year as a visiting tutor was, "trying to get us interested in some of the landmark achievements of radio" (Hendy, 2012). He explores the Welles broadcast precisely because it has often been "invoked in the case of radio," he is careful to add "though not always convincingly"—as evidence for stimulus-response models in which media have narcotising effects on passive audiences (Hendy, 2000, pp. 135, 136). Hendy observes, however, that Cantril's study aids in seeing audience reactions to the broadcast as socially situated responses to the threat of war and other large scale social change going on at the end of the 1930s (Hendy, 2000, pp. 135, 136). He compares the Welles broadcast to Rwandan Genocide broadcasts drawing for the latter on the work of Kellow and Steeves (Hendy, 2000, p. 204), and finds in both cases that radio was the medium invested with the greatest public confidence. Hendy reinterprets Welles broadcast "as an indication, not of mass hysteria so much as how radio had become a taken-for-granted and *trusted* institution in daily life for most Americans" (Hendy, 2000, p. 205).

Tim Crook (1998, 1999, 2012a) has the most extended and intensive engagement with the Welles broadcast of UK radio studies scholars. He heard the broadcast from a recording in a London public library around 1974 or 1975 when he was in his teens (Crook, 2012b), and read literature on Welles when he started producing radio plays in 1987. His academic career meant that he lectured on Welles' radio work in 1991 and since (Crook, 2012b). In a recent book on sound studies (2012a, p. 209) Crook cites the broadcast as leading to "the first academic analysis [by Cantril] of a socio-psychological response to a media broadcast." In the same volume he also identifies the broadcast as the first full use of documentary characteristics, such as reporters responding to unfolding events, cross-cutting between radio studios and outside broadcast locations, and the use of sounds from actuality to flesh out and document the story.

Crook's detailed scholarly analysis of the *War of the Worlds* broadcast provides the best evidence that it has now become quasi-canonic in UK radio studies. Through close attention to the *War of the Worlds* radio text, Crook discovered that Paul Stewart, who played fictional reporter, Karl Phillips, copied the vocal inflections of Herb Morrison in his non-fictional live broadcast, the year before, during the Hindenburg airship disaster (Crook, 1998, pp. 95–6; *The Times*, 1973a,

1986). Crook's most sustained engagement with the broadcast, however, occurs in his book on radio drama, in which it is an object of study, a point of comparison for evaluating other radio plays, and an organising principle and leitmotif for the idea of the book itself (Crook, 1998). Chapter 11 deals with "Blurring fiction with reality," Chapter 12 "Radio drama panics: a cross cultural phenomenon" and chapter 14 with "The *War of the Worlds* effect," which is the creation of radio drama that astonishes, moves or perturbs an audience, despite the fact that radio is at best a secondary medium in contemporary wealthy societies (Crisell, 1986, p. 219).

Conclusion

This chapter has found that the initial UK reception of the *War of the Worlds* broadcast focussed on sensational accounts of the "panic." Some press reports made implicit claims that Americans were more prone to such responses, but mostly press coverage universalized concerns about all listeners in a modern media environment. After 1938, reference to the broadcast in the British press became sporadic until the 1970s in spite of the attention given to the outcome of the Quito, Ecuador, *War of the Worlds* broadcast of 1949, and Welles' own UK television discussion of the broadcast in 1955. It was not until the mid-1970s that popular television and newspaper discussion of the broadcast and publication of memoirs and obituaries of Welles' Mercury Theater colleagues made the broadcast widely known in the UK and thus an object of (educated) cultural literacy. The 1988 UK *Timewatch* documentary confirmed and informed this "cultural literacy" and gave a large scale audiences access to the sounds of the broadcast, mostly for the first time. Though there had been a burgeoning scholarship in media studies in the UK from the later 1960s, it had ignored the broadcast since its focus was very much both on television as the dominant domestic medium and the contemporary UK as the place of concern. From the 1980s, UK radio studies scholars promoted critical knowledge of the broadcast. They drew on the awareness created in the popular media in the UK since the 1970s and made the broadcast canonic—a founding radio text, event and scholarly contribution (Cantril, 1940)—in part to legitimate studying what others could regard as an old, dead medium. The response of these scholars shows both the continuing importance of the medium and the Welles broadcast as a productive text and context and thus amenable to on-going intellectual attention.

Notes

[1] Some UK radio hams did actually receive the *War of the Worlds* broadcast. One told the *Daily Express* (1938a) that he felt "no surprise" that there was a panic since, "*anyone* tuning in after it had started would certainly get the impression it was fact, not fiction, so realistic were the announcers and the effects [my italics]." This listener continued "[t]here was an eyewitness account of bombing planes ... Bombs could be heard dropping."

[2] See Faber (2008) for an excellent account of the failed diplomacy of Neville Chamberlain, then Prime Minister of the United Kingdom, and, in particular, pp. 189–93 for the supportive role played by the UK press, especially the *Daily Express*.

[3] The UK tabloid press was the particular object of an on-going debate about the "pessimism that had settled on Liberal Theory" concerning the role of reason in public life and opinion, in the post WWI world (Scannell and Cardiff, 1991, p. 13).

[4] An anomalous reference going into some detail about the broadcast can be found in a letter written by Burton Paulu to *The Times* (1959). Paulu was a U.S. scholar of British media whose familiarity with the radio play was likely shaped by his experience and training in the U.S. In his letter, he described Cantril's study as documenting, "the astonishing credulity of the public," and he universalized this public credulity by mentioning a range panics—past and present—in the UK (including the Ronald Knox hoax broadcast of 1926), France and Latin America. See further Paulu's first important book on British media (Paulu, 1956, p. 362).

[5] Two exceptions are media education studies published in the UK that had strong American connections (Gorham, 1950, pp. 143, 144; Siepmann, 1950, p. 186).

Acknowledgements

Thanks for precise editorial guidance and the help of Kate Nash, Tim Crook, David Hendy and James McGrath.

References

Barnard, S. (2000). *Studying radio*. London: Arnold.

Barnouw, E. (1968). *The golden web: A history of broadcasting in the United States, Vo.l II: 1933–1953*. New York, NY and Oxford: Oxford University Press.

Bartholomew, R. E., and Evans, H. (2004). *Panic attacks: media, manipulation and mass delusion*. Stroud: Sutton Publishing.
Briggs, A. (1961). *The history of broadcasting in the United Kingdom, volume 1, The birth of broadcasting*. Oxford: Oxford University Press.
Briggs, A. (1965). *The history of broadcasting in the United Kingdom, volume 2, The golden age of wireless*. Oxford: Oxford University Press.
Brown, I. (1938, February 6). The stage in New York—II: How audiences behave / "intellectual adolescence." *The Observer*, p. 13.
Campbell, W. J. (2010). *Getting it wrong: Ten of the greatest misreported stories in American journalism*. Berkeley, Los Angeles and London: University of California Press.
Camporessi, V. (1994). The BBC and American broadcasting, 1922–55. *Media, Culture & Society*, 16(4). pp. 625–639.
Cantril, H. (1940 [2007]). *The invasion from mars: A study in the psychology of panic*. (with the assistance of Hazel Gaudet and Herta Herzog). New Brunswick and London: Transaction Publishers.
Carey, J. (1992). *The intellectuals and the masses: Pride and prejudice among the literary intelligentsia, 1880–1939*. London: Faber and Faber.
Chignell, H. (2009). *Key concepts in radio studies*. London: Sage.
Childs, D. J. (2001). *Modernism and eugenics: Woolf, Eliot, and the culture of degeneration*. Cambridge, UK: Cambridge University Press.
Conboy, M. (2002). *The press and popular culture*. London and Thousand Oaks, CA: Sage.
Crisell, A. (1986). *Understanding radio*. London / New York, NY: Routledge.
Crisell, A. (1997). *An introductory history of British broadcasting*. London / New York, NY: Routledge.
Crisell, A. (ed.). (2009). *Radio: critical concepts in media and cultural studies*. Volumes I-III. London / New York, NY: Routledge.
Crook, T. (1998). *International radio journalism: History, theory and practice*. London / New York, NY: Routledge.
Crook, T. (1999). *Radio drama: Theory and practice*. London / New York, NY: Routledge.
Crook, T. (2012a). *The sound handbook*. London / New York, NY: Routledge.
Crook, T. (2012b, May 23 and June 5). Personal Email Communications with the Author.
Curran, J., and Seaton, J. (1997). *Power without responsibility: the press and broadcasting in Britain* (5th ed.). London / New York, NY: Routledge.
Daily Express, (1938a, November 1). Official inquiry to follow 'war' panic broadcast / Radio firm told to send script. *Daily Express*, p. 3.
Daily Express, (1938b, November 1). Big defence secret out—in 11/- report. *Daily Express*, p. 1.
Daily Express, (1938c, November 2). B.B.C may buy play that scared America. [by Jonah Barrington]. *Daily Express*, p. 1.
Daily Express, (1940, July 8). U.S. destroyer 'torpedoed'—Radio hoax. *Daily Express*,

p. 1.

Daily Express, (1949, September 16). Radio hoax offers free holidays. *Daily Express*, p. 1.

Daily Express, (1977, June 21). Last night's view: Every brain's gone to the moon [James Murray]. *Daily Express*, p. 19.

Daily Express, (1988, February 4). Shares plummet in nuclear scare: £2 bn lost in panic [Daniel McGrory]. *Daily Express*, p. 13.

Daily Express, (1990, August 3). Spaced out aliens. *Daily Express*, p. 30.

Daily Mirror, (1938a, November 1). "War" scare victims flock to doctors with radio shell shock. *Daily Mirror*, p. 2.

Daily Mirror, (1938b, November 1). Girl holds bank for 2 hours at gun point. *Daily Mirror*, p. 1.

Daily Mirror, (1938c, November 14). U.S. say "more of Wells." *Daily Mirror*, p. 25.

Daily Mirror, (1939a, January 11). "Roar" in sky spreads terror. *Daily Mirror*, p. 28.

Daily Mirror, (1939b, July 8). Faked S.O.S. rouses USA. *Daily Mirror*, p. 1.

Donovan, P. (1991). *The radio companion*. London: Harper Collins Publishers.

Faber, D. (2008). *Munich, 1938: Appeasement and World War II*. London: Simon & Schuster.

Freud, S. (2001 [1921]). Group psychology and the analysis of the ego. In *The Standard Edition of the Complete Psychological Works of Sigmund Freud*; Volume XVIII (1920–1922) (pp. 67–44). London: Vintage / The Hogarth Press and the Institute of Psycho-Analysis.

Glevarec, H. (2005). Youth radio as 'social object': the social meaning of 'free radio' shows for young people in France. *Media, Culture & Society, 27*(3), 333–351.

Gorham, M. (1950). *Broadcasting and television since 1900*. London: Andrew Dakers Limited.

Gosling, J. (2009). *Waging the War of the Worlds: A history of the 1938 radio broadcast and resulting panic*. Jefferson, NC and London: MacFarland and Co.

Gray, F. (2004) Fireside issues: Audience, listener, soundscape. In A. Crisell (ed.), *More than a music box: Radio cultures and communities in a multi-media world* (pp. 247–262). Oxford / New York, NY: Bergahn Books.

Guardian, The, (1982, May 19). Television: The Orson Welles story [Nancy Banks-Smith]. *The Guardian*, p. 11.

Guardian, The, (1985, October 11). Citizen Welles [Obituary] [Clancy Sigal]. *The Guardian*, p. 18.

Guardian, The, (1986, October 30). Going against the grain: John Houseman. *The Guardian*, p. 15.

Guardian, The, (1988a, January 30). TV and radio highlights [Val Arnold-Forster]. *The Guardian*, p. 14.

Guardian, The, (1988b, February 3). Watching brief [Francesca Turner]. *The Guardian*, p. 23.

Guardian, The, (1990, January 25). From the shadow [Clancy Sigal]. *The Guardian*, p. 25.

Guardian, The, (1995, July 1). The hiss, crackle and pop of Orson's masterpiece [Richard Boston]. *The Guardian*, p. 29.

Guardian, The, (1997, November 25). William Alland: An obituary from Xanadu [David Thomson]. *The Guardian*, p. 18.

Hall, S. and Whannel, P. (1964). *The popular arts*. London: Hutchison Educational.

Halloran, J.D. (1968). *The effects of mass communication with special reference to television: a survey*. Leicester: Leicester University Press.

Halloran, J. D. (1970). Introduction: studying the effects of television. In J.D.Halloran (ed.), *The effects of television* (pp. 9–23). London: Panther Books.

Halloran, J.D., Brown, R.L., and Chaney, D.C. (1970). *Television and delinquency*. Leicester: Leicester University Press.

Harrison, T. (1941, January 2). The Power of Radio. *The Listener*, p. 27.

Hayes, J. E., and Battles, K. (2011). Exchange and interconnection in US network radio: A reinterpretation of the 1938 *War of the Worlds* broadcast. *The Radio Journal: International Studies in Broadcast and Audio Media. 9*(3), 51–61.

Hendy, D. (2000). *Radio in the global age*. Cambridge. UK: Polity.

Hendy, D. (2012, May 24th). Personal email communication with the author.

Heyer, P. (2005). *The medium and the magician: Orson Welles, the radio years, 1934–1952*. Lanham, MD, New York, NY and Oxford: Rowman and Littlefield.

Hibberd, S. (1950). *"This Is London . . . "*. London: Macdonald and Evans.

Hilmes, M. (1997). *Radio's voices: American broadcasting, 1922–1952*. Minneapolis, MN and London: University of Minnesota Press.

Hilmes, M. (2003). British quality, American chaos: Historical dualisms and what they leave out. *The Radio Journal—International Studies in Broadcast and Audio Media, 1*(1), 13–27.

Hilmes, M. (2011). *Network nations: a transnational history of British and American broadcasting*. New York, NY and London: Routledge.

Hilmes, M., and Loviglio, J. (eds.). (2002). *Radio reader: Essays in the cultural history of Radio*. New York, NY / London: Routledge.

Houseman, J. (1972). *Run-through: a memoir*. New York, NY: Simon and Schuster.

Koch, H. (1970). *The panic broadcast: portrait of an event*. Boston, MA and Toronto: Little-Brown and Company.

Koch, H. (1979). *As time goes by: Memoirs of a writer*. New York, NY / London: Harcourt Brace Jovanovich.

Leaming, B.(1985). *Orson Welles: a biography*. London: Weidenfeld and Nicolson.

Le Bon, G. (2005). *The crowd: A study of the popular mind*. N.p.: Filiquarian Publishing, LLC.

Lewis, P. M., and Booth, J. (1989). *The invisible medium: Public, commercial and community radio*, London: Macmillan.

Loviglio, J. (2005). *Radio's intimate public: Network broadcasting and mass-mediated democracy*. Minneapolis, MN and London: University of Minnesota Press.

McQuail, D. (1977). The influence and effects of mass media. In J. Curran, M. Gurevtich and J. Wollacott (eds.), *Mass communication and society* (pp. 70–94).

London: Edward Arnold / Open University Press.

Manchester Guardian, The, (1938a, November 1). Radio play upsets Americans: "Martian invasion" of United States taken seriously. *The Manchester Guardian*, p. 11.

Manchester Guardian, The, (1938b, November 1). Mr. Wells "deeply concerned": "Unwarranted" rewriting of his novel. *The Manchester Guardian*, p. 11.

Manchester Guardian, The, (1938c, November 2). United States "war" panic: M.P.'s comment. *The Manchester Guardian*, p. .7.

Manchester Guardian, The, (1940, May 27). Miscellany: The "invasion" from mars. *The Manchester Guardian*, p. 3.

Manchester Guardian, The, (1949a, February 4). Panic in Ecuador: Broadcast of Martian invasion. *The Manchester Guardian*, p. 5.

Manchester Guardian, The, (1949b, February 15). Miscellany: Another alarm. *The Manchester Guardian*, p. 3.

Manchester Guardian, The, (1955a, April 26). Mr Orson Welles on commercial TV. *The Manchester Guardian*, p. 9.

Manchester Guardian, The, (1955b, September 24). Last night's tv: Some disappointments in second night of ITV [Bernard Levin]. *The Manchester Guardian*, p. 5.

Morley, D. (1980). *The Nationwide audience: Structure and decoding*. London: British Film Institute.

Observer, The, (1955a, April 24). Dickie Valentine's fans. *The Observer*, p. 9.

Observer, The, (1955b, May 1). Television [Alan Brien]. *The Observer*, p. 14.

Observer, The, (1955c, November 20). Profile: Orson Welles. *The Observer*, p. 5.

Observer, The, (1969, January 12). East German village that went west [Leslie Colitt]. *The Observer*, p. 4.

Observer, The, (1973, February 18). Adventures with Orson [Philip French]. *The Observer*, p. 36.

Observer, The, (1975, December 21). Christmas TV briefing. *The Observer*, p. 26.

Observer, The, (1978, February 12). By the blower to Belfast [Hugh McIlvaney]. *The Observer*, p. 20.

Observer, The, (1985, May 5). Return of citizen Welles [William Scobie]. *The Observer*, p. 21.

Observer, The, (1987, January 4). Television listings. *The Observer*, p. 26.

Observer, The, (1988, January 31). Week in view [Jennifer Selway]. *The Observer*, p. 32.

Observer, The, (1991, July 7). The world's favourite citizen. [Philip French]. *The Observer*, p. 45.

Orson Welles' Sketchbook (1955, June 6). Transcript: Episode 5. BBC Television Programme. www.wellesnet.com/sketchbook5.htm [Accessed 10th May 2012]

Paulu, B. (1956). *British broadcasting: Radio and television in the United Kingdom*. Minneapolis, MN: University of Minnesota Press.

Pickles, W. (1949). *Between you and me*. London: Werner Laurie.

Ruddock, A. (2001). *Understanding audiences*, London / Thousand Oaks, CA / New

Delhi: Sage.

Scannell, P. (1991). Introduction The Relevance of Talk. In P. Scannell (ed.), *Broadcast Talk* (pp. 1–13). London: Sage.

Scannell, P., and Cardiff, D. (1991). *A social history of British broadcasting, Volume 1, 1922–1939: Serving the nation.* Oxford: Basil Blackwell.

Shingler, M., and Wieringa, C. (1998). *On air: Methods and meanings of radio.* London: Arnold.

Siepmann, C. A. (1950). *Radio, television and society.* New York, NY and London: Oxford University Press.

Silvey, R.J.E. (1939, May 11). Taking the American listener's pulse. *The Listener,* p. 985.

Smith, M. (1998). *Democracy in a depression: Britain in the 1920s and 1930s.* Cardiff: University of Wales Press.

Starkey, G. and Crisell, A. (2009). *Radio journalism.* London and New York, NY: Sage.

Sterling, C.H. (2009). War of the Worlds. In C.H. Sterling (ed.), *The Concise Encyclopedia of American Radio* (pp. 819–21). New York, NY and London: Routledge.

Street, S. (2002). *A concise history of British radio, 1922–2002.* Tiverton: Kelly Publications.

Street, S. (2006). *Historical dictionary of British radio.* Lanham / Toronto / Oxford: The Scarecrow Press.

Times, The. (1938a, November 1). Panic caused by broadcast; A Wells fantasy in America; invasion from mars. *The Times,* p. 14.

Times, The. (1938b, November 1). Today's news. *The Times,* p. 15.

Times, The. (1938c, November 2). Less realism in U.S. broadcasts. *The Times,* p. 13.

Times, The. (1946, August 14). Obituary: Mr. H.G.Wells. *The Times,* p. 7.

Times, The. (1959, February 24). Letter: Television plays [Burton Paulu]. *The Times,* p. 11.

Times, The. (1962, August 20). Hollywood man of the theatre; from our special correspondent. *The Times,* p 12.

Times, The. (1973a, January 27). The war of the worlds [John Houseman]. *The Times,* p. 8.

Times, The. (1973b, February 15). Early stirrings of the New York theatre [Ion Trewin]. *The Times,* p. 16.

Times, The. (1975, September 1). John Houseman: Three strings to his bow [Sheridan Morley]. *The Times,* p. 5.

Times, The. (1980, March 8). Saturday review: Orson Welles [Penelope Houston]. *The Times,* p. 6.

Times, The. (1982, July 10). Radio: Fact from fiction [David Wade]. *The Times,* p. 5.

Times, The. (1984, August 27). Yes, Welles would fool us too [Bernard Levin]. *The Times,* p. 8.

Times, The. (1985a, May 6). A screen genius returns [Sebastian Cody]. *The Times,* p. 8.

Times, The. (1985b, October 12). Obituary: Orson Welles; formidable and inventive actor and producer. *The Times,* p. 10.

Times, The. (1986, February 19). Obituary: Paul Stewart. *The Times,* p. 14.

Times, The. (1988a, February 3). Wells and Welles: A fearful match. *The Times*, p. 21.
Times, The. (1988b, October 31). Martians return to spread fresh panic. *The Times*, p. 10.
Times, The. (1988c, November 2). Obituary: John Houseman; the producer, author and actor whose 'men from mars' panicked America. *The Times*, p. 18.
Times, The. (1989, May 3). Don't unfold radio drama [Nick McCarty]. *The Times*, p. 34.
Times, The. (1992, August 1). Hunting for little green men [Nigel Hawkes]. *The Times*, p. 10.
Times, The. (1994a, June 4). £21,000 for Welles script. *The Times*, p. 2.
Times, The. (1994b, November 1). Space 'invasion' alarms US [James Bone]. *The Times*, p. 14.
Times, The. (1995, August 19). Obituary: Howard Koch. *The Times*, p. 17.
Times, The. (1996, October 31). Saying "boo" to a nation. *The Times*, p. 46.
Times, The. (1999, May 27). Welles the myth, the magician, the master. [Geoff Brown]. *The Times*, p. 40.
Times, The. (2000a, April 13). Rebels with a cause [Geoff Brown]. *The Times*, n.p.
Times, The. (2000b, August 28). War of the Welles [Neil Cooper]. *The Times*, n.p.
Times, The. (2001, August 11). Nightmare scenario [Alan Franks]. *The Times*, pp.26–7.
Times, The. (2006). From Kane to Lear, on the trail of Orson [Sam Marlowe]. *The Times*, p. 23.
Tucker, N. (1966). *Understanding the mass media: A practical approach for teaching*. Cambridge, UK: Cambridge University Press.
Tunstall, J. (1977). *The media are American*. London: Constable and Company.
Vaughan, D. (2008) *Battle for the airwaves: Radio and the 1938 Munich crisis*. Prague: Cook Communications and Radioservis.
Washbourne, N. (2010). *Mediating politics: Newspapers, radio, television and the internet*. Maidenhead and New York, NY: Open University Press / McGraw Hill.
Wickham Steed, H. (1938). *The press*. Harmondsworth: Penguin Books.
Williams, K. (1996). *British writers and the media 1930–45*. Houndmills: Macmillan Press.
Williams, K. (2007). *H.G. Wells, modernity and the movies*. Liverpool: University of Liverpool Press.

# PART TWO

Backward and Forward: Media Forms, Conventions, and Crisis

CHAPTER FIVE

Network Radio's Greatest Test: CBS News' Coverage of the D-Day Invasion

WENDY HILTON-MORROW

In this chapter, Hilton-Morrow provides a new perspective on the development of CBS radio news by situating it in relation to the *War of the Worlds* broadcast and larger debates over the public duties and responsibilities of US commercial radio networks. Through an analysis of CBS D-Day recordings and commemorative publications, Hilton-Morrow shows that the legacy of the *War of the Worlds* broadcast remained very real for CBS producers and publicists as they approached wartime news coverage in general, and D-Day coverage in particular.

Introduction

Six years after Orson Welles and the Mercury Theater aired fictional news of a Martian invasion over the CBS network, CBS newsman Bob Trout anchored more than sixteen hours of news coverage of a real-life invasion, the Allied invasion of Normandy. Unlike the *War of the Worlds* broadcast, this invasion coverage did not catch CBS or American listeners off guard. In fact, by the time Allied troops landed on the beaches of Normandy on June 6, 1944, radio networks had spent months preparing to cover this historic event. For the prior fifteen years, radio news had struggled to prove its credibility, particularly during times of crisis. The networks saw the imminent invasion as an opportunity to demonstrate their dedication to serving the democratic good of the nation. By all accounts, they succeeded. *Variety* hailed D-Day as the "Biggest Radio Story" ("Biggest Radio Story," 1944, p. 1), and even the *New York Times*, which rarely championed radio news, conceded that the networks' coverage of D-Day was "Quite a Showing" (Hutchens, 1944, p. X5).

Without downplaying radio's monumental achievement of keeping Americans informed about the developments of D-Day, it is worth examining the ways that CBS used the crisis as an opportunity to solidify its place in the American public sphere. CBS would make its coverage of D-Day almost as newsworthy as the invasion itself by emphasizing the role of technology, the behind-the-scenes experiences of CBS reporters, and the very process of news production. After the fact, CBS would package the story of its D-Day news coverage in manuscript and book form to be shared with advertisers, journalism students, and the wider public. In these sources, CBS actively framed its efforts on D-Day as a great "test," the passage of which validated radio news as vital to American democracy. However, situating CBS's news coverage of the Normandy invasion within the broader context of broadcasting history offers a more complex story of how a moment of crisis provided space for networks to address unsettled tensions over commercial radio broadcasting in the United States. CBS aimed to show how the power of radio could be carefully controlled and exploited by responsible and moral radio newsmen in service of the public interest.

A Context for Radio's Great Test

Radio news in America was growing into its own in a number of ways during World War II. Throughout most of the 1930s, radio had no concerted network news operations.[1] Radio did provide extended coverage of special events like the kidnapping of the Lindberg baby and subsequent trial of Bruno Hauptman, but radio largely relied on wire services for its daily news. That began to change when tensions in Europe prompted networks to develop overseas news bureaus. As a result, Americans increasingly relied on the immediacy of radio broadcasts during the war. For example, during H.V. Kaltenborn's marathon coverage of the Munich crisis in 1938, more radio sets were sold than in any prior three-week period (Douglas, 1999, p. 161). In the process of providing an increasing number of special news reports from overseas, the network radio reporters became familiar and trusted voices for many Americans, contributing to a growing sense that radio was "freer from prejudice" than newspapers (Stott, 1973, p. 80).[2] However, this had not long been the case.

The 1930s was a time during which U.S. network radio was still figuring out the line between entertainment, opinion, and objective news reporting. Since the 1920s, newspapers had clearly differentiated between commentary and reporting, but the line still was blurred by radio commentators like CBS's Boake Carter and NBC's H.V. Kaltenborn, who freely intermixed their own opinions with their reporting of events. Radio came under pressure from many sides to shift to a more objective style of reporting. Advertisers who sponsored news programs feared offending listeners with opinions expressed in news programs associated with their products. In a time of growing concern about the perceived power of radio, particularly when used for propaganda purposes, the National Association of Broadcasters implemented its own standards of objectivity before the government had a chance to impose their own regulations (Hilmes, 2011). The emerging standards of professionalism and objectivity for radio journalism produced the very news conventions mimicked in the *War of the Worlds* broadcast and, as Somerville describes in Chapter 6, taught to journalists today.

Despite the maturation of radio news leading up to and during World War II, some still questioned whether radio was up to the task of covering a major news event. In particular, radio's handling of the Japanese bombing of Pearl Harbor in December 1941 raised questions about commercial radio's ability to serve both its advertisers and the public interest. Caught off guard by the invasion and with no plan in place, CBS restricted almost all of its news coverage to regularly scheduled news reports. In the seventy-two hours following the attack, CBS pre-empted only eight of its 137 commercial programs; five of those program interruptions were for speeches by President Roosevelt and Prime Minister Churchill (Kendrick, 1969). A week later, *New York Times* columnist John Hutchens drew attention to the networks' decision to air entertainment programming during a time of national crisis. He wrote, "After the first impact of the war news, none of the radio's usual features can have seemed important, and a good many of them have seemed impertinent when they were not merely trivial" (Hutchens, 1941, p. X14). If there was any doubt about his veiled criticisms of radio news' handling of Pearl Harbor, Hutchens (1944) later referred to "the confusions and the sorry lapses of taste" in which "sundry fiscal-minded interests could have been suspected, justly or not, of deliberately capitalizing on a catastrophe (p. X5).[3] In response to such criticism, radio networks made certain they would be better prepared for the news event that would come two-and-a-half years later.

Preparations for D-Day

Determined not to be caught between the pull for ongoing news coverage and prior commitments to program sponsors when D-Day came, CBS began warning advertisers in May 1944 that their scheduled programming might be pre-empted by news coverage. The network assured advertisers, though, that they would "be properly reimbursed for the time we seize in the public interest, and we'll be reasonable and not waste time on chaff or gossip" (Hollister & Strunsky, 1945a, p. 5). CBS also agreed to leave it to Paul White, director of news operations, to determine if and when regularly scheduled programming would be pre-empted.

Paul White, who had been hired by William Paley to be CBS's first news director in 1930, was responsible for CBS's growing stronghold on radio journalism and would play a major role in the network's D-Day preparations. White gave Edward R. Murrow the freedom to assemble a news staff with strong journalistic credentials but little to no broadcasting experience. The team that would come to be known as "The Murrow Boys" included Charles Collingwood, William Downs, Richard Hottelet, Larry LeSueur, Eric Sevareid, and William Shirer. By 1944, Murrow had significant experience in coordinating news roundups and was chosen to coordinate a shared reporter pool between the four networks to provide coverage of the invasion when it happened. Of the five hundred American correspondents in London before D-Day, only 28 were chosen to accompany troops for the invasion. Five of those chosen were from CBS; Hottelet was to join Air

Force troops, Collingwood and Willard Shadel were to be with the Navy, and Downs and LeSueur were to land with the Infantry.

Back home, White was busy directing preparations for D-Day coverage. For months before the actual invasion, network executives were meeting twice a week with high-ranking public information officers of the military (Bliss, 1991). By February, White drafted a seven-page memo of guidelines for coverage of the imminent invasion, reminding his staff of his expectations for adhering to professional journalism standards: "No matter what the general tenor of the news, keep an informative, unexcited demeanor at the microphone. . . . Always aim for the listener's confidence and remember that winning the war is a hell of a lot more important than reporting" (p. 152). White's directions demonstrate his well-known aversion to sensationalistic news coverage, the importance of maintaining the audience's trust, and a recognition that radio must not threaten America's national interests.

CBS also began prepping their New York base of operations by installing new technological devices to be used in news coverage of the invasion. Installed on White's desk was what quickly became known as "the piano," a contraption that would allow the user to switch between transatlantic short wave radio channels. On the wall of Studio 9, a new pine cupboard was installed. Inside of it was a microphone with a 60-foot long cable and a switch that would automatically and instantly send the speaker's words over the air to the entire network. By mid-May, the assistant news director, Everett Holles, had drawn up an instruction sheet to brief news staff about using the new pine cupboard when news of the D-Day invasion came across the Associated Press ticker:

> Do not waste time writing a bulletin. And don't waste time in looking for an announcer. After you have pushed down the key, give the bulletin clearly and concisely. Then say you're taking the microphone to our teletypes in the CBS newsroom for more details. The mike has an extension cable. Carry it into the newsroom and read more of the news as it comes over the teletypes. . . . It will be speed and not a polished and professional manner at the mike that will count. . . . Of course, have someone call Production and get an engineer and announcer to Studio 9 as quickly as possible. If there is no one else around, make the call yourself, even realizing the public is listening in. It will all make for additional color. (Bliss, 1999, p. 153)

Hoping to plan for as many details of D-Day broadcasting as possible, White disseminated a 15-page memo to affiliates across the country. The memo included detailed instructions on how the network news department intended to handle invasion coverage (Hollister & Strunsky, 1945a). Leading up to the invasion, CBS even expanded its programming hours to be certain that affiliate stations would be staffed throughout the night.

Despite all of the careful preparations, two days before the real invasion happened, stations in both the United States and Europe committed a major misstep when a false invasion announcement came across the Associated Press wire due to a teletype operator's mistake. The retraction came almost immediately, but too late for announcers who put the news over the air. The gaffe resulted in news coverage in newspapers around the country and CBS's own recognition of the event's similarity to the *War of the Worlds* broadcast in the way that switchboards lit up from angry and confused listeners (Hollister & Strunsky, 1945a). The incident may have been responsible for CBS's overly cautious response to initial reports that the actual invasion had begun two days later.

There can be no doubt that all of this careful preparation resulted in D-Day news coverage that evidenced an increased maturity for radio network news. On-air reporting conventions had solidified into a no-nonsense delivery style, and networks had implemented guidelines for integrating breaking news into the programming schedule. The result was marathon news coverage drawn from shared radio resources in a way that had never been done before. At CBS, Bob Trout spent almost ten consecutive hours on air in New York, transitioning listeners between speeches by national and international leaders, wire reports, live and recorded eye witness reports by embedded reporters, and analysis by military experts. In the 24-hours following first news of the invasion, CBS pre-empted seventeen sponsored programs in order to deliver nearly 16 hours of invasion news and analysis over the course of 113 broadcasts. There is no doubt that radio played a vital role in keeping Americans informed about the developments of D-Day. Without downplaying this monumental achievement, it is worth examining the ways that CBS used the crisis as an opportunity to reify commercial networks' ability to harness the power of radio in the service of the public good.

Inscribing Radio into the History of D-Day

As CBS prepared news operations in anticipation of D-Day, the network actively strategized ways to document its own role in the historic event. Audio recording technologies had improved substantially by 1944, allowing correspondents in the field to submit recorded reports. The new recording capabilities also allowed radio to make a permanent record of its on-air coverage, addressing one of newspapers' major criticisms of radio. Fifteen years earlier, newspapers had pointed to radio broadcasts' ephemeral quality as a disqualifier for the medium to produce reliable news. As a 1929 *New York Times* editorial asserted, "The radio news item is a vibration in the air, without record, without visible responsibility, without that incentive to accuracy that comes with print" ("'News' by Radio," p. 18). By 1944, though, radio was able to provide a full record of its performance, and CBS recognized the marketing potential that could come from these recorded moments of radio history. Those CBS recordings would serve as the basis for accompanying written accounts documenting what CBS would frame as "a day of great test for civilian radio as it was for the armies and navies and air forces themselves" (Hollister & Strunsky, 1945a, p. 1).

Two members of CBS's sales promotion department, Paul Hollister, the Vice President in Charge of Advertising and Sales Promotion and Robert Strunsky, then an advertising copywriter who would eventually become CBS's director of corporate affairs, wrote and edited a mimeographed account of behind-the-scenes activities leading up to and during D-Day. The written account included transcripts drawn from the networks' audio recordings of on-air coverage. The hundred-page volume initially was restricted to CBS employees, affiliates, advertisers and advertising agencies. However, much of the manuscript was included in the 320-page book *From D-Day through Victory in Europe* published by CBS in June 1945. According to CBS promotional material, a hundred thousand copies of the book were printed, resulting in a subsequent book, *From Pearl Harbor into Tokyo*, compiled by Hollister and Strunsky and published by CBS in September 1945. Portions of Hollister and Strunsky's manuscript would also be reprinted without attribution in Paul White's 1947 book written for prospective broadcast journalists, *News on the Air*.[4]

Hollister and Strunsky's written accounts reinforced CBS news' on-air coverage in the 24-hours following the invasion in that both inscribed radio into the history of D-Day. The story told both in the on-air coverage and in Hollister and Strunsky's manuscript emphasized the power of technology, the process of radio news production, and the authority of radio news icons. Not only was CBS able to insure its place in the recorded history of D-Day, it was able to frame the telling as one that seemingly answered any reservations about the power of commercial network radio. After all, less than six years earlier, fears about the power of radio spilled onto the pages of newspapers and magazines following the *War of the Worlds* broadcast event, understood by one *Time* magazine author as a "graphic example of [radio's] power over susceptible multitudes" (quoted in Sconce, 2000, p. 111). The *War of the Worlds* raised questions about the ability of both CBS and its listeners to use radio responsibly. David Goodman (2011) argues that most of the public discourse surrounding the broadcast focused on the failure of American listeners to fulfill their basic civic duty as rational and reasonable citizens (pp. 263, 266). At the same time, however, the *War of the Worlds* also drew attention to the ongoing debate over whether commercial networks could fulfill their own civic obligation to enlighten rather than mislead the people (pp. 18, 275). In this context, CBS actively worked to present its D-Day coverage as indisputable evidence of the network's ability to serve the people and the nation.

As part of this strategy, Hollister and Strunsky's (1945a) behind-the-scenes descriptions of CBS's preparations for D-Day emphasize the role of new technology in their reporting efforts. Their detailed description of the cabinet installed in the studio to be used when the invasion happened gives the technology mystical-like qualities and emphasizes the grave responsibility that comes with this powerful technology:

> Then one day on the wall of Studio 9 appeared not handwriting but a new pine cupboard, about the size of a small medicine cabinet. It was locked. Eleven keys were given to eleven responsible people. If you happened to know one of them, and if he trusted you, he would unlock it. Inside on a hook hung a small hand microphone, attached to a 60-foot length of insulated cable. Above the mike on the hook you saw a small switch, very commonplace. But flip that switch and you cut through all the intermediate

controls, by-passed all the system's elaborate machinery of caution and precaution; you found yourself instantly and automatically on the air of the entire Columbia Network, and inside some 27 million homes; that's why the pine cupboard was locked to all but eleven picked key holders. (pp. 4–5)

Paul White (1947) even went so far as to refer to the pine cupboard as "Pandora's Box," (p. 328) a metaphor that implies the great risks and responsibilities that come with such communicative power. White similarly went into great detail describing the "piano" instrument panel and transmitter that had been installed on his desk, flippantly suggesting it "could do about everything except make a milkshake and eliminate static" (pp. 327–8). These accounts of the pine cupboard and "piano" transmitter emphasized the technological reach of radio, whether across a nation of CBS affiliates or between correspondents half way around the world. Yet, they also explain the safeguards put in place by CBS to ensure that the power of radio does not fall into irresponsible or dangerous hands. Additionally, these guidelines provide assurance that the network will utilize such far-reaching control over affiliate stations in only the most exceptional of instances.

In his on-air coverage on D-Day, Bob Trout also highlighted the role of technology in the newsgathering process. As he brought listeners along to hear the sounds of a radio newsroom operation, Trout made visible the mechanisms by which radio newscasters compile news stories. In doing so, Trout followed to the letter the written choreography that White had distributed via memo to news personnel in the lead-up to the invasion. Just as he had been instructed, Trout made use of the microphone inside the pine cupboard to take listeners into CBS's newsroom across the hall. In this backstage tour, Trout drew listeners' attention to the aural evidence of the news gathering process:

> Incidentally, if at any time in this little tour of the newsroom . . . if you pick out the sounds of the bells in the background, I'd like to explain to you when you hear five bells in rapid succession, that means that one of our many machines—at least one—is notifying us with the signal of five bells that it has a bulletin on its service wire. Of course, if you suddenly hear all the bells go crazy at once, as if it were Christmas and New Year's altogether, that would be a flash, but a flash is not as common in newsrooms as people who do not work in news sometimes believe.

In describing the sounds of the newsroom, Trout simultaneously acknowledges the magnitude of the event being covered while describing routine news procedures followed by CBS news staff as they work to bring listeners the most up-to-date, but credible, information. Following his own guidelines, White also makes audible the behind-the-scenes conversations of news coordination to which listeners generally are not privy. These conversations treat both technical and newsgathering operations as everyday matters. For example, approximately four-and-a-half hours into the invasion coverage, CBS (1944) aired a short-wave radio conversation between White in New York and Murrow in London:

> White: I just thought that perhaps the audience would be interested in how we're setting up these broadcasts, and since we understand there is no more "pool" copy available at this moment I thought we'd have a little conversation with you.
>
> Murrow: Well, Paul, what we're doing is this: we're going to continue to "pool" for the next hour or two, simply trying to move the material as fast as it comes in to all four of the networks. By the way, what kind of a signal are we putting in?
>
> White: Very fine. Congratulations to the engineers over there. Their signal has been uniformly good throughout.
>
> Murrow: Good. Excellent. Things are a little confused over here, you know. Our quarters are a little crowded, and just outside the studio there's an elderly tar woman who's busy scrubbing the floor. She's in some danger of being trampled to death, all the while, but I think she's probably the most unconcerned person in this building. She just goes right on scrubbing.
>
> White: Well, a few moments ago I had a young lady come in here. Now, I say young lady—that is a compliment—with a vacuum cleaner. But (chuckling) she didn't stay very long. . . .

The informal exchange between White and Murrow fulfills a practical function in that it helps to fill airtime in between reports. It also is a way to involve a trusted correspondent who, because of his coordination duties, is unable to file an on-air report until D-Day Plus One. Perhaps most importantly, the exchange illustrates to listeners the way that these seasoned CBS newsmen treat a major coordination of international reporting as a commonplace event. In fact, portions of this conversation apparently were even too mundane for Hollister and Strunsky (1945a) in their manuscript remembrance of the historical events. Their transcribed version of this exchange between

Murrow and White omits the brief discussion of the two cleaning ladies, jumping instead to the rest of the conversation in which Murrow reports to White the current location of CBS newsmen.

Hollister and Strunsky (1945a) take advantage of another informal exchange to marvel at the power of radio. They describe a brief shortwave discussion between White and Charlie Shaw that was shared with listeners. Shaw, who was assisting Murrow in coordinating reports, answers a question from White about what will be coming up in their radio coverage. He tells Shaw, "Well, we know, of course, about the King's broadcast. King George. That ought to reach you at 3 p.m. your time. . . ." Just in case listeners do not recognize the implication of this conversation between Shaw and White, the two marketing men whose job it is to capture the historic magnitude of the day's events make plain its significance:

> To the run-of-the-mill radio man, a good typically-dull routine conversation. If a King of England is going to broadcast on Invasion Day, somebody has to tell somebody, and the Bucknam (sic) Palace cat would do as well as anybody if the Bucknam Palace cat could talk. Instead a radio workman in London says casually to a radio workman in New York –"*by the way, the King's coming up . . .*"

> And that is how America knows that this is the 20th century. When you come down to it, there is no simpler way of saying the King is coming up. You don't need a regiment of mounted trumpets, with tabards—not any more. You just speak into a little contraption in an office in London and you're talking to 30 million non-isolated homes in North America. (Hollister & Strunsky, p. 38)

Hollister and Strunsky's reflection suggests incredulity at the way that radio has compressed the distance between continents and between world leaders and their listeners. However, their blithe tone in reacting to Shaw and White's exchange simultaneously reinforces the routines of such noteworthy events for CBS newsmen.

Hollister and Strunsky's (1945a) account also describes the efforts of CBS's shortwave listening post, made up of eleven "linguist-translator-propaganda-analysts," responsible for intercepting radio transmissions from around the world. The shortwave listeners used the international transmissions as a way to gather and verify reports about the progress of Allied Troops. Hollister and Strunsky herald the work of the listening post, having translated transmissions in fifteen different languages and typed up reports for distribution on the news wires. Their version of events emphasizes CBS's role as trustworthy gatekeeper in this redistribution of information:

> That explains why the front page of your newspaper, and especially the early part of its major war news story, so often says "According to a short wave report heard by the Columbia Broadcasting System. . . ." The practical collaboration between the press and the radio enriching the public news-service of both is a good deal more sportsmanlike and realistic than the business offices, the impatient partisans, or the light-tongued critics of press and radio would sometimes have you believe. (p. 90)

Although their account of events emphasizes the cooperation between newspapers and radio and between the four radio networks, it also emphasizes the leading role of CBS in these partnerships.

Because CBS had the most reporters represented in the overseas reporting pool, its correspondents' voices were the ones heard most often. CBS capitalized on the newsmen's personal accounts, reinscribing their authority in the process. CBS' published transcripts of broadcasts, *From D-Day through Victory in Europe*, were subtitled *The Eye-Witness Story as Told by War Correspondents on the Air* and listed the names of twelve CBS newsmen on the front cover.[5] As Zelizer (2007), notes, the realism of the 1940s emphasized the authority of the "I was there" style of reporting. Radio strengthened this authority with reporters' eyewitness stories told in their own voices. An eye-witness account by Murrow four days after the initial invasion would focus not on the fighting, but on the working conditions in the reporting pool. Hollister and Strunsky (1945a) included a transcript of Murrow's descriptive narrative in their manuscript:

> All the American networks are operating from a basement here in London. It wouldn't be big enough for a vice president's office back in New York. The noise is indescribable. Old newspapermen accustomed to the roar of a city room have put their head in the door and shuddered. . . . Occasionally a burst of gunfire or the roar of a falling bomb sweeps through the room where we do our writing. . . . (p. 88)

Murrow's report uses the same conversational style made familiar to Americans in his London "rooftop reports." Yet, in this case, Murrow's object of description is turned inward to focus on the poor conditions faced by reporters as they work to deliver news from overseas, thus magnifying the authority of the journalist. Although this report by Murrow came days after the height of radio news coverage of the invasion, Hollister and Strunsky's inclusion of it in their written account bundles it into CBS's recorded history of D-Day events.

Solidifying Commercial Radio's Place in History

Radio news' coverage of the D-Day invasion seemingly proved once and for all that commercial networks could handle the responsibilities that came with this new medium. Almost fifty years after the fact, the reports would be remembered as a "media event" that "produced the first defining triumph of modern broadcast journalism" (McDonough, 2001, p. 193). This crisis on the world stage gave radio an opportunity to turn reporting on itself, providing behind-the-scene accounts of the newsgathering process, with particular attention to the power of technology in the hands of trusted radio newsmen to connect people across the country and around the world. In effect, the historic event of Allied troops' invasion of Normandy became intimately tied to in the historic radio coverage of the event. In the months following D-Day, CBS marketers archived this story in written form, making it available for employees, affiliates, advertisers and their agencies, and eventually the broader public.

The story told in these accounts, though, is not just about the success of broadcast *journalism*. It is framed as a "test" passed by *commercial radio networks*. The networks had faced increasing scrutiny from the Federal Communications Commission. As Hilmes (2011) noted, "Chairman James Lawrence Fly, a trusted associate of Roosevelt's, was determined to make commercial broadcasters more accountable to the public interest, wartime cooperation or no" (p. 165). The 1941 *Report on Chain Broadcasting*, a culmination of the FCC's investigation into monopoly practices by the networks, suggested changes to network-affiliate relations and determined that a company could not own more than one network, leaving NBC to relinquish control of NBC Blue. These concerns about the potential for networks to gain monopolistic power came against a backdrop of broader fears about the power of this new medium. These worries remained fresh in the public's minds due to their collective memory of the influence of Welles' *War of the Worlds* broadcast, as well as the events in Europe.

In a clear answer to such concerns, CBS framed its own involvement in D-Day in tones of assurance that the power of the network would only be used in the service of the greater good. Hollister and Strunsky (1945a) conclude their manuscript with this "humble forecast":

> But as all of our years of preparation in news service seemed suddenly that June night to have focused on a supreme test of the ability of a network to serve its country creditably under stress, so now we know that it was indeed (as the tank-colonel said that afternoon) only a "pretty useful dress rehearsal for some *real* news"—only a pledge-by-precept that tomorrow's job will be attacked with readier perception, smoother skill, more daring, rounder perspective.
>
> That goes for the relentless advance, for absolute defeat of Germany, for the ensuing disinfection of the Japanese, and for the long days of peace. To the infinite prolonging of these days, the science, the art, the enterprise and the responsibility of radio communication are irrevocably dedicated. (p. 97)

A moment of crisis such as the much-anticipated D-Day invasion provided the space and focus to allow radio journalism to prove its parity, and even superiority, to print journalism. However, CBS also seized the opportunity to address unsettled tensions over the place and power of radio and commercial radio networks in America.

Notes

1. CBS began the *Columbia News Service* in September 1933 during the height of the press-radio wars, but agreed to shut down the service only six months later as part of a truce agreement between the radio networks and newspapers that led to the formation of the Press-Radio Bureau (Conway, 2009, p. 25).
2. In response to a 1939 Elmo Roper survey sponsored by *Fortune*, almost a full half of respondents answered that radio provided "news freer from prejudice." Just over 17 percent answered newspaper (18.3 percent saw them as being the same and 14.9 percent responded that they didn't know) (Stott, 1973, p. 80).
3. The reference to Pearl Harbor appeared in a column assessing radio's performance on D-Day, suggesting that the medium had "grown up" over the prior two-and-a-half years.
4. White does list Hollister and Strunsky in his "Acknowledgements" as two of many people who gave permission for White to reprint their writings. However, in the chapter in which excerpts from Hollister and Strunsky's manuscript are included, White's accounts are integrated with Hollister and Strunsky's writings with no differentiation between them.

5   The list of correspondents on the book cover ends with George Hicks, a reporter for the NBC Blue Network, whose recording from the bridge on the *U.S.S. Ancon* provided play-by-play description with accompanying actualities of the downing of a Nazi bomber by the *Ancon's* gunners. Hicks' recording would be replayed on radio stations and described by *The New York World Telegram* as "the greatest recording yet to come out of the war" (McDonough, 1994, p. 210). In *From D-Day through Victory in Europe*, Hollister and Strunsky printed the transcript of Hicks' recording with no mention of his network affiliation.

References

Bliss, E. (1991). *Now the news*. New York: Columbia University Press.

Columbia Broadcast System. (1944, June 6). *Complete broadcast day, D-Day*. Retrieved from http://archive.org/details/Complete_Broadcast_Day_D-Day

Conway, M. (2009). *The origins of television news in America: The visualizers of CBS in the 1940s*. New York: Peter Lang.

D-Day biggest radio story. (1944, June 7). *Variety*, pp. 1, 42.

D-Day gives radio greatest opportunity. (1944, June 12). *Broadcasting*, 26(24), 9.

Douglas, S. (1999). *Listening in: Radio and the American imagination*. New York: Times Books.

Goodman, D. (2011). *Radio's civic ambition: American broadcasting and democracy in the 1930s*. New York: Oxford University Press.

Hilmes, M. (2011). *Only connect: A cultural history of broadcasting in the United States* (3rd ed.). Boston, MA: Wadsworth.

Hollister, P., & Strunsky, R. (Eds.). (1945a). *CBS News on D-Day*. New York: Columbia Broadcasting System.

Hollister, P., & Strunsky, R. (Eds.). (1945b). *From D-Day through victory in Europe*. New York: Columbia Broadcasting System.

Hollister, P., & Strunsky, R. (Eds.). (1945c). *From Pearl Harbor to Tokyo*. New York: Columbia Broadcasting System.

Hutchens, J. (1941, December 14). Arms and the radio. *New York Times*, p. X14.

Hutchens, J. (1944, June 11). Quite a showing. *New York Times*, p. X5.

Kendrick, A. (1969). *Prime time: The life of Edward R. Murrow*. Boston: Little, Brown and Company.

McDonough, J. (1994). The longest night: Broadcasting's first invasion. *American Scholar*, 63(2), 193-211.

"News" by radio. (1929, April 19). *New York Times*, p. 18.

Sconce, J. (2000). *Haunted media: Electronic presence from telegraphy to television*. Durham, NC: Duke University Press.

Stott, W. (1973). *Documentary expression and thirties America*. New York: Oxford University Press.

White, P. (1947). *News on the air*. New York: Harcourt, Brace and Company.

Zelizer, B. (2007). On "having been there": "Eyewitnessing" as a journalistic key word. *Critical Studies in Media Communication, 24,* 408-428.

CHAPTER SIX

War of the Worlds as a Radio News Training Tool

KEITH SOMERVILLE

In this chapter, Somerville shows the continuing relevance of the *War of the Worlds* for contemporary broadcast news conventions by describing its use as a training tool for radio news producers. As news organizations geared up for the invasion of Iraq in 2003, the BBC World Service was faced with the need to train dozens of journalists in live radio news coverage. The chapter details how the author put the first fifteen minutes of the *War of the Worlds* broadcast to use in BBC training sessions. Somerville argues that the broadcast provided a simple and stylized model of broadcast news that radio journalists could draw on to build crisis coverage that created a sense of constant contact with the listener.

Introduction

On October 30th, 1938, the CBS radio network broadcast the now infamous dramatization of H.G. Wells's book, the *War of the Worlds*. Despite being introduced as a drama, the play opened with a series of acted-out radio news broadcasts that quickly convinced some Americans listening at home that this was a real story and that the news bulletins were real. The first half hour of the play, in particular, was a highly stylized broadcast aping in a finely tuned but exaggerated fashion the workings of radio networks at the time. The following day, the *New York Times* reported that "mass hysteria" seized the nation as thousands of listeners were persuaded that, "invading Martians [were] spreading wide death and destruction in New Jersey and New York" (Radio Listeners in Panic, October 31,1938, p. 1). Regardless of academic reassessments of the size and extent of the "panic," the Mercury Theater play was a fascinating and professional piece of broadcasting representing a particular style of constant communication with the audience (Hendy, 2000; Hayes and Battles, 2011). It has come—perhaps because of the continuing debate over its effect and over media effects in general—to be a measure against which broadcasting can be assessed.

When you listen to or read the immediately pre-war and wartime broadcasts of key radio reporters like William Shirer or Edward R. Murrow, you cannot help but hear echoes of *War of the Worlds*. This is not because these radio journalists copied the style of the dramatized broadcast; rather, it was because the Mercury Theater performers imitated the style of leading news broadcasters. You can certainly hear echoes of Herb Morrison's famous and very emotional report on the Hindenburg disaster in May 1937 in Carl Phillip's broadcast from Grovers Mill as the dramatic action gained pace (Crook, 1998).

Due to its authentic reproduction of journalistic techniques, its clear signposting of radio conventions, and its stylized and exaggerated nature, the *War of the Worlds* broadcast has become a successful training tool for today's radio producers. It has been used at the BBC World Service and at Brunel University as a means of introducing journalists and students to basic radio reporting and news techniques. It was first used prior to the invasion of Iraq in 2003. This chapter describes how and why the broadcast was uniquely successful in this capacity, and why there was a perceived need for such training.

War of the Worlds and 21ˢᵗ Century Crisis Coverage

When, on October 11th, 2002, the United States Senate and House of Representatives voted to authorize the use of force against Saddam Hussein's Iraq if it failed to give up the weapons of mass destruction (WMD) that the Bush administration said the regime was concealing, it was clear that military action was a distinct possibility. The Bush administration and its allies, notably Britain under Prime Minister Tony Blair, were set on a collision course with Iraq, contending that the regime had developed WMD and was preventing UN weapons inspectors from fully investigating their existence.

Over the next five months, diplomatic pressure increased and military preparations were set in train. When the UN Security Council failed to provide a second resolution giving the green light for the use of force, the United States and its allies decided to proceed with war. Unusually in international affairs, the progress to war was clearly signaled and there was a fairly obvious timescale related to the time to gather forces and the weather in the Gulf. This gave media organizations—notably major international broadcasters like CNN and the BBC—the opportunity to prepare their coverage, gather their resources in the region and, crucially, to provide training for journalists. It also highlighted the growing competition for audiences—at home and abroad—between major networks.

Working as a senior editor at the World Service, I had witnessed the rise of CNN to a point where, despite the differences in media and genre, it was a competitor with BBC World Service radio. Indeed, it was a far more attractive competitor for audiences with access to TV than had been previous competitors such as Voice of America, Deutsche Welle and, up to the fall of communism in the USSR, Radio Moscow. Al Jazeera was also a new competitor. In preparing to cover the war, there was in the back of our minds the question, "how will CNN and Al Jazeera do it" and how can we compete, offer something different and how can we brand ourselves distinctively in a more and more crowded international media environment? This was part of our preparation and was a factor in our training plans.

The need for training covered not just those journalists who would be embedded with combat units, but also those who would be involved in rolling news coverage of the war. This live coverage was termed rolling as it continued without breaks as long as there was news to report—it rolled with the story. Rolling news on TV and radio had developed over the previous 12 years, since the first war against Iraq in January 1991 (following the August 2nd, 1990 invasion of Kuwait by Saddam's army). For the BBC World Service, where I worked from 1988 as a radio producer and then live news program editor, this was a challenge. The general pattern of news coverage was five or ten minute news bulletins on the hour and then built news programs, usually an hour in length, which were presented live and consisted of a mix of live interviews, recorded interviews and features. Teams would have four or five hours to put together the built programming but were equipped to react live on air to breaking stories. On occasions extended live coverage would be provided on an ad hoc basis when major stories broke.

In January 1991, the invasion of Kuwait by US-led armed forces to expel the occupying Iraqis and the subsequent drive into southern Iraq, spawned rolling news coverage for periods on the BBC World Service, BBC TV and BBC domestic radio. The World Service provided live coverage as soon as the invasion of Kuwait began and extended live coverage was provided throughout the two months of the conflict. Network heads did not want to risk missing important developments or to be even minutes late, fearing that audiences would switch to competitors.

On domestic radio, the midnight news on the Radio 4 channel was going out on January 16th when allied forces started bombing Iraq, ahead of the ground invasion. Instead of finishing at the end of the short bulletin, news coverage continued for over four hours. From the following morning, January 17th, a continuous Gulf War news service was broadcast on Radio 4FM. The rolling service became known as "Scud FM" among its own staff and other BBC journalists. It was named after the deadly but rather inaccurate Scud missiles used by Iraq to hit targets in Israel during the conflict. There was a measure of self-deprecation for a hurriedly prepared venture in rolling news—but also a recognition, particularly by BBC staff in the World Service and other news areas, that like the Scud, Radio 4FM did not always hit its news target.

A taste of the perils of live news broadcasting—the pressure to report immediately and to come to rapid conclusions about events even when sufficient information is not available—soon came to the BBC newsroom. Prior to the ground invasion, rolling coverage was proceeding live on air when reports came in from the Gulf from news agencies that there had been an explosion at one of the harbors where allied warships were docked. As I listened prior to starting a nightshift running World Service rolling programming, the team on air reported this but rather than avoiding speculation about the cause, they launched into a discussion with a former army officer who was the on air "expert" on warfare about what could have caused it. The expert opined that it could only be sabotage by pro-Iraqi forces or a Scud missile. This gave the impression of a pre-emptive strike by Iraq. It was not—it was an explosion caused by a leaking gas cylinder left in strong sunlight. The mistake was later corrected on air, and the lessons of this incident were taken on board by journalists and their editors across the BBC as they considered the future of live, rolling news coverage of major events.

As a program editor I learned more lessons about extended rolling coverage on August 19th, 1991. In the early hours of the morning I was putting the final touches to an edition of the live but very short BBC World Service news and current affairs program, *24 Hours*. I was both editor and presenter with a producer and two studio managers (sound technicians). An hour before we were on air with our first edition, the Soviet news agency Tass reported that the Soviet Communist Party's central committee had replaced Mikhail Gorbachev as President and Party leader as he was "unable to perform his presidential duty for health reasons" (BBC On this Day, August 19, 1991). There was no time to get in more staff, as it was 4:00AM, and our first edition was the usual 20 minutes. By the second edition, we had one more producer and the details of the coup were clearer. But we lacked a studio expert and any pre-prepared material to fill any gaps in live coverage. It was a hairy hour on air as presenter. The lesson was that extended or rolling coverage was an effective way to cover major breaking news stories, but journalists and resources had to be prepared ahead of time.

The lessons were put into effect and senior editors at the World Service began to draw up contingency plans for breaking stories—with lists of producers' home phone numbers easily to hand to bring teams in fast. The core of future rolling news had to be constancy, regular updates of the news and recapitulation of what had already happened to keep the audience informed not only of latest events but how the story had developed. In addition, successful and regular branding through the use of a set form of words repeated every 15 minutes or so was a key part of rolling news. Lacking advertisements in its broadcasts, the BBC concentrated heavily on branding to ensure its listeners knew to whom they were listening. These identifying and branding announcement—along the lines of, "You are listening to the

BBC World Service bringing you a special program of news reporting . . ."—were also functional. They communicated the basics of the breaking news story being covered. They also provide short buffers between items, during which fresh scripts could be distributed, guests taken in and out of the studio or presenters briefed.

This approach was successfully used to put on more than 18 hours of rolling coverage following the death of Princess Diana on August 31st, 1997. As overall output editor for the first nine hours, I was able to gather a full program team and presenter at short notice, clear planned programs from the schedule and put on more polished live coverage. Diana's death, as I would strongly argue, lacked the importance or social consequences of war or disaster coverage, but it is undeniable that there was a huge global audience for the story. A similar operation was put in place for the NATO bombing campaign against Serbia in March 1999 during the Kosovo crisis.

BBC editors became increasingly well versed in the protocols of live coverage. They learned how to avoid speculation and how to make the best use of eyewitnesses for developing stories. They also learned to use recaps, regular news bulletins, and station identification announcements to create breathing space for live news teams and presenters. Those editors reacted with skill and amazing calm to the demands of covering the Terrorist Attacks of September 11th, 2001 (9/11), and many were in place in 2003 for the Invasion of Iraq. They were also developing more and more the feel of making even crisis coverage sound like a conversation with the audience. They created a constant communicative contact with listeners through vivid reporting, the use of regular updates, and the method of trailing ahead to major interviews or on-the-spot reports to keep the audience listening over time.

If in 2003 senior editors were prepared for rolling news in the advent of war in Iraq, many newer staff needed training in how to put on rolling coverage, while avoiding the problems of speculation and alarmism. They were keen and had the basic skills of journalists, but had not had the experience of the first Gulf War, Diana's death, the Kosovo crisis or 9/11. In early 2003, as the war against Saddam became inevitable, the BBC World Service along with the wider BBC news organization prepared its combat and Middle Eastern reporting teams in the region, and at Bush House in London, we put together teams prepared to cover the war on a constantly rolling basis. Experienced editors were in place, but younger producers needed training in how to deal with major breaking stories and to put on rolling coverage, avoiding the problems of speculation, or the broadcasting of alarmist, unconfirmed reports. My role was in the newly created post of World Service News Training Editor. I started examining how I could develop real-life scenarios to prepare producers for breaking stories and to give them confidence and the nearest thing to experience ahead of the war. I wrote a number of scenarios that could be rolled out over four or five hours in real-time requiring them to put together live coverage. The question was, how to kick off the sessions and give producers a compelling model to emulate.

Working closely with a colleague, Steve Titherington, we came up with a daylong course that he, as Head of the BBC World Service Newsroom, would introduce with examples of live coverage that would demonstrate how it could be done and where the pitfalls lay. He and I had worked together on live coverage of the Waco siege in Texas and on the rolling programs when Princess Diana died. We were both concerned that if we used past examples of BBC rolling coverage, the producers would get hung up on the actual events, instead of concentrating on basic issues of live reporting. Steve came up with the idea of playing the first 15 minutes and 50 seconds of *War of the Worlds* from the weather bulletin up to the news update following the death of Carl Phillips. The trainees would listen and make notes on aspects of the coverage that they thought were particularly good, bad or requiring explanation or discussion. There would then be an extended discussion of the points raised by the broadcast, with Steve and me pointing up particular issues, techniques or problem areas. I would then use these as key criteria to consider when the trainees embarked on the real-life scenario part of the training.

The reaction was fascination. By taking a dramatized news story and one that had a profound effect on audiences at the time (rather than real news produced by the trainees' colleagues), producers were able to stand back and analyze processes, methods of reporting and language rather than feeling they were picking apart their colleagues' work. Over the period of a month and a half that I ran these sessions, over 50 producers were trained and they all gave feedback that the combination of the *War of the Worlds* exercises followed by a lifelike, real-time news exercise lasting several hours gave them a feel for how rolling news would work and made them more confident in approaching the coverage of the war. The general feeling among editors after the war and the extensive rolling coverage provided, was that the training had helped get over the core points of covering breaking news, alerted journalists to the dangers of rolling coverage, and made them more confident they could deal with them.

After the war, I continued for a year and a half to use this training program to equip new staff and re-acquaint existing staff with the skills needed to cover breaking/rolling news. The lessons from this helped me develop a semi-interactive, real-time online training tool, *The Journalism Tutor*, for the BBC College of Journalism—which trains journalists across the whole range of BBC news and current affairs output (*Journalism Tutor*). The *Tutor* did not use *War of the Worlds* but rather developed versions of the real-time exercises used in the face-to-face training. These would take the form for both uses (live and online interactive) of realistic but invented breaking news stories. Examples of ones used were an airline disaster which turned out to be an incident of insurgents shooting down a civilian airliner, and a scenario involving the death of a major world figure. Prior to the death of Pope John Paul II, I ran several live training sessions practicing what would be done live on air to cover developments. The scenarios would include a whole pack of crafted news dispatches, background information, invented eyewitness accounts, etc., and we would arrange journalists from the newsroom or program teams to play the parts of reporters, pundits or eyewitnesses to be interviewed. There would be regular time-outs in the exercises to discuss how the story was being covered, the style, and also to evaluate the coverage against criteria drawn from *War of the Worlds*.

After moving into academia, I used the broadcast as part of the introductory sessions for BA and MA students on radio journalism modules. Again, the participants in a session would be asked to identify key aspects of the broadcast that related to the fundamentals of radio news journalism.

Forensic Analysis of the *War of the Worlds* Broadcast

How did the *War of the Worlds* broadcast actually work as an example of live news reporting? First, the structure and rhythm of the dramatization accurately reproduced the cadence of breaking news coverage. The Mercury Theater successfully converted H.G. Wells's original story, set in Britain, into a breaking news story reported by a radio station in the eastern United States. After Orson Welles's introductory announcements—which were not played to the trainees or students—an announcer reads a weather report and then sends the audience to a hotel ballroom where Ramon Raquello and his orchestra are playing "La Cumparsita" (*War of the Worlds*, 1938). After a short spell, an announcer interrupts the music with a bulletin from the "Intercontinental Radio News" reporting gas explosions on Mars. The musical program resumes, followed by another bulletin that flags a forthcoming interview with Professor Pierson of the Princeton Observatory. An announcer returns the audience to the music, and then connects them to reporter Carl Phillips on the scene with Professor Pierson.

This opening mimics well the rhythm of radio news when there is a breaking story. Initial reports inserted into the on-air program are followed by a "handover" to a reporter on the scene. Overall, the broadcast creates a typical pattern of radio coverage:
- routine program
- news bulletin
- routine program
- news bulletin and trail ahead (flagging of interesting coverage to come later, used to keep listeners tuned in)
- routine program
- live news report by Phillips

This pattern continues as the play proceeds, with Phillips's live report from Grovers Mill taking the place of bulletins. Phillips also hands back to the normal program when he changes position, and when he is overcome by the attacking Martians.

In our training sessions, producers caught on to this quickly and so were able to discuss how, when there is a breaking story, we would expect them to report factually without speculation and switch to longer coverage of the news story when there is more to say or when we can go live to the scene or to a reporter or expert. So they rapidly got the idea of the structure, tempo and interrupted or nonconstant nature of news as it develops, though emphasizing that the longer coverage is then put in place as we have more to say and can sustain extended coverage.

After this initial, structural analysis of what we can learn from the broadcast, we moved onto an analysis of the organization and wording of the news reports themselves. From the first, they are cautious rather than sensational, attributing the information conveyed; for example, " ... Professor Farrell of the Mount Jennings Observatory, Chicago, Illinois, reports observing several explosions ... Professor Pierson of the Observatory at Princeton confirms Farrell's observation, and describes the phenomenon as, quote, like a jet of blue flame shot from a gun, unquote" (*War of the Worlds*, 1938). The quote is factual but includes the very colorful description of the flame from Pierson, clearly attributed. At no point does the reporter make assumptions, speculate or include un-sourced comment or information. While in modern radio news you would have a more accessibly structured news story, the point was to get across to producers and bulletin writers (who also attended the courses) that factual accuracy, attribution, sourcing and avoidance of speculation or comment were vital aspects of successful breaking news reporting that would be trusted over time by an audience. In today's competitive news environment, in order to impact and "hook" the audience, the exciting development would be put at the top of the story rather than the source. So, a more accessible version for today's market might read: "Several explosions of incandescent gas have been reported on the planet Mars by Professor Farrell of Mount Jennings Observatory, Chicago. They were described as being like a jet of blue flame shot from a gun by Professor Pierson at the Princeton Observatory."

When the music stops again and another news bulletin commences, it starts with the words, "following on the news given in our bulletin a moment ago," signaling clearly that this is further information on a story already reported (*War of the Worlds*, 1938). At the end of the news item, they trail ahead to the plan for an interview with Pierson (already quoted in a news story—and so both a newsmaker and an expert) at the Princeton Observatory. In training terms this was very good in reinforcing the need to keep your audience with you and to stay tuned in for more information on a breaking story—and, there was no attempt to pad out the news with extraneous or questionable detail to keep it running until the program could go to the live interview. This is clearly staged and real life news stories do not break so conveniently, quickly and with experts/participants so easily available. However, as an "ideal type" approach to covering breaking news it enabled us to keep plugging away about accuracy, sourcing, no speculation and both recapping on stories and trailing ahead to the next part of the coverage.

The switch to Carl Phillips at the observatory enabled the development of a strand of training/coaching covering live reporting for radio. Again, the dramatization is very staged and things are more clearly described and signposted than in normal reporting, but the exaggeration enables serious points to be made. One of the main ones is that description of surroundings needs to be clear, noises in the background need to be explained and the tone should be conversational, as it is with Phillips, talking *to* rather than *at* the audience. He gives a very clear picture of the observatory and of what Pierson is doing. Later the announcer and Phillips will use the term "word picture" to describe what they are trying to convey and this is a very good term for radio reporters; we urged our reporters to give the audience a word picture—whether of a military encampment in the Gulf, a burning oil well or a bombed city. Phillips also prepares the audience for likely interruptions—giving dynamism to the scene and continuity and pace to the story.

On the scene, Phillips asks questions that are short, clear and simple—but simple in a good way. Phillips does not try to pack his questions with detail or demonstrate his own knowledge or include his own speculation. Rather, he leaves that to the expert, and avoids presenting an over-complex or jargon-filled interview. Pierson, who would be an ideal interviewee in real life, explains any technical terms he uses and is succinct. There are no attempts to second-guess or to assume knowledge or show-off. Pierson is perhaps rather circumscribed and brief in his answers but they are clear and do not involve speculation, though there is reasoned interpretation.

Another important point is that Pierson is willing to admit when he doesn't know the answer and Phillips does not try to force an answer where one cannot be given without uninformed speculation. For example, when asked about the cause of the gas eruptions, Pierson simply says, "Mr. Phillips, I cannot account for it" (*War of the Worlds*, 1938). This addresses directly the Scud FM problem, outlined above, of experts guessing incorrectly and misleading the audience about the probable cause of an explosion. The only negative point in the interview with Pierson is Phillips's off the cuff remark that forty million miles seems a safe enough distance from Mars. Of course, this proves to be a fatal error and, as trainers, we could point out that potentially speculative off-the-cuff remarks by reporters or presenters should be avoided, although without reducing the broadcasts to non-conversational sterility. Throughout the exercise, we emphasized that a conversational tone allowed the reporter to reach out to the audience and make them feel as though the reporter was in their room with them. This, again, was an advantage of using *War of the Worlds* as an example because of what Hayes and Battles have identified as the importance of constant, two-way communication as a key aspect of the broadcast (Hayes & Battles, 2011, p. 56).

The interview is then interrupted and Phillips eventually reads out the telegram about the seismographic shock, which again Pierson declines to speculate about other than to say it could be a meteorite—a good lesson for journalists about not jumping to unfounded and speculative conclusions on the basis of little information and thereby misleading or alarming the audience. The program then effectively trails ahead to the next development through Pierson's comment that a search will be made for whatever caused the shock as soon as daylight permits. Phillips then hands back to the studio, where the news announcer maintains continuity of communication with a news bulletin highlighting the running story. For good rolling news that grabs and holds the audience the right mix of live reporting, updating the story, recapitulation, analysis and context have all to be included as well as the more subjective element of a conversational communicative style that makes the audience feel that they are involved. Phillips involves the audience well by asking them questions and talking to them as if they are there with him.

The section just discussed at the observatory provides very good pointers for both reporters and producers about how to describe surroundings, set the scene for interviews and conduct clear, conversational but focused interviews. We would write up these criteria on a white board in the training room/mock studio to be consulted during the live scenario exercise. During "time-outs" in the live scenario, trainees would measure their performance in the exercise against some of the criteria or good practices that we had as a group derived from *War of the Worlds*.

When the play moves on from Phillips at the observatory back to the studio, there is a news update which refers back to the "earlier reports received from American observatories" providing continuity and demonstrating, as we emphasized for the trainees, the need to continually relate new developments to what has already been reported to try to present a seamless stream of news rather than a series of rather disjointed reports. The news report updates the information available from Pierson during his interview and trails ahead to the arrival of Carl Phillips and his mobile unit at the scene. At this point the key phrase "word picture" is used to describe Phillips's task when he gets to Grovers Mill. The news update is also branded as from the Intercontinental Radio News. This again is a key aspect of rolling news coverage—constant branding so that the audience knows to whom they are listening and trailing ahead to keep them listening.

These were vital lessons and they were set out for journalists and constantly reinforced in the preparation for the Gulf coverage. The Mercury Theater production was amazingly prescient in its dramatization—divining very accurately how radio (and later TV) would develop as a news and reporting tool. The use of breaks, where the drama returned to music, was also a very good way of us strongly emphasizing that even with breaking news there will be times when there is nothing more to say and you need to return to non-news coverage or to other news stories. He also uses the device—still used in live broadcasting—of reminding the audience that nothing new has happened but when it does happen it will be related rapidly to the listener, again maintaining continuity of contact.

The scene then moves, after a short passage of music, to Grovers Mill where Carl Phillips once more takes up the story. He very usefully, from the point of view of using the broadcast as a training tool, emphasizes that he will "paint for you a word picture of the strange scene before my eyes, like something out of a modern Arabian Nights." As a flight of fancy, Phillips's Arabian Nights comment can be used in training to demonstrate the need to avoid getting carried away with the situation. Phillips then describes carefully and with no attempts at speculation what he can see and gets Pierson to take up the story, giving a clear and factual description of the object in the pit. Phillips usefully tells his audience that he's never seen anything like it rather than trying to develop his own theory or pushing Pierson to do so—a common failing in reporting unfolding events, with journalists desperately trying to provide immediate answers when they are not available. At this stage, we cautioned trainees about not getting too carried away with emotion or overly colorful descriptions.

The interview with the farm owner, Mr. Wilmuth, is a fine example of a difficult eyewitness interviewee and the need for journalists to prepare their interviewees for what they are going to be asked and what is expected of them. This is not a case of coaching eyewitnesses to say what you want them to say, but to try to get them to stick to what they saw, heard, did or experienced rather than waffling on about extraneous events or their unwanted opinions. The Wilmuth example is useful for demonstrating the need to tell the interviewee to speak into the microphone, to be concise, and to get to the point. Phillips has to keep interrupting Wilmuth and verbally nudging him in the right direction until he gets to the description of the impact—then he becomes very clipped and the interviewer has to work to get him to tell the audience what he heard and how he reacted. This provided excellent talking points in the training session about interviewing eyewitnesses who have little or no experience of being interviewed— the need for preparation and patient but firm guidance through questioning.

From the eyewitness interview we progress in radio technique terms to Phillips again telling the audience that he is trying to convey an atmosphere that is quite fantastic. His scene description is clear and takes the events into their listeners' living rooms; making the listeners as near to participants as possible. He describes clearly the scene at the farm and the tussle between the police and onlookers. This is followed by a good example of the conversational technique of reporting: Phillips asks his audience if they hear a noise. When he realizes that the noise is very low, he says he will move the microphone closer and, almost presuming the audience has answered him, says, "Now we're not more than twenty-five feet away. Can you hear it now?" (*War of the Worlds*, 1938). While this is overdone compared to a real news report, the exaggeration enables a trainer to draw out for his/her audience even more effectively the idea of radio not just being a presenter or reporter talking at an audience but of effectively developing a form of dialogue. Although the audience clearly cannot answer, they have unwittingly become participants through the conversational nature of the reporting. In sum, *War of the Worlds* clearly demonstrates the constancy and two-way nature of the conversation that should be developed with the audience in radio reporting.

The following interview with Pierson about the nature of the object—that turns out to be the Martian spacecraft—again demonstrates the need to avoid jumping to conclusions. Pierson is very factual in describing the craft and the materials of which it is made, using the phrase "I don't know what to think" at one stage. While this serves to create an element of suspense and maintain the carefully staged development of the story, it also enables a journalist to appreciate the need to avoid wild speculation. The story soon takes a more sinister turn with the emergence of the alien from the craft. Phillips at first maintains his practice of describing in purely factual detail before giving in to more emotional comments such as "I can hardly force myself to keep looking at it," followed by more lurid description (*War of the Worlds*, 1938). In the training session we discuss Phillips's emotional spells to determine where and to what extent emotion should come into the reports, and how a reporter can convey a scene with empathy without losing balance and distance.

In *War of the Worlds*, the suspense of the emerging Martians is cleverly prolonged by Phillips's decision to stop his report and move position. This cleverly mimics what could happen in real life, although more likely with the need to site cameras than to reposition a microphone. When the announcer returns the listener to the scene, Phillips describes his position and what he can see. As he tells the audience of the police and Professor Pierson approaching the craft, the reporter maintains his calm and factual approach literally up to the point where he meets his untimely end. This is the point at which the training session moves from listening to discussing the drama.

The Lessons of *War of the Worlds* for Journalists

As described above, the first 15 minutes of *War of the Worlds* can be used to demonstrate key elements of the task of reporting a breaking story for radio news. Clearly, many aspects are exaggerated or portrayed in a simplified and heavily emphatic way but the basic elements are all there:

- Clear, factual reporting
- Recapping the story when you return to it
- Branding your news service—identify the station regularly
- Trailing ahead to keep your audience tuned in—maintain the conversation
- Sourcing and attribution of key elements of the story
- Constant development and regular updates—constancy of communication
- On-the-spot reporting
- Utilization of expert opinion
- Avoidance of speculation
- Eyewitness material
- Involving the audience—making the reporting into a personal conversation rather than a lecture. It should be a two-way process

These are all core factors or skills in news reporting that were emphasized in the BBC breaking news sessions. These skills then informed the performance of the teams during the live exercise, and were used as points for discussion during time-outs or in the concluding session. The *War of the Worlds* broadcast, in itself, did not teach journalists news skills. It did, however, provide a clear and compelling example that helped journalists identify key elements of rolling coverage and develop confidence in reporting major breaking news stories.

At Brunel University, the broadcast was used in the first session of both the undergraduate and postgraduate radio journalism modules for the BA and MA in Journalism and the MA in International Journalism. The majority of students had little if any experience other than as listeners and had not thought in depth about the techniques and methods of news or reporting for the ear. The simplified and emphatic approach to the basics of reporting provided by the *War of the Worlds* was ideal in introducing students to the basics of radio news in an entertaining and engaging way—it meant that students could concentrate on the basic skills rather than the content of the story. It also intrigued them as it was something they were not expecting.

But why does the broadcast work so well as a training tool? Firstly, the *War of the Worlds* broadcast captured the conversational, friendly, and trusted nature of radio. As Lewis argues in his work on radio and radio techniques, the medium "plays a significant and intimate role as a friend, trusted informant and soundtrack for living in the everyday life of listeners" (Lewis). In the broadcast, this aspect of the medium was conveyed in the news bulletins and reports that emphasized the interconnection between broadcasters and listeners—particularly through the effective, conversational nature of Phillips's reporting. A rethinking of the history of radio propaganda reveals numerous cases where a model of exchange and interconnection between broadcasters and audiences provides a better way of interpreting the role of radio—in contexts as different as WWII and Rwanda—than a model of the dominating power of the medium (Somerville, 2012).

Secondly, the broadcast crystallized the basic conventions of radio communication through its stylized use of new reporting techniques. It seized upon the very fact that radio works, as Crissel has written, through auditory codes "consisting of speech, music, sounds and silence ... their deployment has to be relatively simple" (Crissel, 1986, p. 5). Welles's deployment was imaginative but basically simple and he attained a "technically convincing realism" (Hendy, 2000, p. 204). For this reason it works well as a training tool. The emphasis on some of these codes, the slightly repetitive nature of the reporting style (repeat of the term "word picture," for example) and the way that the reporter describes what he is doing and why he is doing it now, all work to provide an ideal type broadcast that can be analyzed and deconstructed to provide a toolbox of techniques for the radio journalist.

References

BBC On this day (1991, August 19). Hardliners launch coup against Gorbachev. *BBC On this day*. Retrieved from http://news.bbc.co.uk/onthisday/hi/dates/stories/august/19/newsid_2499000/2499453.stm

Crissel, A. (1986). *Understanding radio*. London: Routledge.

Crook, T. (1998). *International radio journalism: History, theory and practice*. London / New York, NY: Routledge.

Hayes, J.E., & Battles, K. (2011). Exchange and interconnection in US network radio: A reinterpretation of the 1938 *War of the Worlds* broadcast. *The Radio Journal, 9*(3), 51–62.

Hendy, D (2000). *Radio in the global age*. Cambridge, UK: Polity Press.

Journalism Tutor, The. (n.d.). BBC College of Journalism. Retrieved from http://www.bbc.co.uk/journalism/skills/writing-styles/journalism-tutor/

Kellow, C.L., & Steeves, H.L. (1998). The role of radio in the Rwandan genocide. *Journal of Communication, 48*(3), 107–28.

Lewis, P.M. (n.d.). In *Radio theory and community radio*. Retrieved from http://www.sosci.ku.nl/LRT/LRTpapers/lewis.htm

Radio 5 launches non-stop news. (n.d.). In *BBC Newswatch*. Retrieved from http://news.bbc.co.uk/1/shared/spl/hi/newswatch/history/noflash/html/1990s.stm

Radio Listeners in Panic, Taking War Drama as Fact (1938, October 31). *New York Times*, p. 1.

Somerville, K. (2012). *Radio propaganda and the broadcasting of hatred: Historical development and definitions*. London: Palgrave.

War of the worlds (1938). CBS Radio Network, Sunday October 30th.

CHAPTER SEVEN

Body Contact: Interconnection and Embodiment in Howard Stern's 9/11 Radio Broadcast

JOY ELIZABETH HAYES AND DANA GRAVESEN

In this chapter, Hayes and Gravesen explore the relevance of the *War of the Worlds* broadcast for understanding radio coverage of the Terrorist Attacks of September 11th, 2001 (9/11). Rather than looking at traditional news coverage, the chapter analyzes shock jock Howard Stern's radio broadcast from New York City on the morning of 9/11. The chapter focuses on the way that Stern's coverage highlighted the two-way potential of radio and positioned his body as a medium through which the public could experience the crisis. Hayes and Gravesen show how the broadcast was continuous in form and content with the broadcast era of *War of the Worlds*, at the same time that it prefigured the social media era in its coordination of multiple media and creation of an interactive web of communication.

Introduction

Although various forms of Internet communication shaped people's experiences of the terrorist attacks of September 11th, 2001—from email messages and images to Internet forums, websites, and instant messaging—broadcasting and cable dominated 9/11 coverage. Indeed, the televisual accounts of the attacks are arguably the most recognizable media artifacts of the last half-century. Rosemary V. Hathaway (2005) and others have identified the visual nature of planes colliding with the World Trade Center towers in New York City and the fires and explosions at the Pentagon in Washington, D.C. as dominant in both national and international narratives and sense-making of the events (see Abel, 2003; Jaworski, Fitzgerald, and Constantinou, 2005; Muntean, 2009). These images represent a "unified" country under attack, universally affected and victimized. They are exemplary of what Jesús Martín-Barbero (1993) has claimed as the homogenization of experience by television as a medium.

In contrast to the televisual focus of most 9/11 studies, we argue that radio played a key role in the way the event was experienced both at the time and in the months and years following.[1] Radio technology was at the heart of the 9/11 crisis in the flawed emergency communication systems used by first responders in New York City, the mobile phones and two-way radios used by civilians and officials during the attacks, the ground-to-air communication systems that monitored the hijacked planes, and the radio stations that covered the events. There is evidence that Americans turned increasingly to radio to understand the impact and meaning of 9/11. Radio listening grew in the 2000s as people tuned into NPR and other traditional news programs, as well as national conservative (and for a short time liberal) talk radio shows (Sherman, 2005). 9/11, war in Iraq and Afghanistan, and numerous subsequent natural and human-made disasters in the 2000s and 2010s revealed the continued relevance of radio broadcasting in the era of social media.[2]

Radio, then, offers a unique window onto how Americans experienced the 9/11 crisis. More importantly for our purposes, however, is the way that the crisis of 9/11 provides a new perspective on the form and content of radio at the beginning of the new millennium. In particular, we analyze shock jock Howard Stern's coverage of the event during his talk radio program originating from New York City on the morning of September 11th, 2001.[3] This chapter focuses on two main aspects of the show's coverage of the 9/11 crisis: the way it highlighted the inherent interconnectivity and interactivity of the radio medium; and the way it positioned Stern's body as a public medium through which to experience this event of national crisis. The crisis of 9/11 emphasized the central role played by Stern's "radio body" as a medium or node of exchange between media, broadcasters, and listeners. At the same time, it exposed radio's interconnectivity much in the way the "performed" crisis of the *War of the Worlds* broadcast did.

Hovering on the cusp of the social media era, Stern's coverage of the 9/11 attacks invites comparisons with both network radio of the 1930s and social media of the 2000s. In a broader sense, the mediated event of 9/11 resembled the broadcast event of *War of the Worlds* on many levels: as a sneak attack by a distant and obscure enemy at a time of social insecurity; as an event of such unexpected horror that it both demanded and defied belief; and as a communication event that was primarily experienced via traditional broadcast media. As will be detailed below, Stern's coverage followed the model of dispatch employed in the *War of the Worlds* dramatization (Hayes & Battles, 2011, p. 56). As with *War of the Worlds*, Stern's broadcast integrated communication from different media and relayed those communications to the audience via radio. On the other hand, the speed and scope of interactivity between broadcasters and listeners was greatly increased by the use of mobile phones and digital technology.

Our analysis of Stern's 9/11 broadcast indicates that the show's listeners became increasingly active "users" of the medium as the crisis unfolded and looked less and less like mass media "audiences." Although early 21st century listeners had access to new technologies for talking back to the radio, we claim that radio has always been a medium of social interaction via its technology, mode of address, and interconnection with other means of communication from face-to-face to letters to telephone to Internet. While the concept of para-social interaction theorizes the sense of connection that audiences have with mass media as an "illusion of intimacy" or "compensatory" sense of false sociability (Horton & Wohl, 2006), we contend that audiences build real connections with media through the social networks that shape their reception of, and response to, media content. In the case of the *Howard Stern Show*, we argue that the program built a web of intercommunication between Stern, his crew, his audience, and other media that resembled social media in its interactivity, networking, and blurring of private and public communication. In order to clarify the continuities and discontinuities between Stern's show and both broadcasting and social media, it is helpful to begin with an historical perspective on talk radio at the turn of the 21st century.

Shock, Talk, and the Reinvention of Radio

The emergence of talk radio in the 1980s represents a third moment of reinvention of radio broadcasting in the post-war period (the first being the rise of the disc jockey format in the 1950s, and the second being the FM revolution of the late 1960s and early 1970s—see Douglas, 1999). While the shock jock format is most strongly associated with Howard Stern, other national and regional practitioners include Don Imus, Oppie and Anthony, Bubba the Love Sponge, Mancow Muller, and Tom Likus. Lawrence Soley views shock radio as a hybrid of sexually oriented "topless radio" developed in the 1970s and aggressive "insult radio" pioneered by Joe Pyne in the 1960s (Soley, 2007, p. 78). Susan Douglas describes Stern and Imus as "horny, insubordinate twelve-year old boys" who drew largely male audiences with self-consciously aggressive and vulgar jokes and talk about sex, bodily functions, violence, ethnic or racial identity, gender and, occasionally, politics (Douglas, 1999, pp. 292, 318). Stern and other shock jocks exemplified a rejection of buttondown, bourgeois masculinity and a celebration of an uninhibited "boy-man" identity (Cross, 2008, p. 6; Douglas, 1999, p. 289).

A number of economic, political, social, and technological factors influenced the rise of talk radio in the 1980s and its continued expansion in the 1990s and 2000s.[4] While post-Watergate political disenchantment and economic dislocation fuelled the turn to talk, Douglas identifies a backlash against the feminist movement as key to the explosion of conservative male voices on the airwaves (Douglas, 1999). Both conservative talkers, epitomized by Rush Limbaugh, and the more libertarian shock jocks voiced a kind of "macho populism" that repudiated gender equality along with all forms of "political correctness" (Douglas, 1999, pp. 293, 304–306).

The use of satellite technology for program distribution reduced the cost of talk programming and encouraged national syndication, at the same time that increased commuter drive times and mobile phone technology promoted captive and responsive audiences (Douglas, 1999, pp. 295–299). At the same time, deregulation removed many federal controls on the ownership and content of broadcasting (including the Fairness Doctrine) and reduced the limits on crossownership of media. This process of deregulation, which both reflected and fuelled industry consolidation, culminated in the Telecommunications Act of 1996, which removed all national limits on station ownership (Fairchild, 1999). Industry concentration created radio conglomerates like Infinity Broadcasting (now CBS Radio) that nurtured the political talk and shock jock genres as profitable formats for national syndication (Soley, 2007).

Between the mid-1980s and mid-2000s, shock jocks drew large audiences in major U.S. radio markets. Although Stern's national listenership appears to have peaked in the early-to-mid-1990s, definitive national ratings are difficult to find. A number of station managers interviewed during the mid-1990s claimed that airing Stern would virtually guarantee a station a top three rating in its market (Petrozzello, 1996, p. 43). Although Stern's listenership fluctuated over the next decade, his ad revenue continued to rise despite concerns over offensive content and FCC indecency rulings (Flint, 2000). In 2004, Arbitron reported that 8.5 million people listened to Stern weekly on 35 U.S. stations; and New York City market data indicated that three-quarters of those listeners were men and half were in the 18–44 age bracket (MacBride, 2004, p. B1). Although the broader talk radio format remained second to country music during the 1990s, by late 2010 talk had become the nation's most popular radio format.[5] Ironically, although they were important to the ascendancy of talk radio, most shock jocks had left broadcasting for satellite radio by 2010 due to their increasingly shocking content and enhanced FCC enforcement.

Interconnection

Mediated Intimacy

While the shock jock genre of talk radio is a unique product of the late 20th century, it has important points of continuity with golden age radio in terms of its construction of mediated intimacy. The mediated intimacy generated by radio broadcasting, we argue, is a product of the very real interactivity that characterizes the medium. After first reviewing the history and theory of mediated intimacy, we analyze Howard Stern's 9/11 broadcast in order to show the kind of interactivity that radio enables, particularly in times of crisis.

From the very beginning, most observers viewed radio broadcasting as requiring a personal and intimate style of communication. Performers no longer had to amplify and project their speech, drama or music across public space to reach their congregated audiences. In fact, they faced the opposite problem. As Rudolph Arnheim (1936) observed,

> Anyone who does not possess [an] unaffected personal way of speaking suited to the short distance between the source of sound and the microphone, and to the isolated position of the individual listener, will never have his text understood by the listener.... (pp. 73–74)

Leading practitioners concluded early on that an intimate conversational tone was the best way to negotiate what they perceived as radio's "intrusion into the private sphere" (Lacey, 1994, p. 593). With deference to the genteel, "feminized" middle-class home, advertising experts encouraged radio speakers to communicate, "just as you would if you were seated before a cheery log fire or chatting over a cup of tea" (Marchand, 1985, p. 353). This personal, conversational approach was adopted by politicians as well as performers, and epitomized in FDR's famous Fireside Chat broadcasts (Jamieson, 1988; Lacey, 1994).

While mediated intimacy is sometimes viewed as an explicit strategy to "offset the inherent impersonality of the media" and mask mass address with an interpersonal veneer (Horton & Wohl, 2006; Munson, 2000, p. 115), this is an overly negative view of mass communication. Rather, as Jason Loviglio observes, "Radio voices were thrilling because they moved with impunity back and forth from private to public modes of performance" (Loviglio, p. xvii). Along with radio's intimacy, listeners enjoyed radio's ability to connect them with a community of listeners. This was particularly clear in the case of listener letters sent in response to President Roosevelt's (and even President Hoover's) radio addresses in which listeners expressed both a sense of personal connection with the speaker, and a feeling of communion with the thousands of others who simultaneously shared their listening experience. In Loviglio's terms, letter writers alternately identified themselves as particular subjects and "meta subjects" of the speech and the nation. Evidence from listener letters suggests that the "massness" enabled by radio could be as important as the sense of intimacy it created (Hayes, 2000; Loviglio, pp. xv, 5).

Paddy Scannell (2000) theorizes this double character of radio address as a "for-anyone-as-someone structure," that is, a mode of address that simultaneously speaks to the listener as an impersonal "anyone" and a personal "someone" (p. 9). In this mode of communication, he argues, the listener feels that she or he is being addressed personally, but also knows that other listeners are sharing this same experience (p. 11). Drawing on Heidegger, Scannell argues that "anyone" is an impersonal category defined by the mass-production of an object or address and the interchangeability of users or listeners. He later observes, however, that mass communication entails a sociability or "we-ness" that is experienced as communion with other listeners (Scannell, 2000, pp. 9, 12).

We argue that listeners recognize common ground with both the speaker and other listeners because all communication (including mass communication) must be addressed to someone. As V.N. Voloshinov (1986) observes, "there is no such thing as an abstract addressee" (p. 85). He continues:

> Orientation of the word toward the addressee has an extremely high significance. In point of fact, *word is a two-sided act*. It is determined equally by *whose* word it is and *for whom* it is meant. As word, it is precisely *the product of the reciprocal relationship between speaker and listener, addresser and addressee*. (p. 86)

As an act that is both addressed and answerable (Bakhtin, 1990), communication is always a product of interconnection and reciprocity. Mass communication may not be personal in the sense of knowing specifically to whom one speaks; however, it is addressed to, and is intelligible to, a culturally-, historically- and linguistically-specific group of listeners. In the case of the Fireside Chats, news, and other nonfiction programming, the listener is often addressed as a member of a national community, and that is the basis of the "we-ness" that she or he experiences (Billig, 1995; Hayes, 2000). Mediated intimacy, then, builds interconnections between listeners and speakers that are multidirectional and blur the line between private and public.

Masculine Intimacy in the *Howard Stern Show*

Interconnections between Stern and his crew, his guests, his listeners and a variety of other communication media were built into the show's daily formula. On the morning of September 11th, 2001, the show had been airing over New York City station WXRK for over 15 years and was nationally syndicated by station owner Infinity Broadcasting (now CBS Radio). Along with his ever-present co-host, Robin Quivers, Howard amassed a crew of participants who regularly joined him in the studio or from around the city via mobile phones. Stern's crew created an environment where unruly male voices offered mostly crude and offensive commentary on celebrities, sex, current events, or in-studio guests (usually women who were invited to sexually self-disclose and physically disrobe). Stern's interactions with his crew, guests, and listeners intentionally blurred the line between listeners and participants and added to the feeling of many listeners—even female listeners—that they "knew" Stern and could relate to him as "just one of the guys" (Zechowski, 2002, pp. 130, 157).

Stern's program format combined personal intimacy with a kind of "clubhouse" environment that gave listeners a sense of interconnection and community. Stern's deep, breathy voice spoke intimately into the microphone for the ear of the listener alone (often to share his own emotional response or describe his bodily arousal). At the same time, however, he created a shared space of "macho" camaraderie. Commentators have described listening to Stern as an experience of "loitering" in a men's locker room or bus station men's room (Douglas, 1999, p. 302). The *Howard Stern Show*, then, created multiple connections between Stern, his crew, his guests, and his listeners.

On the morning of 9/11, about two hours into his broadcast, Howard and the gang were having a typical locker-room-style conversation about his recent sexual contact, or lack thereof, with Pamela Anderson. Members of Stern's crew were trying to find out "how far" he had gotten with Anderson and admonishing him for not "sealing the deal" with her when he had the chance. Stern's access to Anderson signaled his own celebrity status at the time, which was based on his radio notoriety, his best-selling books *Private Parts* (1993) and *Miss America* (1995), his various media ventures, and his 1997 film version of *Private Parts*. Howard was casually bantering with his gang in the studio and via call-ins when he interrupted the conversation to relay the news that a plane had crashed into the World Trade Center.

The *Howard Stern Show*'s coverage of the crisis of the World Trade Center attacks highlights the interconnection of different modes of communication that are a regular part of the show (e.g., television, Internet, computer interface and satellite, landline and mobile phones). With the exception of the telephone, these means of communication are rarely mentioned at all, let alone fore-grounded, in talk radio. During the 9/11 crisis, however, the interactive potential of radio broadcasting was laid bare. Stern's show became a medium for dispatching and relaying communications between media, between listeners and media, and between listeners themselves.

To begin, the way that the news initially broke on the show revealed talk radio's interconnection with other media. After Howard interrupted the Pamela Anderson discussion with news of the plane crash, there was a brief discussion of the fire at the World Trade Center and what could be seen of it from the window of Stern's studio. Show regular, Ralph, who was on the phone from Brooklyn, reported that he could see a huge fire from his building. After some more talk about the World Trade Center, however, the conversation returned to Anderson for another several minutes until Howard's producer interrupted him to say: "Howard, you gotta watch your monitor. They're gonna play back; there was just an explosion!" The presence of the TV monitor in the studio is an indicator of the way that the show regularly incorporated a range of different kinds of communication and media into its broadcasts. More specifically, Stern's producer mentioned the need to pay attention to incoming communications in order to interpret, mediate, and dispatch them to his listeners.

Over the course of the rest of the radio show Howard and his crew stayed in constant contact with TV coverage of the event via sister station CBS Chanel 2, sometimes turning up the sound so that listeners could hear the TV report. They were initially quite confused about the visual footage being broadcast and the sketchy information being reported. However, they continued to respond to, discuss, and relay that information to the radio audience. Also notable was the way that listeners called in to relay information from other media—in a process similar to the posting and re-posting of mass media content on social media sites like Twitter, Facebook, and YouTube. For example, the producer informed Howard that, "somebody just called and said that on CNN, a *second* plane just crashed. . . . " Similarly, Matt called in with a report from another media channel:

> I'm watching FOX, uh, network here, and I just saw, uh, saw a thing, and on the thing it said that the FBI is, uh, almost verified that there's been a hijacking early this morning before the crash.

Given the failure of television and mobile telephone for at least some of the New York area audience, callers "posted" information from CNN and FOX on Stern's show in order to share it with Stern and his listeners. The permeability of the broadcast to reports and relays from other media appeared to increase as the crisis deepened.

Howard's interconnection with listeners via landline and mobile phones—a ubiquitous part of his and most other talk radio shows—also became newly "visible" during the 9/11 crisis. Normally these calls brought different voices into the conversation and relayed the opinions of different participants to Howard's crew and the listeners. However, the proximity of the World Trade Center attacks and the fact that they disrupted communications (including television and mobile phones in the New York area) meant that these calls took on a new role of relaying descriptions of events and updates on conditions in various parts of the city. Along with Ralph's eyewitness account from Brooklyn, Joey Boots called in from downtown with this emotional description:

> Howard, I'm looking at it from here ... you, you couldn't even believe the sight. I mean, I've never seen anything like this before. We heard the first explosion. It rocked my friend's apartment, and he lives — eh — West 4th Street, and that's downtown, and we could see the twin towers right from here, there's smoke billowing out of the side of the, the building, there's a hole in the side, then we saw the other plane flyin' around after we were out there watching it for a few minutes, and that plane disappeared into the building, and it blew up!

These calls relayed the state of physical and emotional conditions on the ground. Indeed, show regulars called to express their anger, frustration, and desire for violent retribution for the attacks.

By the second half of the broadcast, the show's role in relaying and dispatching information expanded to the point where the program became a hybrid of one-way and two-way communication.

In one case, Stern's show became a node of relay between one caller and another:

> CALLER: Hello. Could I, um, could I talk to, uh, to Cabbie?
>
> HOWARD: Yeah. Go ahead, he's on.
>
> CABBIE: Yeah, what's up?
>
> CALLER: Cabbie, um, what is Brooklyn look like? My, my girlfriend's some place in there. What — is that OK out there?
>
> CABBIE: Yeah, Brooklyn's fine. It's, ah, i— i— they're not, it appears they're not letting anybody into the city. All the bridges out are, are filled with cars. Um, people are trying to walk across the, uh, there's a walkway goin' into the city, and it looks like they're being turned back, and told they cannot go into the city.

Stern did not object to the caller's request to speak to Cabbie, and treated the relay as unremarkable. The caller used Stern's telephone connection to Cabbie as a way to learn about his girlfriend and Brooklyn in general. Stern appeared comfortable with the show's role as a kind of message board or node of two-way communication during the crisis.

At a couple of points during the broadcast when Stern considered leaving the air, his producer, Gary Dell'Abate, convinced him that he should continue mediating events and dispatching important information to listeners. Local affiliates were still airing the show, he argued, and Stern was a comforting presence and reminder of normalcy. In the final hour of the broadcast, Dell'Abate described Stern's marathon show as a "good service to the public," harkening back to radio's original mandate to serve the "public interest, convenience and necessity." During the 9/11 crisis, Stern played a hybrid role of being a familiar and dominating radio presence, and acting as a medium of two-way exchange and interconnection.

Embodiment

Sincerity and Reciprocity

Another important point of continuity between the *Howard Stern Show* and golden age radio was the host's use of embodiment as a means of conveying sincerity and communicative reciprocity with listeners. Our concept of embodiment is drawn from Linda William's notion of body genre and from M.M. Bakhtin's theorization of the grotesque body. Williams' work examines film genres that are premised upon, "the spectacle of a body caught in the grip of intense sensation or emotion." These genres, namely melodrama, horror, and pornography, are defined not only by the excessive display of bodily functions or emotions, but by, "the perception that the body of the spectator is caught up in an almost involuntary mimicry of the emotion or sensation of the body on the screen ... " (Williams, 1991, p. 4). In other words, the intent of a body genre text is to elicit a physical reaction from the spectator: orgasm, ejaculation, hairs standing up, screams, accelerated pulses, tears.

Although Williams' framework has been applied, critiqued, and expanded in film studies (e.g., Case, 2000; Hills, 2005; Hunt, 2000; Keith, 2007; Showalter, 2000; Williams, 1999, 2002), it has yet to be applied to broadcasting. Following Williams, we use the concept of embodiment to describe the performance of bodily excess (emotional or physical) over the radio with the intent to produce a commensurate and reciprocal response on the part of listeners. While embodiment has been a regular strategy of U.S. commercial radio from the beginning, we argue that the shock jock radio genre represents a kind of high water mark of bodily excess. The shock jock's emotional outbursts, use of offensive language (racist, sexist, etc.), and frank discussions of sexual bodies and acts are designed to produce similar bodily reactions in listeners. The fact that shock jocks can directly interact with their listeners, however, adds a dimension of interaction and exchange that is not possible with a film text.

Bakhtin's theory of the grotesque body is also relevant for analyzing shock jock radio because it connects bodily excess to popular resistance, and because it focuses on the body as a medium of social interaction. In *Rabelais and His World* (1984), Bakhtin argues that grotesque embodiment ignores the smooth, impenetrable surfaces of the body, and zeroes in on the "convexities and orifices"—the genital organs, the anus and buttocks, the belly, the mouth and the nose (p. 319). The focus on the "lower strata" of the body, Bakhtin argues, offers a socially situated critique of "official culture" and respectability (1984, p. 437). Indeed, several studies of the shock jock phenomenon have suggested that the grotesque content of Stern's show can be read as a working class or populist critique of bourgeois civility (Douglas, 1999; Zechowski, 2002). In addition, the grotesque body is not an individuated or isolated body, but an excessive body that comes together with other bodies, shares fluids, and produces new kinds of social contact. Grotesque embodiment focuses on zones of stimulation and interaction between bodies, in the same way that body genres emphasize reciprocal excess on the part of performers and audiences.

A concept of embodiment enriches our understanding of the perceived sincerity of radio voices. In his study of British wartime crooner, Vera Lynn, Scannell declares: "Sincerity mediates intimacy; it is its medium of communication." Although Scannell defines sincerity as "self-disclosure without concealment," he outlines a couple of different ways that radio performers can be read as sincere. First, they can appear to be genuine; that is, to give listeners access to themselves as real people rather than performers. Second, they can willingly conduct interpersonal intimacy with others (Scannell, 1996, p. 65). While noting the paradox in sincerity between disclosure and performance, Scannell appears to come down on the side of performance when he concludes that audiences perceive sincerity when the singer, "performs as if she believes what she sings" (p. 67). The ability of performers to act as if they believe in their own performances, then, seems to provide the best evidence of sincerity.

In their famous study of U.S. singer Kate Smith, researchers Robert K. Merton, Marjorie Fiske, and Alberta Curtis found that Smith's perceived sincerity was key in persuading listeners to buy war bonds (Merton, Fiske & Curtis, 1946). In particular, listeners responded to the way that Smith's radio voice communicated (both described and performed) her physical exhaustion and bodily sacrifice in staying on the air for so many hours during her bond drive marathon. Her sacrifice inspired listeners to make sacrifices of their own and commit their limited funds to purchase war bonds. Merton, Fiske, and Curtis argued that the view of Smith's embodied radio performance as sincere was augmented by a more general perception of her body as a sign of sincerity or lack of artifice. As one participant observed, "she's just fat, plain Kate Smith" (Merton et al., 1946, p. 147). Embodiment, then, could enhance radio performers' appearance of sincerity.

Howard Stern's resonant radio voice similarly conveyed sincerity by describing and performing its own bodily responses and attempting to invoke bodily responses in listeners. In this, he followed in a long line of male singers and talkers who used their excessive "radio bodies" to "touch" listeners and evoke strong reactions (see McCracken, 1999). Arthur Godfrey and Ted Malone were two marathon talkers who had long careers on national radio based on their embodied intimacy. Stern's commanding, macho voice is reminiscent of Godfrey's, while his use of the medium for sensual contact is reminiscent of Malone. Malone read poetry and chatted intimately with daytime listeners over the CBS network during the 1930s-1950s, and the fan mail he received became the subject of Elihu Katz's 1950 master's thesis (Simonson, 2012). In 1935 he described his relationship with female listeners to *Newsweek* in the following terms: "Sometimes I play games with them. . . . Sometimes I make love. If I blow softly across the microphone, their eardrums will vibrate just as though I'd blown in their ears" (Dunning, 1998, p. 82). Malone understood his sentimental and aural excess as a means of physically stimulating his listeners and producing a sensual response on their part.

In the film version of *Private Parts* (1997), one scene depicts a radio bit in which a woman attempts to have sex with Stern over the radio. Stern tells the woman to place her stereo speaker on the floor of her apartment, max out the volume, turn the bass all the way up and the treble all the way down, and straddle the speaker. The woman complies. She removes her panties, straddles the speakers, and begins to pleasure herself while Stern vibrates his lips into his studio microphone. In the film, the woman climaxes from the experience, screaming out "Howard," ripping her top, exposing her breasts, and dropping the phone. But the event never actually happened over the airwaves. A few months after the film's premiere, an attempt by Stern to reenact the scene with a female caller resulted in failure. Stern and the caller had trouble communicating with one another given the extensive delay imposed on Stern's show by corporate parent Infinity broadcasting. Listeners had to contend with overhearing the "live" broadcast (already delayed), the caller speaking into her phone, and the sound of the minutes-delayed Stern show, pumped up to full volume, through the woman's phone and then rebroadcast. Stern ends up hanging up on the woman after asking, "Who's stupider, her or me?" Although a failed attempt, the intent of the segment was to bring the woman to orgasm using Stern's voice and radio technology—a combination of voice, vibration, and the human body.

Stern's Radio Body

In his daily radio show, Stern not only described his own bodily responses to in-studio sexual escapades, he also performed various bodily functions and responses for the microphone, including belching and farting. Excessive bodily responses were a regular part of his everyday humor and sex talk. Stern's embodied response to the 9/11 crisis, however, unfolded gradually as the nature and scope of the attacks became evident. On the morning of the broadcast, when Howard and his crew first realized that planes had crashed into both towers of the World Trade Center, Howard exclaimed "Oh My God," and his voice began to sound angry, but contained. After watching video of the second plane hitting the tower, Howard's voice rose with alarm: "We're under attack! We're under attack! It's war. C'mon!"

Initially, Stern seemed reluctant to express his emotions fully, and he tried to describe his anger in a dispassionate way by saying, "Oh, this is so aggravating," and, "Yeah, I am speechless." Stern's apparent calm stood out in contrast to caller Joey Boots, who became audibly upset after describing the collision of the second plane. His voice was threaded with anger when he cried, "This, this is them towel-head bastards!" He added, "It's about time we take these towel-head bastards, and throw 'em out of the damn country!" In response, Howard said, "Well, don't over react, kid," and both he and Robin tried to diffuse Joey's statements. Joey's voice started to break as he cried, "I just want to hurt somebody now!"

While Howard and Robin expressed sympathy with Joey's anger, they may have been concerned that his outburst would be construed as inciting violence against Arab Americans. Stern appeared to exercise some caution in terms of how far he could go in broadcasting incendiary racist and xenophobic statements. While Stern worked to contain outbursts involving violence on the domestic scene, he became increasingly expressive with regards to violence against Arabs on foreign soil. With a quiet anger he observed that, "The Israelis could kill everyone over there. They got the, they got the manpower, they got the bomb, they got everything." He complained that George Bush did not have the "chutzpah" to bomb the terrorists and stated, "We need a guy who didn't grow up rich, a guy like me who will bomb things because he is angry."

Stern's anger became more audible and embodied as the nature of the attack began to unfold. Following the Pearl Harbor analogy, Stern ranted that the U.S. should use nuclear weapons on the Arab World and "burn their eyes out with atomic bombs." He also began to describe his body's reaction to the crisis: "I swear to you I'm getting queasy ... I'm having trouble breathin.' I'm very angry! I feel that people need to suffer now." While Howard's wrath was focused on countries in the Middle East rather than on Arab Americans, he began to echo Joey Boot's emotional language and call for immediate violence. After Cabbie called in to express his feelings of shock, disgust, and anger, Howard stated, "I'm in shock too, and I tell ya one thing ... I'm getting increasingly, uh, woozy from this." Stern's bodily response signaled the sincerity of his revulsion and anger, and provided listeners with a medium through which to share their own somatic responses to the crisis.

Not surprisingly, the collapse of the first World Trade Center tower elicited a particularly strong emotional response from Stern and his crew. Even before the collapse, Stern's anti-Arab rhetoric had escalated as he described "animal countries" that needed to be taught the lesson that, "we are the boss, and you are going to be our dogs, and you have gotta be spanked." Although show regular, Dominick, asked him to, "not be the leader of these thoughts right now," Stern's shrill rhetoric did not abate. Again, however, we see Stern and his crew make a clear distinction between violence at home and violence abroad. When Zolar called in to encourage listeners to attack Arab Americans, Howard, Robin, and others in the studio shouted him down:

> ZOLAR: I'm going to go out there and start going to those A-rab stores and I'm going to start kickin'—
>
> (raised voices)

HOWARD: No, you don't want to do that, you don't want to do that, don't say that Zolar!

ZOLAR: I implore all Americans to get your arms together baby, get out there on the streets, and go to your local freakin' deli —

(raised voices)

HOWARD: Alright, I got him ... He's just upset.

Howard cut off Zolar's call, but simultaneously expressed sympathy with his bigoted anger and call for violence. As in the case of Joey Boots, Stern was careful not to endorse domestic attacks, while he continued to vilify Arabs in general and advocate full-on war against Arab countries.

Throughout the over-five-hour-long broadcast, Stern's "radio body" expressed a range of emotional and physical states, from controlled anger, to speechlessness, to nausea, to virulent anger. Towards the end of the broadcast, Stern stated, "And I'm angry. I'm angry right now and I'm not tryin' tuh — I don't care how the radio show sounds or not, I mean, I just genuinely feel this way." He did not try to contain his bodily excess (whether it be sexual arousal during his routine broadcasts or violent anger during the 9/11 crisis). Rather, Stern's physical and emotional excess created a zone of "body contact" between himself and his listeners. In addition, Stern's bodily excess acted as a witness to his sincerity, and intimacy, with his broadcast listeners.

Conclusion

This chapter examines two key elements of the *Howard Stern Show's* coverage of the 9/11 crisis: the way it highlighted the interactive potential of the radio medium; and the way it positioned Stern's body as a medium through which listeners could experience the national crisis. As in the *War of the Worlds* broadcast, Stern used his show as a kind of "crisis headquarters" where incoming information about the attacks could be relayed or dispatched to a network of participants and listeners. Stern's show differed from the *War of the Worlds* radio drama, however, in that listeners contributed to the dispatch of information in real time. In this way, the broadcast resembled a social networking platform that circulated user-generated information and posted content from other mass media. Also following the pattern of *War of the Worlds*, Stern's 9/11 broadcast increasingly incorporated elements of two-way communication as the show wore on. This occurred when a caller asked to be connected to another caller, and when Stern and his producers openly discussed the program's interconnection and exchange with other radio stations as well as other media.

During the 9/11 broadcast, Stern did not stop being a domineering "shock jock" who controlled the conversation, determined the hawkish ideology espoused by the show, and limited callers' access to the air (as witnessed by his hang-up on Zolar). For good or ill or both, Stern channeled the violent retribution demanded by himself, his crew and callers away from the domestic front and toward foreign soil. He committed a great deal of his time and energy during the broadcast to calling for an all-out war against Middle-Eastern countries that supported terrorism, even advocating the use of nuclear weapons. Ultimately, Stern created a hybrid role for himself during the crisis that combined his strong-willed shock jock personality with an increasing openness to two-way exchange and interconnection as the crisis deepened.

The role of embodiment in the Stern broadcast is both continuous and discontinuous with early radio broadcasting. As explored above, Stern followed in the footsteps of early talkers like Godfrey and Malone who could "touch" listeners with their somatic radio voices. Similarly, Stern's response to the 9/11 attacks—including excitement, anger and nausea—resembled Carl Philips's embodied reaction to the Martian attack in *War of the Worlds*. The response of the play's fictional reporter, in turn, was modeled on Herb Morrison's live report on the 1937 Hindenburg disaster, in which Morrison registered his powerful emotional and physical shock while continuing to describe and monitor the impact of the explosion (Crook, 1998). Stern's bodily response signaled the sincerity of his revulsion and anger, and provided listeners with a medium through which to share their own embodied responses to the crisis.

Shock jocks like Stern, however, distinguished themselves from early broadcasters by engaging in a new extreme of bodily excess. The shock jock's emotional outbursts, use of offensive language (racist, sexist, etc.), and frank discussions of sexual bodies and acts were designed to produce similar bodily reactions in listeners. Bakhtin's concept of the grotesque body and Williams' theory of body genres offer a framework for interpreting the form, content, and potential impact of this important broadcasting practice, which remains glaringly understudied.

Notes

[1] In terms of media access, New Yorkers might have experienced 9/11 differently than the rest of the nation because, "Seconds after the attack began at the World Trade Center, six of the city's eight major television stations, whose broadcast antennas were on the 300-foot mast atop the north tower, lost their signals" (Blair, 2001, n.p.).

[2] Large-scale disasters of this era include the Indian Ocean Tsunami in 2004, Hurricane Katrina in 2005, the Deepwater Horizon Oil Spill of 2010, and the Fukushima Daiichi nuclear disaster of 2011.

[3] Our analysis is based on a digital copy (5 hours and 21 minutes long) of the original broadcast of the 9/11 *Howard Stern Show* recorded from Boston station WBCN (now off the air) and a transcript made from one of the rebroadcasts of the original show. Unofficial recordings of the broadcast are readily available online, and by using two different sources we are able to check them against each other in order to verify their content.

[4] Despite all of these reasons explaining the growth of talk radio in the U.S., it is important to note that the explosion of talk radio was also a global phenomenon. Thus the rise of talk radio should be linked to broader global changes, such as the spread of automobiles and mobile phones and the rise of large urban centers where commute times for workers are ever increasing.

[5] The website *Inside Radio* recognizes a decade-long (2001–2010) decrease in the combined AM and FM stations that identify as "country" and a simultaneous increase in those that identify as "news/talk." By 2011, talk radio had taken the lead over country music—for years the nation's most popular format—in format counts (see http://goo.gl/6cWsN).

References

Abel, M. (2003). Don DeLillo's "In the Ruins of the Future": Literature, images, and the rhetoric of seeing 9/11. *PMLA, 118*, 1236–1250.

Appel, E.C. (2003). Rush to judgment: Burlesque, tragedy, and hierarchal alchemy in the rhetoric of America's foremost political talk show host. *Southern Communication Journal, 68*, 217–230.

Arnheim, R., Ludwig, M., & Read, H. (1936). *Radio*. London: Faber & Faber.

Bakhtin, M. M. (1984). *Rabelais and his world* (H. Iswolsky Trans.). Bloomington, IN:

Indiana University Press.

Bakthin, M. M. (1990). In M. Holquist M.& V. Liapudov (eds.), *Art and answerability*. Austin, TX: University of Texas Press.

Billig, M. (1995). *Banal nationalism*. Thousand Oaks, CA: Sage.

Blair, J. (2001, September 22). A nation challenged: notebook: TV reception problems. *New York Times*. Retrieved from http://goo.gl/Fe10C.

Case, S. (2000). Tracking the vampire. In K. Gelder (ed.), *The horror reader* (198–209). New York, NY: Routledge.

Crook, T. (1998). *International radio journalism: History, theory and practice*. London / New York, NY: Routledge.

Cross, G.S. (2008). *Men to boys: The making of modern immaturity*. New York, NY: Columbia University Press.

Douglas, S. J. (1999). *Listening In: Radio and the American Imagination*. London, UK: University of Minnesota Press, 1999. Print.

Dunning, J. (1998). *On the air: The encyclopedia of old-time radio*. New York, NY: Oxford University Press.

Fairchild, C. (1999). Deterritorializing radio: Deregulation and the continuing triumph of the corporatist perspective ... *Media, Culture & Society, 21*(4), 549–13.

Fiske, J. (1996). *Media matters: Race and gender in U.S. politics*. Minneapolis, MN: University of Minnesota Press.

Fiske, J. (1987). *Television culture*. London, UK: Methuen.

Flint, J. (2000, 07 September). FM's shock jock loses listeners. *Wall Street Journal*, pp. B1.

Hathaway, R.V. (2005). Life in the TV: The visual nature of 9/11 lore and its impact on vernacular response. *Journal of Folklore Research, 42*, 33–56.

Hayes, J. E. (2000). Did Herbert Hoover broadcast the first fireside chat? Rethinking the origins of Roosevelt's radio genius. *Journal of Radio Studies, 7*(1), 76–92.

Hills, M. (2005). *The pleasures of horror*. New York, NY: Continuum.

Horton, D., & Wohl, R. R. (2006). Mass communication and para-social interaction: Observations on intimacy at a distance. [Originally published in *Psychiatry* in 1954.] *Particip@tions, 3*(1). Retrieved from http://www.participations.org/-volume%203/issue%201/3_01_hortonwohl.htm

Hunt, L. (2000). A (sadistic) night at the *opera*: Notes on the Italian horror film. In K. Gelder (ed.), *The horror reader* (198–209). New York, NY: Routledge.

Jamieson, K.H., & Cappella. J.N. (2008). *Echo chamber: Rush Limbaugh and the conservative media establishment*. New York, NY: Oxford University Press.

Jamieson, K.H. (1988). *Eloquence in an electronic age: The transformation of political speechmaking*. New York, NY: Oxford Univ. Press.

Jaworski, A., Fitzgerald, R., & Constantinou, O. (2005) Busy saying nothing new: Live silence in TV reporting of 9/11. *Multilingua, 24*, 121–144.

Keith, B. (2007). *Film genre: From iconography to ideology*. New York, NY: Wallflower.

Lacey, K. (1994). From *Plauderie* to propaganda: on women's radio in Germany, 1924–1935. *Media, Culture & Society, 16*, 589–607.

Lee, G., & Cappella. J.N. (2001). The effects of political talk radio on political attitude formation: Exposure versus knowledge. *Political Communication, 18*, 369–394.

Loviglio, J. (2005). *Radio's intimate public: Network broadcasting and mass-mediated democracy*. Minneapolis, MN: University of Minnesota Press.

Marchand, R. (1985). *Advertising the American dream: Making way for modernity, 1920–1940*. Los Angeles, CA: University of California Press.

Martín-Barbero, J. (1993). *Communication, culture and hegemony: From the media to mediations*. Thousand Oaks, CA: Sage.

McBride, S. (2004, 08 March). He 'is what he is': Advertisers stand by Howard Stern. *Wall Street Journal*, p. B1.

McCracken, A. (1999). "God's gift to us girls:" Crooning, gender, and the re-creation of American popular song, 1928–1933. *American Music, 17*(4), 365–395.

Merton, R. K., Lowenthal, M. F., & Curtis, A. (2004). *Mass persuasion: The social psychology of a war bond drive* (1st Howard Fertig pbk. ed.). New York, NY: H. Fertig.

Munson, W. (1993). *All talk: The talkshow in media culture*. Philadelphia, PA: Temple University Press.

Muntean, N. (2009). "It was just like a movie": Trauma, memory, and the mediation of 9/11. *Journal of Popular Film and Television, 37*, 50–59.

Petrozzello, D. (1996). Will Howard Stern play in Peoria? *Broadcasting & Cable, 126*(12), 42–44.

Scannell, P. (2000). "For-anyone-as-someone Structures." *Media, Culture & Society, 22*(5), 5–24.

Sherman, S. (2005). Good, gray NPR. *Nation, 280*(20), 34–40.

Showalter, E. (2000). Dr. Jekyll's closet. In K. Gelder (ed.), *The horror reader* (pp. 190–197). New York, NY: Routledge.

Simonson, P. (2012). Mail and females at the Bureau: The happiness game in the gendered contexts of early U.S. communications research. *International Journal of Communication, 6*, 1277–1289.

Soley, L. (2007). Sex and shock jocks: An analysis of the Howard Stern and Bob & Tom Shows. *Journal of Promotion Management, 13*(1), 75. doi:10.1300/J057v13n0106

Stern, H. (1995). *Miss America*. New York, NY: Regan Books.

Voloshinov, V. N. (1986). *Marxism and the philosophy of language*. Cambridge, UK: Harvard University Press.

Williams, L. (2002). *Playing the race card: Melodramas of black & white from Uncle Tom to O.J. Simpson*. Princeton, NJ: Princeton University Press.

Williams, L. (1999). *Hard core: Power, pleasure and the "frenzy of the visible."* Berkeley, CA: Universtiy of California Press.

Williams, L. (1991). Film bodies: Gender, genre, and excess. *Film Quarterly, 44*, 2–13.

Zechowski, S. (2002). *Howard Stern and the women who love him: Working-class subjectivity and the discourse of male talk.* (Ph.D., Ohio University).

CHAPTER EIGHT

Mediating Misinformation: Hoaxes and the Digital Turn

ZACK STIEGLER AND BRANDON SZUMINSKY

In this chapter, Stiegler and Szuminsky trace the history of media hoaxes from the era of traditional mass media to the age of social media. The chapter reviews the debated status of the *War of the Worlds* as a media hoax and explores changes in the form and content of media hoaxes across "old" and "new" media. Stiegler and Szuminsky argue that the success of media hoaxes in both mass media and social media depends on trust, intimacy, or a combination of both. With social media, however, the opportunities for hoaxes have increased due to the possibility of user-generated hoaxes and the tendency of media users to prioritize speed over accuracy.

Introduction

Defined as mediated information with an intent to deceive, media hoaxes have historically called into question the legitimacy of media institutions, the circulation of information, and audiences' critical faculty. Hoaxes have been a consistent presence of our media landscape, despite seismic shifts in the ways that we consume, share, and process information. In fact, just as legitimate media content has had to adapt to the fundamentally different structures of new media, hoaxes have had to follow suit.

This chapter examines media hoaxes with respect to their traversal of the shift from mass to social media. In doing so, we pay particular attention to the impact of changes in culture, technology, and information flows. While some mechanics of hoaxes persist from the era of mass media, the transition to social media brought with it significant changes that have altered the way that media hoaxes operate: an increased opportunity for user-generated hoaxes, adoption of user-generated aesthetics by institutional media outlets, as well as the very structure of social media.

Collectively, these three factors speak to changes in cultural flows of information in a broad sense. However, they have also significantly altered the ways in which media hoaxes operate in the twenty-first century. This turn creates a clear demarcation between distinct eras of mass and social media, both of which facilitated hoaxes via their respective communication technologies.

Understanding Hoaxes

There are numerous instances of news media reporting false or exaggerated stories that subsequently produce fear and discomfort among audiences. Fears of noxious gasses in the tail of Halley's Comet, an alleged outbreak of slayings in the name of Satanic ritual, as well as reports of rape and murder in the Houston Astrodome in the wake of hurricane Katrina are but a few such examples (see Bartholomew and Radford, 2012). These cases exemplify news media's proclivity to latch onto sensational news stories without adequate fact checking. While they did scare media audiences, such stories appear to have had honest intentions, even as they neglected journalistic standards. Importantly, however, such inadvertent scares are fundamentally distinct from media hoaxes. Rather than simply misunderstood, erroneously reported, or miscommunicated information, hoaxes are consciously fabricated with the intent to deceive their audiences (Fedler, 1989, p. xii). In fact, such motives are apparent in the earliest recorded uses of the term in the nineteenth century.[1]

Similar to hoaxes are pranks, which McLeod (2005) argues "involve cooking up a story or an event in order to make a larger, satirical point" (p. 119). Both hoaxes and pranks set out to fool their audiences. Thus, pranks are a type of hoax, albeit one which seeks to have an impact beyond the story or event itself. We discuss such examples in this chapter, although we collapse them into a broader definition of "hoax." This broader scope grants a flexibility to the concept of hoaxes that is particularly useful in our historical approach.

To be sure, hoaxes resist simple classification, situating themselves in a space somewhere in between news and entertainment. Here, hoaxes conflate entertainment and news, mixing and manipulating elements of each. Certainly, hoaxes are not alone in occupying this liminal space. Infotainment staples, including hyperbolic talk show hosts, celebrity gossip, and soft news programs are its more common inhabitants. Yet, hoaxes provide a particularly vibrant example of media phenomena that blur the lines between news and entertainment as well as those between fact and fiction. Still, it is the intent to deceive or trick audiences that distinguishes hoaxes from other forms of misinformation and panic generated by media outlets.

Beyond intent, the particular media technologies utilized directly shape not only the transmission of hoaxes, but also their scope, impact, reception, and audiences' level of engagement with them. In short, the medium matters. Marshall McLuhan's well-worn adage that "the medium is the message" illuminates our understanding of how shifts in the media landscape affect the nature of media hoaxes as well as how they function socially.

McLuhan (1964) famously argued that what is significant about media technologies is not the messages that they contain, but their larger impact on society — "the change of scale or pace or pattern that it introduces into human affairs [...] it is the medium that shapes and controls the scale and form of human association and action" (p. 24). This macro-level perspective emphasizes that the significance of mass media is both social and historical, a point that is especially evident when contrasting the eras of mass and social media. Mass media hoaxes illustrate the "scale and form[s] of human association and action" within these eras, underscoring the characteristics of specific media technologies as well as the ways in which they shape our social relations. It is those social relations that led McLuhan to characterize media as "extensions of man," which for him was nowhere more apparent than in mass media.

Hoaxes in the Age of Mass Media

Despite its heavy usage, the very term "mass media" can be quite vague. Here, we use "mass media" to refer to centrally produced, and often commercial media content distributed to large scale mass audiences. Consequently, we use "mass media era" to compartmentalize the historical epoch in which these media flourished, encompassing the mid-19th century through the whole of the 20th. Mass media allowed the few to communicate with the many, disseminating important news and information at a hitherto unprecedented speed. Yet, mass media also allowed mass communication technologies to be used as a means of manipulating, persuading, and fooling the public through the spread of hoaxes and misinformation.

Newspaper Hoaxes

Mass media hoaxes had their first iterations in newspapers of the 19th century. The content, form, and impact of newspaper hoaxes are products of both cultural and technological characteristics. Newspapers in the 19th century were a fiercely competitive media business, faced with constant pressures of competition for a limited readership and, by extension, advertising dollars.

As advances in technology made production cheaper, presses began to offer their papers for a penny, meaning publishers were unable to undercut competitors' prices. As such, content became the primary competitive battleground. No longer the sole province of the erudite, newspapers now vied for audiences by featuring crime, scandal, sensationalism, sex, and human interest stories. The pressure to stand out among competitors also encouraged journalists to embellish or bend the truth, at times even falsifying information for the sake of producing a better story. In effect, the age of yellow journalism at the turn of the century normalized such press sensationalism. Thus, by the time some newspapers engaged in full-blown hoaxes, the content, language, and tone of the articles in question were already familiar to audiences.

This familiarity aided in audiences' acceptance of the *Sun*'s publication of perhaps the most notorious media hoax of its time (Bartholomew and Radford, 2012, pp. 79–80). Presented over the course of six days in the *Sun*, journalist Richard Adams Locke presented several "findings" culled from the defunct *Edinburgh Journal of Science*. The hoax began rather innocuously, reporting the discovery of vegetation on the moon. But with each day's report the articles grew increasingly detailed and fantastical, culminating in his most incredible discovery:

creatures that resembled men in stature but were anatomically more kindred to bats.[2]

Locke's series produced the desired effect. Sales skyrocketed, making the *Sun* the world's most widely circulated newspaper. Other papers unknowingly perpetuated the hoax by printing their own stories based on Locke's reports. The hoax drew on the longstanding belief of educated individuals in the West that life existed on the moon, planets and other heavenly bodies. According to Copeland (2007), people had been waiting for proof, and the work of astronomer William Hershel promised to reveal conclusively that life existed on the moon. Locke built his famous story around Hershel's son's well-publicized failed attempt to see Halley's Comet from South Africa, giving it a strong ring of truth (Copeland, 2007).

So strong was the acceptance of Locke's stories that when some rivals called out the story as a hoax, readers thought such critics jealous of the *Sun*'s newfound success (Fedler, 1989, p. 64). Faced with the difficulty of furnishing evidence to skeptics as well as a stream of requests for republication rights, Locke and the *Sun* came clean about the stories' falsity a month after publication. Despite this eventual confession, Locke's moon hoax was incredibly successful both at fooling audiences and gaining greater exposure for the *Sun*.

Whereas Locke's moon hoax was a self-serving venture to boost sales, other newspaper journalists employed sensationalist hoaxes to raise awareness of social issues. For example, in 1874, the *New York Herald* reported that due to poor maintenance of cages and locks, wild animals had escaped from the Central Park Zoo and were freely roaming the streets. An imagined bloodbath ensued as lions, bears, panthers, rhinos, tigers, and wolves rampaged through New York City, maiming, mutilating, and killing citizen bystanders (Bartholomew and Radford, 2011, pp. 84–86).

The *Chicago Times* published a similar hoax in 1875, in which Wilbur Storey fabricated a story of a blaze erupting at a local theater. Lacking side doors, the theater bottlenecked the endangered crowd, who perished in the flames (Fedler, 1989, pp. 98–103). Both the *Herald*'s Central Park Zoo hoax and the *Times*' piece on the Chicago theater fire announced their true nature within the text of their respective articles, exposing the deception as well as explaining the intent to raise awareness of legitimate public safety concerns.[3] Yet, both articles failed in that mission, as most readers did not look past the alarmist opening paragraphs, and thus took them to be true.

Today it seems implausible that large segments of a newspaper's audience would accept stories based entirely on false accounts. Yet, one must take into consideration characteristics of the medium itself, as well as the contemporary socio-cultural context. The minimal degree of media interconnectedness in the mid-late 19th century meant that communities lived in relative isolation. The filtered, gatekeeping local newspapers thus provided an intermediary between isolated communities and outside information.

The technological nature of print media also hampered the swiftness of information diffusion. Even as the penetration of the telegraph and telephone increased in the late 19th century, the pre-broadcast era had an inherent communication lag, which presented audiences with few opportunities to check one information source against others. Later technological developments would more easily allow for verification checks via switching to another broadcast station, up-to-the-minute news updates on 24-hour cable news, or instantaneous access to a seemingly unlimited pool of real-time information sources online. Absent these technologies, the print era's lack of fact-checking capacity facilitated audiences' acceptance of media hoaxes. As Bartholomew and Radford (2012) simply put it, "Verification was much slower" (p. 80).

Radio Hoaxes

Although relative isolation and lack of swiftness in the print age greatly contributed to believability, the immediacy and interconnectedness afforded by broadcast media did not diminish the effectiveness of media hoaxes. In fact, the increased speed of radio broadcasting sometimes served only to spread them more quickly.

As noted by Cantril, Herzog, and Gaudet (2008), the aesthetics of *War of the Worlds* greatly facilitated audiences' acceptance of the drama as true. Yet, beyond aesthetics, radio's structural and technological characteristics also play a significant role in the believability of hoaxes carried out on that medium. Radio's immediacy significantly eroded barriers of both time and distance in information dissemination. Coupled with radio's liveness, broadcasting up-to-the-minute news and information places a great deal of responsibility on radio stations. This is especially true of emergency and breaking news broadcasts, the aesthetics of which Welles and the Mercury Theater writers so meticulously studied. In turn, radio's role as a purveyor of up-to-the-minute news and information generates a high level of audience reliance upon and trust in the medium.

Radio is also unique in that it engenders a much more personal relationship with the listener than do newspapers or television. As Scannell (1996) explains, broadcast media operate as for-anyone-as-someone structures; they at once address an anonymous mass, but do so by addressing audience members individually (p. 14).[4] This manner of addressing mass audiences fosters a sense of intimacy between listeners and program hosts. To an admittedly limited extent, media audiences feel as if they "know" program hosts. In many ways, they do: daily, program hosts share their interests, passions, personality, and values with audiences. These projections may very well be affected constructions. However, their constructed nature does not particularly matter, for these are the personalities to which listeners attach themselves; these are the personalities that we feel we "know." Coupled with the trust engendered by radio stations' role as communicators of public information, this intimacy creates a unique relationship between broadcasters and audiences, and it is this sense of intimacy and trust that radio broadcasters exploit in their execution of media hoaxes.

An entire class of radio hoaxes capitalized on this perceived intimacy by directly involving popular disc jockeys. In an effort to generate publicity, Tuscon's KIKX orchestrated a hoax involving the supposed kidnapping of disc jockey Dennis Gropen in 1974. KIKX broadcast the news of Gropen's abduction, supported with fake police interviews. Even as other local media reported the kidnapping as a hoax, KIKX maintained the story's veracity. Once revealed as a hoax however, public sentiment was so strongly negative that the FCC refused to renew the station's license in 1980 (Federal Communications Commission, 1980).

Deejays at Los Angeles' KROQ hoaxed their listening audiences in 1999. In a segment inviting listeners to share their confessions on-air, one caller confessed to murdering his girlfriend, then promptly hung up. The call was staged by the program's hosts, but was so believable that local authorities initiated a homicide investigation. It wasn't until the *LA Times* exposed the hoax ten months later that KROQ came clean (Bartholomew and Radford, 2012, p. 28).

In contrast to the relatively insular KIKX and KROQ examples, many radio hoaxes convey a sense of danger to the larger community, which often produces a heightened reaction among audiences. In

1973, a small community radio station in Barsebäck, Sweden reported an accident at a local nuclear power plant. The broadcast went on to report that the accident created radioactive leaks that now threatened air quality and public safety. A subsequent audience study found that an alarming 70% of listeners believed the broadcast to be true (Bartholomew and Radford, 2012, footnote 1, chapter 5). As with the Chicago theater fire and Central Park Zoo stories, the motivation behind the Barseback hoax was not simply to dupe listeners, but to initiate dialogue, in this case about the safety of nuclear power (Bartholomew and Radford, p. 31).

Radio's lack of any visual component also aids its perpetration of hoaxes. A hoax as elaborate as *War of the Worlds* is significantly more difficult to execute on television, as audiences generally expect some sort of visual accompaniment to such "big" stories. Further, the hoaxes mentioned in this section capitalized on the perceived intimacy and trust that audiences placed in radio as source for breaking news and information. Indeed, the exploitation of broadcast's immediacy is also characteristic of television hoaxes.

Television Hoaxes

In contrast to radio, television's emphasis on the visual limits its ability to perpetrate hoaxes, as constructing a believable televisual aesthetic is much more difficult to achieve than one that is purely aural or textual in nature. Consequently, television has produced far fewer hoaxes than newspapers and radio.

This is not to say that TV's history has been absent successful hoaxes, however. There are, for example, a number of made-for-TV movies that significant numbers of viewers took to be legitimate news broadcasts. Taking a cue from *War of the Worlds*, these TV movies appropriated the aesthetics of legitimate news broadcasts so familiar to audiences, which no doubt aided their believability. NBC's 1983 film *Special Bulletin* presented a fictionalized narrative about a terrorist threat in Charleston, South Carolina. The movie included fictionalized live feeds from the terrorists as well as reports from the White House, Pentagon, Congress, and major news centers such as New York, which also lent an air of authenticity to the broadcast. To give *Special Bulletin* a greater semblance of broadcast aesthetics, producers recorded onto tape rather than film (Bartholomew and Radford, 2012, p. 38).

CBS's 1994 movie *Without Warning* took a related approach by including fictionalized news reports of an asteroid's pending collision with Earth. Capitalizing upon audiences' trust in reporters with whom they are familiar, *Without Warning* utilized real TV journalists playing themselves rather than fictionalized characters (Bartholomew and Radford, 2012, p. 40). In the cases of both *Special Bulletin* and *Without Warning*, segments of the TV audience took the fictional narratives to be legitimate news broadcasts, fueling concern and fear among some viewers ("WDAF Gets Calls"; "War of the Worlds Revisited"). Regarding *Without Warning* however, CBS later admitted receiving "more calls from reporters seeing if we'd received any calls than calls [from viewers themselves]" (Cox, 1994, 1).

As the examples chronicled here suggest, media hoaxes tend to emanate from media producers. Foreshadowing the characteristics of the digital turn, however, a recent television saga shows that hoaxes can generate from outside the media industries. In October 2009, the Heene family of Colorado made a panicked call to local KUSA-TV, claiming that a prototype hot air balloon had carried away their six-year-old son. Other news media soon picked up the "balloon boy" story, with CNN airing live footage nationally. After five hours of breathless news coverage, the boy emerged from his parents' attic to reveal that the entire ordeal had been a ruse.[5]

The balloon boy hoax is unique in that it was not the product of a media institution, although it spread via local and national news coverage. Unlike the Chicago fire hoax, *War of the Worlds*, or *Special Report*, the balloon boy hoax generated from a media consumer who successfully manipulated communication channels that traditionally restrict audiences to receptive roles. The balloon boy hoax upsets the traditional dynamic of mass media hoaxes, more closely resembling that of online and social media in recent decades.

In his exhaustive 1989 survey of mass media hoaxes, Fred Fedler (1989) comments that, "Americans no longer seem to enjoy hoaxes, nor that type of stunt and practical joking. People have changed, and so have the conditions that, for years, encouraged journalists to create the hoaxes" (p. xxv). Published a few short years ahead of the Internet revolution, Fedler's assessment cum eulogy for media hoaxes was premature. In fact, media hoaxes are alive and well in the twenty-first century, although the drastic changes in media technology have fundamentally changed their form and scale.

The Digital Turn: Hoaxes and Social Media

While hoaxes have long been a part of our mediated environs, several characteristics unique to social media have reshaped these messages: a) the increased opportunity for user-generated hoaxes; b) the adoption of user-generated aesthetics by institutional media, muddying the distinction between user- and institutionally-generated media messages; and c) the structure of social media as compared to traditional forms of media. In particular, social media have dramatically altered the way that hoaxes spread. Hoaxes don't always originate on social networks, but they spread rapidly there, at once sharing some characteristics with their mass media brethren while also drawing stark distinctions between them.

The most interesting social network in terms of hoaxes is the microblogging service Twitter. Created in 2007, Twitter enables users to send and receive text messages called "tweets" composed of a maximum of 140 characters. Like other social networks, Twitter allows users to designate other users that they would like to subscribe to (or "follow" in Twitter parlance) in order to view their activity on the network. In addition to "tweeting" their own content or sharing hyperlinks to off-network content, Twitter users can "retweet" others' messages, spreading the message to their own followers (Bakshy, Hofman, Mason, and Watts, 2011; Cha, Haddadi, Benevenuto, and Gummad, 2010). The retweet structure of Twitter is so powerful, in fact, that in their study of 106 million tweets by 41.7 million users, Kwak, Lee, Park, and Moon (2010) found that any retweeted link reaches an average of 1,000 users. Retweeted messages are quickly retweeted and retweeted again, creating a snowball effect (Ghosh and Lerman, 2011; Lerman and Ghosh, 2010). This is a key factor in Twitter's effectiveness at spreading hoaxes in the age of social media: the retweet mechanism empowers users to spread information far beyond the reach of the original tweeter's followers.[6]

Increased Opportunity

The rise of the Internet and advances in production technology dramatically lowered the barriers of entry to potentially reach a mass audience. Previously, the collection, production and dissemination of news and information came with high costs (Bandari, Asur, and Huberman, 2012). To perpetuate any large-scale hoax during the broadcasting era, a would-be scammer needed access to a printing press or a broadcast license; today, a would-be hoaxer needs only a working Internet connection.

Moreover, creating a believable aesthetic is simpler than ever, as advances in technology have led to affordable production tools of professional quality. As such, it is not uncommon to see amateur video, audio, and websites that rival the quality of those generated by institutional outlets. The rise of social networks, meanwhile, creates a ready-made means of reaching a potentially mass audience that was once only the domain of institutional media. And since these networks are designed for sharing between users, a hoaxer can easily exploit them to pass along misinformation.

Meanwhile, audiences grow increasingly accustomed to using these online networks for information. According to a survey by the Pew Research Center (2005), the Web is the most important resource for news for those under 30, while the general population ranks it second only to television. Most notably, more than half of audiences (52%) report using social media for news (Pew Research Center, 2012), where the line is far from clear between user-generated and institutional content. Information is also commonly spreading from peer-to-peer online, as 59% of individuals say they frequently share online content with others (Allsop, Bassett, and Hoskins, 2007). And when it comes to audiences sniffing out hoaxes, as sharing of digital content becomes the new norm, audiences are less likely to treat information gathered from these new methods of dissemination with skepticism (Phelps, 2012, Morris, Counts, Roseway, Hoff, and Schwarz, 2012).

Social Media Hoaxes in Practice

The mass media hoaxes detailed earlier in this chapter share a common theme of largeness — fittingly so, considering the size of the audiences that these media outlets reach. Yet, social media have reduced the scope and scale of hoaxes compared to their predecessors, often trading fake incidents of substantial impact—alien invasions, huge fires, stampedes through crowds, for example—and replacing them with comparatively minor tales of celebrity deaths and other fictionalized stories meant to pique interest rather than inspire fear or panic. Because any hoax involving a large-scale event would be easily debunked by verification checks of any of the hundreds of media options available to today's audience, hoaxers stick to the type of story that will pique interest and encourage sharing, but not dominate the mainstream news cycle.

This disparity in content between mass and social media hoaxes also suggests a substantially different relationship between these media and their audiences. Mass media hoaxes alarmed audiences to geographically proximate calamities (a nuclear meltdown, rampaging zoo animals) or national disasters (alien invasions, terrorist threats to national security). Even where they do not make a personal appeal to audiences, the narratives of mass media hoaxes are such that audience members can conceive that the story may directly affect them or someone that they know. A good friend may have been at the theater that burned down. Loved ones living near the power plant may be in danger. The entire nation may fall at the hands of Martian invaders. In short, the narratives of mass media hoaxes can establish stronger connections to audience members based on the threat that such hoaxes allegedly pose to audience members.

In contrast, social media hoaxes rarely involve direct threats to users. Although Twitter offers an arguably more participatory medium where users connect with one another, the types of hoaxes that proliferate there tend not to connect with audiences on a personal level. Rather than raising concern over the safety of friends, family, and self, Twitter death hoaxes and falsified historical accounts are fairly innocuous. Put simply, audiences' stake in the veracity of a celebrity death hoax on Twitter is significantly different than a mother's sense of alarm that her son may have been mauled by a lion or charred in a theater blaze. These lower stakes may in part account for the tendency of Twitter users to retweet information without verification.

Blogger and habitual hoaxer Nate St. Pierre initiated such a hoax when thousands shared his blog post about Abe Lincoln founding a 19th century version of Facebook. The hoax spread on Facebook and Twitter, garnering attention from major media outlets, but was of relatively slight importance so as to not garner too much skepticism. After the hoax was debunked, St. Pierre told *The Atlantic* that he believes the Internet's obsession with speed undermines audiences' inclination to verify information before spreading it:

> Web people especially, but even news sources, will fall all over themselves to be first, especially on something cool, especially on something tech, especially on something that's in the news that combines a couple

interesting famous people. They'll share first and answer questions later. And by the time anyone knows it's not real, it's too late. (Garber, 2012)[7]

This prioritization of speed over accuracy fosters a media culture ripe for the spread of hoaxes and misinformation, a tendency further complicated by individual users' biases, which also influence the information that they spread.

People are much more likely to retweet information that they want to be true (Lotan, 2012), will share content to reduce dissonance (Peters and Kashima, 2007), and even after a hoax has been uncovered, the correction will fall on deaf ears if it concerns "ideologically sensitive topics" (Nyhan and Reifler, 2010). The old journalism credo, "if it bleeds, it leads" still applies online: the more outlandish or provocative the story, the more likely it is to receive audiences' attention. There is also a link here between virality and emotions (Berger and Milkman, 2012; Heath, Bell, and Sternberg, 2001). Messages that evoke strong emotions, either positive (awe, patriotism) or negative (anger, anxiety) are more likely to be shared (Berger and Milkman, 2012), and spreading such emotionally charged content can help users deepen social connections (Rime, Mesquita, Philippot, and Boca, 1991). In short, the stronger the emotion tied to a message, the more likely people are to transmit it socially. This may also explain why even though most Twitter hoaxes are debunked rather quickly, the correction does not receive the same viral spread that the original misinformation did (Silverman, 2012a): a dry, factual correction is simply not affecting enough to warrant much attention.

Compounding matters, while the lack of interconnectedness facilitated hoaxes' believability during newspapers' heyday, the issue today is a media ecosystem that is highly connected; the natural cyclical nature of news reporting has been transformed by major and minor outlets alike into an echo chamber that only reinforces itself (Myers, 2010). On social media, however, it is not just journalists who can get caught up in the excitement, since people tend to retweet others with whom they agree (Menczer, 2012). This creates ample opportunity for like-minded individuals to further circulate untruths simply because they hear the same messages repeatedly from sources they associate themselves with. If a user sees a story from enough other users (which again, is easy enough considering the ease and power of the retweet), they are likely to share the story too, so as to not seem out of the loop.

Real-life events are also a factor in the spread of hoaxes and false information on Twitter. Research into activity during disaster and breaking news found that Twitter takes on an altered state during such events (Toriumi, Shinoda, Kurihara, Sakai, Kazama, and Noda, 2011; Heverin and Zach, 2010) and that false rumors are more likely to spread if there is a vacuum of firsthand information from traditional news outlets (Mendoza, Poblete, and Castillo, 2010). At other times, hoaxers simply take advantage of our natural tendency for pattern recognition, capitalizing on real-life events to spread similarly themed misinformation. The Twitter death hoax is perhaps the most common manifestation of this phenomenon, as false reports of celebrity deaths spring up around other notable deaths in the news (Tsukayama, 2011b). The deaths of Ed McMahon, Farrah Fawcett and Michael Jackson in June 2009 prompted a particularly concentrated torrent of hoax death reports, including Jeff Goldblum, Harrison Ford, George Clooney, Miley Cyrus, Natalie Portman, Ellen DeGeneres, Britney Spears, and Louie Anderson (Corcoran, 2009).

As the glut of celebrity death hoaxes surrounding real celebrity deaths suggests, media hoaxes do not exist inside of a vacuum. In some fashion, they are products of their cultural, social, and technological environments. *War of the Worlds* succeeded in part due to broadcast conventions established by coverage of the European conflict; the Chicago Theater fire hoax succeeded due to the popularity of the theater as well as its known safety shortcomings; notable and newsworthy deaths allow for an increased believability of celebrity death hoaxes. As we have seen in surveying mass media hoaxes, the communicative structure of a particular medium also affects its ability to disseminate and perpetuate hoaxes.

User-generated Aesthetics and Institutional Media

Even in the social media world, many hoaxers rely on the established ethos of institutional media. Some hoaxes utilize images doctored to resemble major media outlets (Tsukayama, 2011a), while others simply lie about being sourced from them (Levin, 2010). Some hoaxes are carried out by fake accounts posing as real-world luminaries (Kington, 2012; Castillo, Mendoza, and Poblete, 2011). In one particular case, hoaxers dispensed with pretending to be a major media outlet and simply took one over. In 2011, hoaxers hacked Fox News' Twitter account and posted false information that President

Obama had been assassinated (Jackson, 2011). Using the power of institutional media as a tool for chicanery is an effective hoaxing tactic, as 73–80% of users find established media reliable and accurate, compared to only 9–16% who say the same about information from individuals (USC Annenberg Center for the Digital Future, 2012).

However, as audiences migrate to the Web, institutional outlets actively blur the lines between producer and consumer. With the rise of social media changing audience expectations for interactivity, institutional media increasingly carry user-generated content (UGC) in the same vein as it once carried professionally reported and vetted content. It is common for major media outlets such as cable news channels to read audience tweets on-air or showcase viral YouTube videos, for example. This promotion of audience content and Twitter's lack of hierarchy has brought the institutional outlets down to the masses, causing difficulty for those who seek to differentiate the sourcing of information circulated on social media networks.

This trend raises questions of how to evaluate the credibility of citizen reporting (Mustafaraj, Metaxas, Finn, and Monroy-Hernandez, 2012), as this information lacks the internal modes of evaluation present in institutional media (Flanagin and Metzger, 2007). While not hoaxes by our definition, institutional media have passed along erroneous information by relying on this type of crowd-sourced content (Myers, 2010; Sonderman, 2011). For example, in 2011 a CNBC reporter was fooled into reporting on the owner of an escort service who had seen a decrease in clientele with the NBA lockout. The owner was really a "bored" teenager who responded to the reporter's open call on Twitter for sources affected by the lockout. The reporter failed to verify any of the claims or the teen's identity before publishing the information (Silverman, 2012b). As established outlets continue to carry less credible UGC, they may very well lose the ability to differentiate themselves from other, less reliable, sources of information online.

Hoaxers have always followed media innovation. First with newspapers, then radio and television and now the Internet and social media, these purposeful attempts to deceive the public continue to find fertile ground. With their unique structure and wide reach, social media are well poised to be a breeding ground for hoaxes, a trend that is likely to continue as the mobility and popularity of social media continue to grow.

Conclusion

More than 170 years after the *Sun* published its tales of bat-men living on the moon, media hoaxes are perhaps more prolific than ever, albeit with varying degrees of impact. In this chapter we've outlined unique characteristics of the mass and social media eras to show how technological features directly shape the creation, execution, and reception of hoaxes. Yet a more direct comparison between hoaxes of the mass and social media eras illuminates what makes hoaxes successful and thus, helps to account for their continued prominence in our media culture.

What often made early hoaxes successful was audiences' sense of trust in newspapers. This overwhelming trust in journalists as disseminators of news and information allowed newspapers to manipulate audiences. Broadcast media added a dimension of perceived intimacy between audiences and on-air personalities that served to reinforce audiences' faith in the integrity and veracity of broadcast information. Successful hoaxes generated by broadcast media manipulate the perceived intimacy of para-social relationships, most clearly in those hoaxes that engage the names and identities of established broadcast journalists.[8] In short, what made mass media hoaxes successful was a sense of trust (as in newspaper hoaxes) and intimacy (as in broadcast hoaxes).

Functionally speaking, hoaxes in the era of social media represent a convergence of these characteristics. That is, what facilitates the success of social media hoaxes is a combination of trust and intimacy. As noted above, there is a tendency for social media users to trust information shared by sources that they know. There are two dimensions to this intimacy within social media: a mirroring of relationships from our personal lives, and the perceived intimacy that social media fosters with celebrities, institutions, and others with whom we have at best weak social ties. Even so, intimacy on social media—be it real or perceived—cultivates a sense of trust for many users, creating a fertile environment in which hoaxes and misinformation can be readily accepted.

Introducing this chapter, we defined hoaxes as having a deliberate intent to deceive, although there are often additional motives unique to the medium utilized. For hoaxes of the mass media era, deception was not the end goal, but a means to some other end. Those motives ranged from the virtuous (raising awareness of a social issue) to the self-interested (increasing profits). To date, social media hoaxes lack such ulterior motives; their objective tends to be the deceit itself, and the satisfaction of having pulled one over on other users and in some cases, mainstream media institutions.

Hoaxes proliferate online with varying results. Some gain significant attention; others fail to gain traction. While most of these hoaxes are fairly harmless, they highlight a danger in our contemporary media culture: the devaluation of accuracy in favor of immediacy. The primacy placed on speed over accuracy is disconcerting in two ways.

First, it encourages the reporting of unchecked information by institutional outlets. Recent gaffes by NPR, Fox News, CNN, and others illustrate how the failure to verify information can result in potentially pernicious misinformation being reported to the masses (Lee, 2012; Schonfeld, 2012). This not only violates the trust that audiences place upon established media institutions, but also serves to delegitimize them. These highly public incidents jeopardize the credibility of news organizations, which is particularly troublesome in light of other factors battering "traditional" media. To wit, newspapers struggle to maintain profitability in a virtual world, while broadcast media continue to consolidate under corporate ownership and content homogenization. The rising frequency of misreported information by institutional media does little to recoup their reputability in an environment where it is increasingly questioned.

Secondly, the success and proliferation of social media hoaxes suggests that audiences tend not to verify information encountered online. Consumers' decreasing engagement of critical faculty online is fueled by our own obsession with timeliness, and the ability for the constant online engagement provided by mobile devices. As the availability and popularity of mobile devices continues to increase, this constant connection to digital and social media is likely to continue.

The question thus becomes not how to prevent the creation and execution of social media hoaxes, but how to foster a digital culture wherein users take a more critical stance in evaluating the daily barrage of information that they encounter. Recent literature emphasizes the important role that media literacy programs can have in helping consumers navigate our media-saturated world. Much of this body of work focuses on fomenting a critical stance toward media representations of body image, gender dynamics, racial identity, sexual orientation, and media violence (see, for example, Durham, 2008 and Hobbs,

2006). The virtue of such projects is that they seek to effect change in social relations by engendering a critical approach to media content among audiences.

Lacking from this growing body of work, however, is a program seeking to make social media users more self-aware of their own habits while pushing them to more critically evaluate the information that they encounter on sites such as Facebook and Twitter. Such an approach does not preclude the execution of hoaxes and pranksterism online. Instead, such initiatives should encourage users to evaluate social media messages rather than indiscriminately accepting them to be true and spreading them to other users. Social media users taking a more critical approach to online information also have the potential to reverse the prioritization of speed over accuracy, which may in turn encourage institutional outlets to follow suit.

The accessibility, mobility, and speed of social media have proven to be a boon for the circulation of crucial information. Beyond especially prominent examples such as the Arab Spring and the #occupy movement, the ability to report and transmit information from virtually any location has undoubtedly been beneficial in keeping citizens informed while drastically reducing the lag inherent in information relay of the mass media era. Yet, accessibility and currency can come at the cost of accuracy. By actively engaging media literacy programs that promote the engagement of critical ability among social media users, we foster a digital culture that remains accessible and open, but also critically engages users, ultimately enhancing the value of social media as a platform for news and information exchange.

Notes

[1] In his 1875 novel *The Story of Sevenoaks*, James Holland makes an early reference to media hoaxes when he describes "a paper with more enterprise than brains, more brains than candor, and with no conscience at all; a paper which manufactured hoaxes and vended them for news, bought and sold scandals by the sheet as if they were country gingerbread, and damaged reputations one day for the privilege and profit of mending them the next" (p. 201). For etymology, see "hoax" in the *Oxford English Dictionary*.

[2] The series of articles was later published as a mass marketed pamphlet. See Locke and Nicollet (n.d.).

[3] Nineteen years after the hoax's publication, Chicago's Iroquois Theater erupted in flames due to structural and safety faults similar to those featured in Storey's

hoax; 571 people died in the fire, while another 350 suffered injuries. Every theater in Chicago was subsequently closed to undergo mandatory renovations—just the kind of widespread reform that Storey had called for nearly two decades earlier (Fedler, 1989, p. 108).

4 For a fuller explication of this concept, see Scannell (2000).

5 As events unfolded over the following days, Heene disclosed that the hoax was intended to generate attention in the interest of the family's aspirations for a reality TV show.

6 It is also the reason Kwak et al. (2010) classified Twitter as a new medium.

7 In the rush to break news stories, even mainstream outlets have erred in their reportage of significant events. When Arizona Congresswoman Gabrielle Giffords was shot at a 2011 public appearance, NPR, CNN, Fox, MSNBC, and the *New York Times* erroneously reported that the shooting had been fatal. When the US Supreme Court issued its controversial ruling on the Controversial Care Act in 2012, both CNN and Fox News misreported that the Court had struck down the law's individual mandate, when in fact the ruling upheld that provision.

8 On para-social relationships with mass media, see Horton and Wohl (1956).

References

Allsop, D.T., Bassett, B.R., and Hoskins, J.A. (2007). Word-of-mouth research: Principles and applications. *Journal of Advertising Research*, 47, 388–411.

Bakshy, E., Hofman, J.M., Mason, W.A., and Watts, D.J. (2011). Everyone's an influencer: Quantifying influence on Twitter. In *Proceedings of WSDM 2011*, 65–74.

Bandari, R., Asur, S., and Huberman, B. A. (2012). The pulse of news in social media: Forecasting popularity. Retrieved from http://www.hpl.hp.com/research/scl/papers/newsprediction/pulse.pdf

Bartholomew, R. E., and Radford, B. (2012). *The Martians have landed! A history of media-driven panics and hoaxes*. Jefferson, NC: McFarland and Company.

Berger, J., and Milkman, K. (2012). Social transmission, emotion, and the virality of online content. *Journal of Marketing Research*, 49(2), 192–205.

Cantril, H., Herzog, H. and Gaudet, H. (2008). *The invasion from mars; a study in the psychology of panic*. New Brunswick, NJ and London: Transaction

Castillo, C., Mendoza, M., and Poblete, B. (2011). Information credibility on Twitter. In *Proceedings of the World Wide Web (WWW) Conference 2011*, March 28-April 1, 2011, Hyderabad, India.

Cha, M., Haddadi, H., Benevenuto, F., and Gummad, K. P. (2010) Measuring user influence on twitter: The million follower fallacy. In *Proceedings of 4th Int'l AAAI Conference on Weblogs and Social Media*, Washington, DC, 2010.

Copeland, D. (2007). A series of fortunate events: Why people believed Richard Adams Locke's "moon moax." *Journalism History*, 33 (3), 140–150.

Corcoran, M. (2009, July 10). Death by a cliff plunge, with a push from Twitter. *The New York Times*. Retrieved from http://www.nytimes.com/2009/07/12/fashion/12hoax.html

Cox, T. (1994, November 7). "Without Warning no War of the Worlds." *Daily Herald*.

Durham, M. G. (2008). *The Lolita effect: The media sexualization of young girls and what we can do about it*. New York: Overlook Press.

Federal Communications Commission. (1980). *Arizona license memorandum opinion and order*. 83 F.C.C. 2d 440, para 6, 48 Rad. Reg.2d (P&F) 1006.

Fedler, F. (1989). *Media hoaxes*. Ames: Iowa State University Press.

Flanagin, A.J., and Metzger, M.J. (2007). The role of site features, user attributes, and information verification behaviors on the perceived credibility of web-based information. *New Media Society*, 9(2), 319–342.

Garber, M. (2012, May 9). Abraham Lincoln did not invent Facebook: How a guy and his blog fooled the whole wide Internet. *The Atlantic*. Retrieved from http://www.theatlantic.com/technology/archive/2012/05/abraham-lincoln-did-not-invent-facebook-how-a-guy-and-his-blog-fooled-the-whole-wide-internet/256945/

Ghosh, R., and Lerman, K. (2011). A framework for quantitative analysis of cascades on networks. In *Proceedings of ACM Web Search and Data Mining Conference* (WSDM), 665–674.

Heath, C., Bell, C., and Sternberg, E. (2001). Emotional selection in memes: The case of urban legends. *Journal of Personality and Social Psychology*, 81, 1028–1041.

Heverin, T., and Zach, L. (2010). Microblogging for crisis communication: An examination of Twitter use in response to a 2009 violent crisis in Seattle-Tacoma. In *Proceedings of the Seventh International ISCRAM Conference*, Seattle, Washington. Retrieved from http://www.thomasheverin.com/uploads/4/6/5/8/4658640/heverin_iscram_2010.pdf

Hoax. (n.d.). *Oxford English Dictionary*. Retrieved from www.oed.com.

Hobbs, R. (2006). *Reading the media: Media literacy in high school English*. New York: Teachers College Press.

Holland. J.G. (1875). *Sevenoaks: A story of today*. New York: Scribner, Armstrong & Co.

Horton, D., and Wohl, R. (1956). Mass communication and para-social interaction: Observations on intimacy at a distance. *Psychiatry*, 19, 215–29.

Jackson, D. (2011, July 4). Fox News Twitter feed hacked; Obama death hoax. *USA Today*. Retrieved from http://content.usatoday.com/communities/theoval/post/2011/07/fox-news-twitter-feed-hacked-obama-death-hoax/1#.T-fgn7W4_-s

Kington. (2012, March 30). Twitter hoaxer comes clean and says: I did it to expose weak media. *The Guardian*. Retrieved from http://www.guardian.co.uk/technology/2012/mar/30/twitter-hoaxer-tommaso-de-benedetti

Kwak, H., Lee, C., Park, H., and Moon, S. (2010). What is Twitter, a social network or news media? In *Proceedings of the World Wide Web (WWW) Conference 2010*, Raleigh, NC: ACM Press.

Lee, Kristin. (2012). CNN and FOX blow health care ruling coverage. *New York Daily News*. Retrieved from http://articles.nydailynews.com/2012–06–

28/news/32461198_1_individual-mandate-health-care-tweet

Lerman, K., and Ghosh, R. (2010). Information contagion: An empirical study of the spread of news on Digg and Twitter social networks. In *Proceedings of the 4th International Conference on Weblogs and Social Media*, 2010.

Levin, J. (2010, December 16). The man behind Morgan Freeman's fake death. *Slate*. Retrieved from http://www.slate.com/blogs/browbeat/2010/12/16/the_man_behind_morgan_freeman_s_fake_death.html

Locke, J.A., and Nicollet, J. N. (n.d.). *The moon hoax, or a discovery that the moon has a vast population of human beings*. Charleston, SC: Bibliobazaar.

Lotan, G. (2012). A tale of three rumors. Truthiness in digital media blog. Retrieved from http://blogs.law.harvard.edu/truthiness/2012/03/05/541/#more-541

McLeod, K. (2005). *Freedom of expression: Overzealous copyright bozos and other enemies of creativity*. New York: Doubleday.

McLuhan, M. (1964). *Understanding media: The extensions of men*. New York: Signet.

Menczer, F. (2012). New Media 360: Abundant, promiscuous, questionable, & fast moving. [Video File]. Retrieved from http://www.youtube.com/watch?v=plAJXVUgibw&feature=player_embedded

Mendoza, M., Poblete, B., and Castillo, C. (2010). Twitter under crisis: Can we trust what we RT? In the *Proceedings of the 2010 Social Media Analytics Workshop* (SOMA). July 15, 2010, Washington, D.C.

Morris, M.R., Counts, S., Roseway, A., Hoff, A., and Schwarz, J. (2012). Tweeting is believing? Understanding microblog credibility perceptions. In *Proceedings of CSCW 2012*, February 11–15, 2012, Seattle, WA: ACM Press. Retrieved from http://research.microsoft.com/pubs/155374/tweet_credibility_cscw2012.pdf

Mustafaraj, E., Metaxas, P., Finn, S., and Monroy-Hernandez, A. (2012). Hiding in plain sight: A tale of trust and mistrust inside a community of citizen reporters. Retrieved from http://cs.wellesley.edu/~pmetaxas/mustafaraj_icwsm2012.pdf

Myers, S. (2010, September 20). 5 lessons for journalists & consumers in statue of liberty tornado photo. *Poynter*. Retrieved from http://www.poynter.org/latest-news/making-sense-of-news/105752/6-lessons-for-journalists-consumers-in-statue-of-liberty-tornado-photo/

Nyhan, B., and Reifler, J. (2010). When corrections fail: The persistence of political misperceptions. *Political Behavior, 32*(2), 303–330.

Peters, K., and Kashima, Y. (2007). From social talk to social action: Shaping the social triad with emotion sharing. *Journal of Personality and Social Psychology, 93*, 780–797.

Pew Research Center. (2008). Internet overtakes newspapers as news outlet. Retrieved from http://pewresearch.org/pubs/1066/internet-overtakes-newspapers-as-news-source-2008

Pew Research Center. (2012). State of the media. Retrieved from http://stateofthemedia.org/

Phelps, A. (2012, March 16). Think fast: Is that tweet true or false? How we use credibility cues to make decisions. Neiman Journalism Lab. Retrieved from http://www.niemanlab.org/2012/03/think-fast-is-that-tweet-true-or-false-how-we-use-credibility-cues-to-make-decisions/

Rime, B., Mesquita, B., Philippot, P., and Boca, S. (1991). Beyond the emotional event: Six studies on the social sharing of emotion. *Cognition and Emotion*, 5 (September-November), 435–465.

Scannell, P. (1996). *Radio, television & public life*. Oxford: Blackwell Publishing.

Scannell, P. (2000). For-anyone-as-someone-structures. *Media, Culture and Society*, 22 (1), 5–24.

Schonfeld, R. (2012). CNN killed Gabrielle Giffords, but we didn't kill Jim Brady. *The Huffington Post*. Retrieved from http://www.huffingtonpost.com/reese-schonfeld/who-killed-gabrielle-giff_b_807333.html

Silverman, C. (2012a, June 6). CNBC reporter apologizes after falling for teenager's hoax. *Poynter*. Retrieved from http://www.poynter.org/latest-news/regret-the-error/176383/cnbc-reporter-apologizes-after-falling-for-teenagers-hoax/

Silverman, C. (2012b, March 7). Visualized: Incorrect information travels farther, faster on Twitter than corrections. *Poynter*. Retrieved from http://www.poynter.org/latest-news/regret-the-error/165654/visualized-incorrect-information-travels-farther-faster-on-twitter-than-corrections/

Sonderman, J. (2011, July 8). How to verify—and when to publish—news accounts posted on social media. *Poynter*. Retrieved from http://www.poynter.org/how-tos/newsgathering-storytelling/138495/how-to-verify-and-when-to-publish-news-accounts-posted-on-social-media/

Toriumi, F., Shinoda, K., Kurihara, S., Sakai, T., Kazama, K., and Noda, I. (2011). How disaster changes social media. In *Proceedings of the JWEIN '11 Conference*.

Tsukayama, H. (2011a, March 30). Jackie Chan lives, but so do Twitter death hoaxes. *The Washington Post*. Retrieved from http://www.washingtonpost.com/blogs/fasterforward/post/jackie_chan_lives_but_so_do_twitter_death_hoaxes/2011/03/30/AFx4lH3B_blog.html?wprss=rss_business

Tsukayama, H. (2011b, December 20). Jon Bon Jovi: The latest Twitter death hoax. *The Washington Post*. Retrieved from http://www.washingtonpost.com/business/technology/jon-bon-jovi-the-latest-twitter-death-hoax/2011/12/20/gIQAzrFn6O_story.html

USC Annenberg Center for the Digital Future. (2012). Special report: America at the digital turning point. Los Angeles, CA: USC Annenberg School for Communication & Journalism.

"War of the Worlds Revisited—Almost." *The Chronicle-Telegram*. October 31, 1994, p. A3.

"WDAF Gets Calls on 'Special Bulletin.'" *The Chillicothe Constitution*. March 21, 1983.

PART THREE

Looking Forward: *War of the Worlds* and Social Media

CHAPTER NINE

War of Worlds? Alternative and Mainstream Journalistic Practices in Coverage of the "Arab Spring" Protests

DIANA BOSSIO AND SABA BEBAWI

In this chapter, Bossio and Bebawi offer a comparative case study of online coverage of pro-democracy demonstrations in Egypt and Libya on six separate days in early 2011. They identify tensions between "old" and "new" journalistic coverage of the crisis similar to those shaping reactions to the *War of the Worlds* broadcast event. Despite these tensions, however, Bossio and Bebawi argue that shared interest in the struggle for democracy and the welfare of innocent people spurred cooperation between professional and citizen journalists during the crises.

Introduction

The *War of the Worlds* broadcast has become an iconic example of how new communication technologies affect the distribution and reception of news and information. On the seventy-fifth anniversary of the original broadcast, we take an opportunity to establish some conceptual connections between *War of the Worlds* and contemporary issues about the application of new communication technologies in crisis situations. For example, recent public demonstrations in various countries across the Middle East are notable for the way in which new communication technologies were used to report and to distribute news and information both locally and across the world. The so-called Arab Spring describes a range of revolutionary movements across many Arabic-speaking states in North Africa and the Middle East. These protests began in Tunisia in December 2010 and unseated the government there. The demonstrations then seemingly "spread" to Egypt, Libya and Yemen. Serious uprisings occurred in Syria, Bahrain and Algeria; while minor protests were recorded in Iraq, Jordan, Kuwait, Morocco, Saudi Arabia and Lebanon, among others. The mostly youth-driven civil nature of this resistance, which used social media technologies not only to organize but also to raise awareness across the Arab world and to distribute news and information across global networks, has been labeled the Arab Spring.

This chapter takes the clash between "old" and "new" media at the heart of the *War of the Worlds* event as a comparison point for interpreting the role of new media practices in coverage of the Arab Spring crises. Specifically, this chapter illustrates how social media platforms influence more traditional forms of journalistic practice in crisis situations. To do so, we investigate the interactions between alternative and mainstream journalism and the impact of such interactions on crisis situation reporting. Interactions are defined as moments when the two modes of journalism inform and modify each other via reporting on each other's practices, information sharing and collaborative reporting.

We argue that the interactions between mainstream and alternative journalistic practice during the Arab Spring were more complex and contingent than recent scholarship has generally suggested. Some scholarship within journalism disciplines has suggested that the professionalism of journalism as an institution has been under attack from social media's more subjective and immediate content (see Brodin, 2011; Rosen, 2009). The two media "worlds" have been segregated by the supposed authenticity, authority and credibility of traditional journalistic modes and the efficiencies and audience-driven content of alternative media practice (see Cenite et al., 2011; Mitchelstein & Boczkowski, 2009; Singer, 1998). When we examined the supposed "discontinuities" between the two worlds, however, we found that the two modes of journalistic practice actually relied upon each other in recent times of crisis. Indeed, the recent (and continuing) Arab Spring protests have illustrated that the relationship between mainstream and alternative journalistic practice is not the "war of worlds" that many have suggested but instead a more complex relationship of "diplomatic tensions." During the protests, both mainstream and alternative reporters, activists and protesters utilized digital and social media to share information across both alternative and traditional media platforms. This is what we might term a "diplomatic" interaction to incorporate new modes of journalistic practice in crisis situations between the two fields. Nonetheless, moments of "friction" were evident in the language of mainstream reporting, especially when their authenticity, credibility and authority appeared to be challenged by new practices and practitioners.

Our study utilizes a comparative case study of online coverage of pro-democracy demonstrations in Egypt and Libya on six separate days in 2011. The analysis covers forms of alternative and mainstream reporting distributed through social media and blogs. This is compared to "mainstream" journalistic content productions, including online text, video and audio reporting on CNN, BBC and Al Jazeera. Within the analysis, we provide evidence of the interaction between social media and mainstream media reporting and explore the ways in which traditional and alternative journalistic practices were used during crisis situations over the six days covered by the analysis. With this analysis, we aim to show that while what we consider "professional" or "mainstream" journalistic practice has changed in accordance with the collaborative and engagement potential of online media, there is no discursive practice to describe that change within journalistic reporting. The tensions result from differences in the language each uses to report to its respective audiences and to position itself within the public sphere. Thus, we illustrate that the various uses of social media by different media practitioners indicate the complex and contingent social and cultural effects that new media technologies bring to the reporting of and dissemination of news and information during crises.

Conceptualizing Mainstream and Alternative Journalistic Practice in Contemporary Media

Contemporary academic readings of the "most famous radio show of all time" (Fisher, 1998, p. 52) have contextualized the broadcast as a clash between the "reliable" tradition of newspaper reporting and the "panic" wrought by new radio technologies in the 1930s. Campbell (2010) suggests that the *War of the Worlds* broadcast, "offered American newspapers at the time an exceptional and irresistible opportunity to rebuke radio—then an increasingly important rival source for news and advertising—as unreliable and untrustworthy" (p. 28). This tension between the relative authority and responsibility of "old" and "new" media, we argue, manifested itself again in the 1990s-2010s with the clash between print, broadcast and digital news media. As print and broadcast journalists faced increasing competition in the online environment, some voiced a similar rebuke of the perceived threat that alternative modes of journalistic practice posed to professional journalistic standards.

There is no doubt that local and international news coverage has been influenced by the greater number of online communication channels, as well as the number of people who are willing to create and distribute their own news via those channels. Heinrich (2011) suggests that, "the news sphere has undergone a shift from a fairly organized, linear news flow structure, to chaotic organization of information flows produced and disseminated globally by an uncountable number of information transmitters" (p. 62). Bruns (2005) calls this a "paradigm shift" toward "the collaborative, iterative and user-led production of content by participants in a hybrid user-producer, or *'produser'* role" (p. 275). However, Heinrich (2011) suggests that we lack a conceptual approach to understand the role of these new "reporters" and where they fit within the traditional field of journalism. In response, she suggests navigating between journalists who are fearful of "online invasions," those who treat alternative journalistic practitioners simply as sources, and those who attempt to integrate new forms of reporting into journalistic practice.

Heinrich's (2011) criticism suggests there might still be a somewhat derisory tone in discipline-specific research around these supposed interactions. Much of this derision centers on the training, accountability and professionalism that alternative journalists apparently lack. This focus on the either/or effects of alternative journalistic practice suggests that a theoretical framework to conceptualize a positive or productive interaction between mainstream journalists and alternative media practitioners is lacking in journalism disciplines despite some examples of how this interaction has occurred. The either/or approach used to describe these interactions suggests that amateur journalists working within online spaces are being unfairly compared to mainstream practitioners with the benefit of institutionalized training and support. This means that interactions between the two kinds of journalists are being formulated along the old lines of journalist-source relations rather than through a theoretical framework where a productive, symbiotic relationship could occur. Indeed, until recently, the dominant research approach has been very much encapsulated by the "threat" felt from shrinking newsrooms and the failure of traditional media business models in a digital age.

The rise of user-generated content has begun to circumvent traditional mass media control of news and information (Hartley, 2005; Livingstone, 1999), and this has even led some to question the concept of needing a "professional" journalist to report the news (Berkman & Shumway, 2003). Others (see Brodin, 2011; Livingstone, 1999) have continued to highlight the need for trained or professional journalists who can verify information and adhere to particular institutional and ethical guidelines in an online arena. While traditional scholarship about alternative journalism has centered on its deviance from mainstream journalism's economic, institutional and social structures, the field lacks clear demarcation around what alternative journalism encompasses and how it differs from other journalistic practices. Downing (2001, p. ix) has defined alternative journalistic practice as "radical," "grassroots" or "community" media, although these definitions have been forwarded more as a structure for information dissemination and practice not purely focused on journalism. Another popular term used to describe alternative journalistic practices has been "citizen" journalism, linking alternative news practice to forms of citizenship practice and empowerment in the everyday lives of citizens (see Rodríguez, 2001, p. 20). Atton (2002, p. 9) uses the term "alternative media" generally to suggest a practice that provides information and interpretations of the world that would not be found anywhere else. Atton and Hamilton (2008, p. 4) describe alternative journalism as the "journalism of politics and empowerment," which suggests not only its political imperative but also its economic and institutional imperative because it is produced "outside mainstream media institutions and networks" and by amateurs "who typically have little or no training or professional qualifications as journalists" (2008, p. 1).

While these formulations are helpful in thinking about individual practice modes, more contemporary theoretical frameworks suggest ways to encourage productive interactions. By defining a framework for understanding new types of news work, media production and journalism as an integrated whole, Mark Deuze (2003), for example, has investigated how online and converged media have been incorporated into journalism. He suggests (2003, p. 206) that digital and networked journalism cannot always be tied to the work that defines the salaried media practitioners in traditional media formats. Downing (2001, p. ix) has suggested that there has been a tendency in the field to assume a dichotomy between mainstream and alternative journalistic practices, without considering the relationship between them. He suggests instead that "the edges are almost always blurred" between the demarcation of alternative and mainstream journalistic practices and functions. Likewise, Harcup (2005, p. 362), in reference to Downing (2005), suggests that there has been a realization that alternative and mainstream media are not binary opposites.

During the protests in Egypt, for example, there were many people involved in what we might call journalistic practices: eyewitness reporting of events; analysis of those events in the larger political context; and video, audio and social media information updates. Some were paid as journalists for Egyptian media outlets, others considered themselves journalists despite being unpaid, some collaborated with mainstream news organizations and others defined what they were doing simply as important information dissemination in a time of crisis. Some were reporting from outside Egypt itself, using online resources to "cover" the protest, whereas others participated through other online networks. In any case, only some people identified their activities as "journalism" or media production. The complexity of this situation demonstrates why "alternative journalism" is an incomplete term to describe the ways in which news coverage may occur outside the realms of paid journalistic activity. These descriptions have in common, as Heinrich argues, that they describe the potential of globalized networks of interaction between mainstream and alternative modes of journalistic practice, but they are not applied to a conceptual model of practical interaction (Heinrich, 2011, p. 58). How can we illustrate these practices to better represent the complexities of the kinds of people and professionals contributing to news coverage, as well as their institutional, political and personal interests in doing so?

The Arab Spring is a recent example of the ways in which practical interaction between mainstream and alternative modes of journalistic practice have led to new ways of disseminating news during crisis situations. To illustrate this, we utilized a thematic analysis within a comparative case study of online coverage of pro-democracy demonstrations in Egypt and Libya on six separate days at the beginning of the protests in 2011. We chose to focus our analysis on the initial days of the protests because we believed this might yield better examples of interaction between different modes of practice as different journalists initially set up their own investigations of the crisis. We chose to analyze politically significant days where a) major governmental action occurred, b) a sizeable protest occurred or c) large-scale violence was reported. As a point of comparison, we also tried to identify days when journalistic practice may have been more difficult because of governmental curfews, threats of violence or logistical difficulty.

The "unhindered" days during the Egyptian crisis that we chose for analysis were January 26, 2011 (one of the first days of mass protests), January 31 (the infamous "March of the Millions"), and February 7 (Mubarak agrees to constitutional change). The "hindered" days we chose for analysis were January 27 (internet and phone connection stoppages), January 28 (Friday of Rage protests and violence), and February 3 (gunmen reportedly firing on anti-government protesters in Cairo). In Libya the dates chosen for the unhindered analysis were: February 17, 2011 (the "Day of Rage" protests), February 20 (African mercenaries kill Libyan protesters), and February 22 (Gaddafi makes a rare media appearance). Only three days of analysis are included because reporting was incomplete or so small on the initial days of the protests that an adequate data sample could not be garnered.

The analysis covers what we considered "mainstream" and "alternative" forms of reporting distributed through Twitter, blogs and other social media. We define alternative journalistic practices similarly to Rodríguez (2001) as a set of media reporting, production and dissemination practices, which are embedded within the everyday lives of people specific to a historical, political and cultural context. We do not suggest these practices are solely the domain of "citizens" because global online networks allow collaboration beyond the borders of nation-states and citizenship identification. Instead, we maintain that alternative journalistic practices demarcate themselves (from the professionalized and institutionalized practices of mainstream media) in that their interests are solely committed to the audience and issues within a specific context. In serving those interests, alternative journalistic practices emphasize overt advocacy, first-person and eyewitness accounts, populist styles of presentation and collective organization and reporting practice (see Rodríguez, 2001). Unlike alternative journalistic practices, mainstream journalism operates accord-according to particular professional and discursive practice codes, as well as a particular economic model. Their economic imperative means that mainstream media are disseminated via the largest distribution channels and are likely to be encountered by a larger number of consumers. This demarcation is not to suggest an either/or distinction between alternative and mainstream reporting practices, however. Following Downing (2001), we suggest that a continuum of journalistic practices exists, which ranges from simply uploading video content onto YouTube to the professionalized practices of investigative journalism. This demarcation separates the types of journalistic practice evident during the Arab Spring protests, but it also attempts to acknowledge that a productive interaction can occur—albeit as part of a larger power relation—between types of media production and distribution. We located "alternative" journalists by identifying authors within the most widely accessed Egyptian and Libyan non-governmental blogs, Twitter and Facebook sites. We then collected all text, video and audio material from those sites on the six days we had chosen. Next, we compared these alternative selections to online text, video and audio reporting by CNN, BBC and Al Jazeera.

The individual analyses were reviewed together to compare how emergent themes occurred across the differing protests, as well as the different media and practitioners. The thematic analysis follows Orbe and Kinefuchi (2008) in utilizing three criteria in a discursive analysis to elicit emergent themes from diverse communication sources. An initial reading allowed the themes to emerge from the articles themselves, rather than guiding the search through pre-defined themes. Next, the text was read closely, organizing items relating to similar topics into categories or "proto-themes." Lastly, proto-themes were categorized and given a particular significance according to how each had emerged from the text. We also measured how many alternative forms of journalism were used by mainstream journalistic practitioners and vice versa in the form of linking, footnoting, Twitter, Facebook, Youtube videos and excerpts from blogs in reporting. This analytical process allowed for a systematic qualitative analysis, even where there was no consistency or agreement among the various texts analysed. This is important given the variety of materials selected for analysis and the different societal, political and cultural roles of both the communication technologies and their users. The individual analyses were reviewed together to compare how the emergent themes occurred across the differing protests, as well as the different media and practitioners. The goal of the analysis was to determine how alternative and mainstream journalistic practice interacted and to identify the kinds of outcomes and discourses these interactions created. We found that changes in the traditional practices of journalism were occurring in order to investigate and disseminate news and information in difficult communications environments.

Building Bridges Between Two Worlds: An Analysis of Reporting During the Egyptian and Libyan Arab Spring

The repercussions of technological change, such as blogging, citizen journalism and alternative media, have meant that citizens, rather than professional journalists, have often been credited for reporting, analyzing and disseminating information on a global scale (Bowman & Willis, 2003, p. 9). In more recent times, both alternative and mainstream modes of journalistic practice have interacted to serve the vested interests of both commercial and particular audiences; nowhere has this been more obvious than during the Arab Spring. Our analysis found that both mainstream and alternative journalistic modes of practice interacted in different ways to source, confirm and disseminate information to both local and global audiences. This mutually beneficial practice led to two major changes in how the two modes of practice interacted. The first seemed to be the level of cooperation—aided by social media—between the different modes of journalistic practice to report on the crisis. The second was the amount of mainstream news reporting that incorporated these first hand accounts, allowing alternative practitioners to disseminate their own view of the crisis.

Initial alternative coverage of the Egyptian and Libyan protests illustrated that individual bloggers conveyed information to their readers using links to mainstream news coverage. Twitter users also frequently retweeted coverage from the mainstream press, occasionally criticizing the coverage, but in the main using it as a source of credible information. This is not a new practice; many analyses of alternative journalism have shown that bloggers link to mainstream news to confirm their own reporting as credible or to criticize mainstream news (see Bruns, 2005; Jenkins, 2006). However, we noted a more interesting change in how mainstream modes of journalistic practice were using more social media especially tweets and YouTube footage, as a major aspect of their investigation and reporting.

Mainstream journalistic practice was still represented by traditional reports of "breaking" news from correspondents on location. However these correspondents were using a greater variety of techniques to source the news. This was especially evident in the number of references to Twitter, Facebook and other social media platforms; blog posts from "citizen journalists" and activists; the websites of NGO's in addition to the traditional use of official media representatives. We also noted instances of mainstream journalists encouraging local voices to phone or email updates, such as a journalist from the BBC who tweeted in Libya on February 15: "BBC WS wants to speak with anyone in #Benghazi #Libya at the moment, pls email me bard.aune@bbe.co.uk or call +44 207 557 3714." Others supplemented their own reporting with their personal views, such as when Anderson Cooper from CNN tweeted "Situation on ground in #egypt very tense. Vehicle I was in attacked. My window smashed. All ok." Mainstream journalists in Cairo also used social media to get around media blackouts. During the first days of the Egyptian protests, Egyptian journalist Sarah El Sirgany reported that she simply tweeted the news from her phone all day after the Daily News Egypt website was shut down (Get to know, 2011).

Reliance on social media for reporting was particularly evident during Internet and communication blackouts and during the days when it was too dangerous for journalists to report using their true identities. Both CNN and Al Jazeera lacked media access to Libya at the beginning of the protests. Al Jazeera correspondents said that "[v]erifying news from Libya has been difficult since the protests began, because of restrictions on journalists entering the country, as well as internet and mobile phone blackouts imposed by the government" (Uprising flares, 2011). In Egypt, both CNN and BBC reported that interruptions to Internet and mobile phone signals made it difficult to report, given that it was often dangerous to be on the streets when riot police had been deployed in Cairo (Egyptian-American, 2011; Holmes, 2011). As such, reporters often relied on social media and media-savvy witnesses to help them report the crisis. The BBC, for example, sourced information about the Libyan protests from what they termed "dissident websites" and from three main tweeters: "Feb

17 voices," "shabablibya" and "enoughgaddafi," although information was often presented as unverified.

However, one of the most important changes to traditional reporting practice was the level of cooperation with other journalistic practitioners. For example, The Arab Forum (McArthur, 2011) described Al Jazeera's journalistic process in Egypt:

> When Al Jazeera's signal was cut by authorities in the country, and the network's journalists were forced to hide their identities whilst reporting, it became a case of demonstrators calling up news channels to report as well. During the first few days of protests, when the Egyptian government cut the internet to the whole country, residents were speaking to friends abroad via landline, and in turn those friends would share information via Facebook, Twitter etc.

Thus the inherently dangerous crisis situation and the communications blocks meant that witnesses, activists and alternative journalistic practitioners often described events for mainstream journalists. For example, El-Hamalawy, who tweeted from the protests in Egypt every day, acknowledged that he would come home from the demonstrations at 11pm to find that Al Jazeera had used his pictures and videos in its news report: "A lot of my tweets had been broadcasted on Al Jazeera, or they would call me and confirm if something was actually happening" (El-Hamalawy cited in Rabie, 2011). Natasha Tynes, director of the International Centre for Journalists' Middle Eastern programs, argued that the two forms of media practice both complemented and corroborated each another to provide international coverage during media blackouts and journalist/protester arrests: "During the internet outage ... people tuned in to mainstream media such as TV news channels. Afterward, during the crackdown on journalists that began on February 2, mainstream news outlets relied on online activists, with tweets and emails frequently quoted in articles and live blogs" (Tynes cited in Rabie, 2011).

These contributions often were subsequently aggregated into a format that enabled listeners or viewers to access a broad overview of the situation. For example, Mashable (What the Arab Spring, 2011) describes the blogs and "curated" Twitter, YouTube and Facebook posts, all of which were part of mainstream coverage of the uprisings in Egypt and Libya, and sometimes the only coverage, particularly during the state crackdown on journalists in Egypt and for the early days of the Libyan revolution. In fact, the Al Jazeera live blog covering the Libyan revolution went as far as crediting the "Libya 17 voices" social media group as a main source of news coverage during the early days of the conflict. Al Jazeera also established a permanent link on its site to a livestream set up by a protester in Benghazi. The Arab Media forum (Hunter, 2011) describes this participation as a process of co-operation:

> When internet coverage was blocked, twenty-four-hour news channel Al Jazeera—a news outlet using the old media platform of T.V.—curated and collected the raw, immediate content citizens were sharing from each and every country, and made all that content available to television viewers as fast as possible. According to the Allied Media Corporation, Al Jazeera reaches 40 million viewers in the Arab world. Their extensive coverage of the Arab Revolution and willingness to broadcast both original citizen journalism and diverse views allowed Arab citizens without computers to see the digital content being shared by their neighbours and countrymen.

Our analysis also showed an increase in the amount of alternative journalism that mainstream news outlets included in their coverage of the Libyan and Egyptian protests. For example, some major news stories were actually broken by activists calling into mainstream news organizations to describe the crisis, to report on violence and to rectify misinformation. This practice was encouraged during the protests because it helped mainstream journalists collect information. For example, Al Jazeera allowed a "celebrity" activist and author of a bestselling book in Egypt, Alaa al-Aswany, to report on the protests in his own words (Fresh anti-govt, 2011). Another article on the BBC featured the prominent activist and blogger Gigi Ibrahim as an expert correspondent from Tahrir Square (Egypt unrest, 2011).

Social media was also a vital tool in allowing news organizations to report witness testimony from the crisis without endangering their safety. For example, a CNN report about the Egyptian "Friday of Rage" protests shows YouTube footage posted on social media websites without a source or verification (Cairo Protests, 2011) and another "eyewitness" was given prominence without being named in a video about the planned protests (Cairo protests, 2011). Similarly in Libya, CNN used an unnamed "medical source" who reported deaths via mobile phone during the protests (Get to Know, 2011). In these examples, the organization used informants without naming them due to the dangers associated with identification during the protests.

The variety of interactions demonstrate the high level of co-operation between different forms of journalistic practice—and how each action appears to satisfy the different vested interests of each group. For alternative media practitioners, the value of interaction with mainstream reporting was the dissemination of information about the crisis on a global scale. For mainstream news reporters, the value of the interaction was to obtain news and images quickly in a crisis situation. Such information would have been difficult to obtain given the instability of the political situation and the inherent danger associated with being on the streets of Libya and Egypt.

War in a New World? Tensions in Mainstream Reporting About Alternative Modes of Journalistic Practice

In what seemed like a largely diplomatic and mutually beneficial relationship between the two modes of journalistic practice, moments of friction nonetheless appeared in the language of mainstream reporting. In particular, mainstream coverage was marked by concerns to maintain authority and credibility, despite the dominant role of alternative modes of journalistic practice in informing mainstream reporting. While the use of social media could suggest mainstream reporting was simply appropriating alternative practices to continue its domination of the media landscape (particularly as it did not always credit "citizen journalists" for their work), this was not the case. In fact, as Natasha Tynes (cited in Rabie, 2011) suggests, "[m]any mainstream media outlets were caught off guard as they realized that citizen journalists were filling major holes found in the coverage of professional journalists."

A second focus of our analysis concerned the discourses presented within alternative modes of journalistic practice. We found that alternative journalists did not predominantly aim to confirm or inform mainstream journalistic practice. Instead, they, aided mainly by social media and online networks, created a communications and media environment all of their own. This environment served mainly to inform protesters at the local level. However, savvy alternative journalists also used it to shape mainstream reporting, and to disseminate their activism to a global audience. The global distribution and availability of social media platforms, and their linkages to mainstream media, brought alternative news coverage of local protests to a wider national, regional and international community.

Typically, alternative forms of journalistic practice used social media to mobilize protesters and to "amplify" news in real time. For example, during the Libyan protests, much social media reporting was used to communicate among activists, protesters and locals. Tripolitanian in Libya tweeted: "#Benghazi hospital has run out of anaesthesia a day ago, have to perform surgery without painkillers, please send supplies." Twitter appeared to be the best resource for alternative modes of journalistic practice inside Libya, although Facebook was initially used to mobilize the movement.

We identified four main types of reporting on Twitter. The first type of tweet was mainly descriptive of events that the person sending the message had directly experienced or witnessed. This was an important form of information dissemination, widely utilized by mainstream modes of journalistic practice. For example, Shabablibya tweeted: "#Benghazi protesters burnt down the radio station and taken the media and will make announcements shortly!! BREAKING URGENT #Libya." This tweet was then used in reporting in Al Jazeera's news blogs. The second form of tweet confirmed or retweeted what had been reported in mainstream media organizations with or without additional commentary. The third commented directly on previous communication blocks, and the last type of tweet confirmed reports by other protesters through retweet or further evidence. For example, Habibh (a well-known entrepreneur and activist) tweeted: "Egypt gets its Tiananmen square moment. Man bravely stands in front of armoured vehicle! Must watch!" These tweets, while serving an important communicative role for those participating in the protests, were also widely reported verbatim in the mainstream press.

Alternative practitioners embraced the information dissemination possibilities of new technologies and demonstrated personal investment in the protest outcomes, which yielded more subjective, first-person accounts. Mainstream journalists—who reported on the use of new digital technologies both as insiders (users of social media) and as outsiders (observing the use of social media by others)—attempted to maintain a professionally distant and objective discursive style. Furthermore, most of the description and audio and visual components produced by alternative modes of journalistic practice were not professionally produced, edited or censored, providing more of a lived experience of the protests than that of mainstream coverage. For example, Egyptian activist Mahmoud Salem wrote in his blog, Rantings of a Sandmonkey, about his own experiences of the protests. On February 3, he wrote a moving report of his fatigue after being on the protest frontline, moving between friends' houses to rest and avoid police: "We were being collectively punished for daring to say that we deserve democracy and rights, and to keep it up, they withdrew the police, and then sent them out dressed as civilians to terrorize our neighborhoods. I was shot at twice that day, one of which with a semi-automatic by a dude in a car that we the people took joy in pummeling" (Salem, 2011). Interestingly, alternative media reports also appeared (at times) to be more joyous, humorous and celebratory in their representation of what they considered to be a "youth" revolution. For example, Mosaaberizing, a photographer who lived in Tahrir Square during the protests, tweeted: "I kid you not. A group of us are practicing baseball with the stones they're throwing. Bats and all. Fun revolution :)" These intimate and personal modes of news reporting illustrated new practices by new practitioners; alternative media practitioners in both countries were deeply involved in activism, set up reliable communication channels and were often more efficient and credible sources of information than their mainstream counterparts.

Within this atmosphere of networked, collaborative and instantaneous news coverage, the authority, credibility and, most importantly, the need for mainstream news services was no longer immediately obvious. This manifested as a tension within the discourse of mainstream news coverage, where new journalistic practices were appropriated for news coverage but simultaneously constrained as a threat against the authority of traditional media. This was evident in the language of mainstream news reports that appeared to incorporate new media sources but nonetheless juxtaposed mainstream news against "protestors" using "social media." This method allowed mainstream journalistic practice to be represented as more credible and quality news reporting than amateur, unverified information presented by alternative modes of journalistic practice.

This effort to distinguish "authentic" from "inauthentic" journalism had a significant impact on mainstream news outlets' use of language and politicization of sources. For foreign journalists covering the Arab Spring, the need to source information meant speaking to those who were organizing, participating in and witnessing the uprisings. The word "protester," for example, did not always adequately describe the source of information or the kind of interaction that led to the report. In addition, much of the information sourced from those participating in the Arab Spring was done in an online environment via social media, adding another layer of complexity to the relationship. However, within mainstream coverage, it appears that the term "protester" became the catch-all descriptor for those who participated in the protests, despite their varied roles within the crisis, their expertise, their professional and activist associations and their normal occupations. This is problematic because using the generalized term "protester" relegated the person to the role of non-expert source, or eyewitness, even if she or he was an alternative journalistic practitioner, political expert or activist leader. It also suggests that mainstream journalists were on the street talking to eyewitnesses, when this was not always the case. Some "eyewitness" source material actually came from monitoring social media or from protesters' efforts to contact journalists. While this might not seem like an overtly political action, it is worth mentioning in light of the fact that Al Jazeera chose to use the more politically charged description "pro-democracy protesters," whereas BBC and CNN began their coverage on the Arab Spring with the more negative sounding "anti-government protesters." In one Al Jazeera article, this term appeared seven times. In comparison, both BBC and CNN began using the term "anti-government protesters" with some repetition, although CNN changed to the term "pro-democracy demonstrators" in later reporting (Fahmy, 2011).

The desire to distinguish traditional journalism from non-traditional practices also shaped the use of social media by mainstream news practitioners. Whereas alternative practitioners embraced the information dissemination possibilities of new technologies (and were also personally invested in the outcome of the protests), mainstream journalists reported new digital technology use as both insiders (users of social media) and outsiders (observing the use of social media by others). Much coverage questioned what the use of social media meant for the practice of journalism as a profession and how its use affected the quality of the information provided. Many feature articles in the mainstream media discussed the phenomenon with several points raised, but the most prominent discourse questioned the credibility of social media as a mode of reporting during times of crisis. This was evidenced in the coverage of the Egyptian and Libyan protests, when most social media accounts were reported with a caveat that the footage or reports could not be verified. One former CNN journalist, who had covered the Iranian demonstrations in 2009, said: "The information we received from the public was very important—however, any information or footage had to be thoroughly checked and analyzed by our team" (Rabie, 2011). That is, journalists relied on social media reporting by alternative journalistic practitioners, but ironically, did not credit it as journalism because they viewed it as lacking the credibility and authority of professional news practices.

Much of the criticism in mainstream media discourse centered on verification issues in using social media: One article about the protests in Egypt suggested, "There is as much misinformation as information. But social media can help tip off journalists about developments in places they can't get to" (Lister & Smith, 2011). This distrust of social media was also evidenced in mainstream journalistic practice; reporting almost always sought official channels to confirm information. For example, the BBC used the Swedish-based website, Bambuser, to confirm that communications had been blocked by government officials rather than relying upon eyewitnesses Much of the social media used in mainstream forms of journalistic practice also came with the caveat that the information "could not be verified"; thus, mainstream journalists disseminated the information but would not take professional responsibility for its veracity.

Another popular trope in mainstream coverage was the attempt to temper the positive fervor surrounding social media and blogging. Some journalists who questioned the use of social media were quick to contextualize it as an extension of simple information-sharing communication, such as the telephone. For example, one feature story suggested that critics were "rightly pointing out that it becomes tempting for analysts to give more credit to the new and sexy tools than they actually deserve" (Twitter blocked, 2011). Similarly, another feature asked, "is the internet only one tool in this process—nothing more than the modern version of the telephone?" (Making sense, 2011). Both journalists appear to put alternative media practices "in their place." They establish a hierarchy that affirms mainstream journalistic practice as the "real" reporting, and describes use of the Internet by protesters as merely a means of information sharing.

These efforts to "contain" the challenge of new media resonate with responses to the upstart medium of radio in the 1930s. Just as broadsheet newspapers eagerly reported radio's "unreliability" after the *War of the Worlds* broadcast, mainstream news organizations emphasized that the only "true" reporting during the Arab Spring came from recognized news outlets. Professional journalists described citizens' news reports via social media as "source material," rather than recognizing it as an alternative mode of journalistic practice. A sense of competition between "old" and "new" media practices influenced mainstream journalists to frame themselves as the only authoritative and credible sources of information during the crisis. Despite the diplomatic interactions between the two modes of journalistic practice during the protests, the Arab Spring has shown that traditional frames of journalistic discourse do not yet have the language to describe the changes wrought by the digital age.

Conclusion

In the 75 years since the *War of the Worlds* aired, print and broadcast platforms have individually capitalized on their specific attributes; print allows for in-depth, reporting and feature writing whereas broadcasting allows rich visualization and immediacy of the news. Audiences see these processes as complementary rather than competitive within an integrated news "diet." Thus the debate around which is the more credible news source has dissipated to discussions of individual issues posed by each medium's news practice. In the digital age, however, the news process is once again in a state of upheaval. Not only have print and broadcast news practices become integrated online, but social media and online communication platforms have revolutionized the investigation of and dissemination of news. Although most contemporary scholarship about journalistic practices rejects the dichotomous representation of the threat that alternative forms pose to professionalized processes, tensions remain.

Our analysis illustrates that the two modes of journalistic practice rely upon each other to source, inform and confirm news in a crisis and collaborate to ensure that vital information is disseminated across both local and global audiences. It can be argued that these interactions were spurred by the specific vested interest of each mode of journalism, the informational and activist motivations of alternative journalism and the competitive and commercial interests of mainstream journalism. Nonetheless, the motivating factor of crisis—the need to promote awareness of a political moment of upheaval and the struggles of innocent people—seemed to spur relations between the two modes of practice. Whatever the motivation, the Arab Spring protests have illustrated changes that have occurred in traditional journalistic practice. The inability of traditional frameworks of discursive representation to acknowledge these changes mirrors the tensions evident between media platforms during the 1930s. While the changes in investigating and disseminating the news suggest the war between the two media modes has ended, the battles over representation have only just begun.

Acknowledgement

Authors of this chapter would like to acknowledge the research assistance supplied by Amelia Johns and project funding given by the Faculty of Life and Social Sciences at Swinburne University.

References

Atton C. (2002). *Alternative media* London: Sage Publications.

Atton, C., & Hamilton, J. (2008). *Alternative journalism*. London: Sage Publications.

Bardoel, J., & Deuze, M. (2001). Network journalism: Converging competencies of old and new media professionals. *Australian Journalism Review*, 23(3), 91–103.

Beckett, C., & Mansell. R. (2008). Crossing boundaries: New media and networked journalism. *Communication, Culture & Critique*, 1(1), 92–104.

Berkman, R., & Shumway, C. (2003). *Digital dilemmas: Ethical issues for online media professionals*. Ames: Iowa State University Press.

Bowman, S., & Willis, C. (2003). We media: How audiences are shaping the future of news and information. *NDN website*. Retrieved from www.ndn.org/webdata/we_media.htm.

Boyd-Barrett, O. (2007). Alternative reframing of mainstream media frames in *Media on the move: Global flow and contra-flow*, Daya Kishan Thussu (Ed.) London: Routledge, 178–194.

Brodin, S. (2011, October 21). In the aftermath of the Arab Spring revolutions, journalists ask, who is a journalist? *European Journalism Centre Magazine*. Retrieved from www.ejc.net/magazine.

Bruns, A. (2003). Gatewatching, not gatekeeping: Collaborative online news'. *Media International Australia Incorporating Culture and Policy*, 107, 31–44.

Bruns, A. (2005). *Gatewatching: Collaborative online news production*. New York: Peter Lang.

Cairo protests: Eyewitness account. (2011, January 28). *BBC*. Retrieved from www.bbc.co.uk.

Campbell, W. (2010). *Getting it wrong: Ten of the greatest misreported stories in American journalism*. Berkeley: University of California Press.

Cenite, M., Detenber, B., Koh, A., Lim, A., & Soon, N. (2011). Doing the right thing online: A survey of bloggers' ethical beliefs and practices. *New Media and Society, 11*(4), 575–597.

Deuze, M. (2003). The web and its journalisms: Considering the consequences of different types of news media online. *New Media and Society, 5*(2), 203–230.

Downing, J. (2001). *Radical media: Rebellious communication and social movements.* London: Sage.

Downing, J. (2007). Grassroots media: Establishing priorities for the years ahead. *Global Media Journal, 1*(1). Retrieved from: www.commarts.uws.edu.au/gmjau/.

Egypt unrest: Day nine as it happened. (2011, 3 February). *BBC.* Retrieved from www.bbc.co.uk.

Egyptian-American leaders call for US support of 'Lotus Revolution.' (2011, January 28). *CNN.* Retrieved from: www.cnn.com.

Fahmy, M. (2011, December 18). Outrage over women's beating fuels new Egypt protests. *CNN.* Retrieved from http://articles.cnn.com/2011-12-18/africa/world_africa_egyptunrest_1_egyptian-police-tahrir-square-police-officers?_s=PM:AFRICA.

Fisher, L. (1988, 29 October). Orson Welles' '38 shocker remade. *New York Times,* p. 52.

Fresh anti-govt protests in Egypt. (2001, January 26). *Al Jazeera.* Retrieved from: http://English.aljazeera.net/news.

Get to know Piers Morgan. (2011, January 31). *CNN.* Retrieved from: www.cnn.com.

Harcup, T. (2005). I'm doing this to change the world: Journalism in alternative and mainstream media. *Journalism Studies, 6*(3), 361–374.

Hartley, J. (2005). *Creative Industries.* USA: Blackwell.

Hayes, J.E., & Battles, K. (2011). Exchange and interconnection in US network radio: A reinterpretation of the 1938 *War of the Worlds* broadcast. *The Radio Journal International Studies in Broadcast and Audio Media, 9*(1), 51–62.

Heinrich, A. (2011). *Network journalism: Journalistic practice in interactive spheres.* Hoboken, N.J.: Routledge.

Holmes, S. (2011, January 28). Is today a turning point for Egypt? *BBC.* Retrieved from: www.bbc.co.uk.

Hunter, E. (2011, February 24). The Arab revolution and social media. Flip the media: At the crossroads of media, culture and technology. Retrieved from http://flipthemedia.com/2011/02/the-arab-revolution-and-social-media/.

Jenkins, H. (2006). *Convergence culture: Where old and new media collide.* New York: New York University Press.

Lister, T., & Smith, E. (2011, January 27). Social media @ the front line in Egypt. *CNN.* Retrieved from http://articles.cnn.com/20110127/world/egypt.protests.social.media_1_social-media-twitter-entry-muslimbrotherhood?_s=PM:WORLD.

Livingstone, S. (1999). New media, new audiences? *New Media and Society, 1*(1), 59–66.

Livingstone, S. & Asmolov, G. (2010). Networks and the future of foreign affairs reporting. *Journalism Studies, 11*(5), 745–760.

Making sense of the internet and Egypt. (2011, January 31). *CNN*. Retrieved from www.cnn.com.

McArthur, S. (2011, May 18). Arab media forum 2011, Day Two. *Arabian bytes: Digital and tech trends in the Middle East*. Retrieved from: http://arabianbytes.com/tag/news-2/.

Mitchelstein, E. and Boczkowski, P. J. (2009). Between tradition and change: A review of recent research on online news production, *Journalism*, 10(5), 562–586.

Orbe M. P., & Kinefuchi E. (2008). Crash under investigation Engaging complications of complicity, coherence and implicature through critical analysis. *Critical Studies in Media Communication*, 25, 135–156.

Rabie, P. (2011, March 1). The cyber revolution. *Egypt Today*. Retrieved from: http://www.egypttoday.com/news/display/article/artId:198/The-CyberRevolution/secId:46.

Rodríguez, C. (2001). *Fissures in the mediascape: An international study of citizens' media*. New York: Hampton Press.

Rosen, J. (2009, January 12). Audience atomisation overcome: Why the internet weakens the authority of the press. *Pressthink*. Retrieved from: http://archive.pressthink.org/2009/01/12/atomization.html.

Salem, M. (n.d). *Rantings of a sandmonkey*. Retrieved from www.sandmonkey.org.

Singer, J.B. (1998). Online journalists: Foundations for research into their changing roles. *Journal of computer-mediated communication*, 78(1), 65–80.

Twitter blocked in Egypt amid street protests. (2011, January 26). *CNN*. Retrieved from www.cnn.com.

Uprising flares in Libyan city. (2011, February 11). *Al Jazeera*. Retrieved from: http://www.aljazeera.com/news/africa/2011/02/201122014259976293.html.

What the Arab Spring taught journalists about social media in 2011. (2011, December 21) *Mashable*. Retrieved from: http://mashable.com/2011/12/21/arab-spring-lessons/.

CHAPTER TEN

Social Media Curation and Journalistic Reporting on the "Arab Spring"

VITTORIA SACCO, MARCO GIARDINA AND
KATARINA STANOEVSKA-SLABEVA

In this chapter, Sacco, Giardina and Staneovska-Slabeva investigate the way that media professionals and amateurs use an emerging media content curation platform, Storify, to cover events of the so-called "Arab Spring." They argue that Storify demonstrates continuities with the broadcasting technique of "dispatch" highlighted in the *War of the Worlds*, but goes beyond dispatch to offer a platform for users to assemble and contextualize diverse messages spread throughout social media. The chapter explores the framing and sourcing of Storify stories in times of crisis, finding that they both perpetuate and depart from traditional news reporting practices.

Introduction

Recently, Arab uprisings have demonstrated the extent to which social media can support digital activism, which shows their power to coordinate communication, facilitate action around the world and make everyone a reporter (Eltantawy, 2011). During the Arab Spring, information, pictures and videos were distributed not only by media organizations or group leaders but also by protesters themselves (Eltantawy, 2011). Challenging journalists, social media have turned out to be important sources of information (eyewitnesses' information) and distribution channels for breaking news, which are employed by media organizations and users (Jarvis, 2008; Newman, 2011). However, in the context of digital activism, social media have raised concerns with respect to the efforts needed for extracting the best content in real time. Often, people only have access to the information posted by their small communities, causing them to lack an overall picture of the recent events discussed on social media. Immersed in events, activists may not know what is happening elsewhere on the same day.

Consequently, media content curation practices have emerged to make sense of the information stream posted on social media. In this study, the term "media content curation" means the curation of any social or traditional online media content. Based on the old principal of museum curation, media content curation knits technological and human skills for selecting, classifying, preserving, contextualizing and crafting traditional media sources and social media content into curated narratives (Fincham, 2011; Rosenbaum, 2011). Curation platforms enable the collection of content from different sources, the reorganization of that content into one's own story and the publication of that story (Scoble, 2010). The role of curators is to collect and organize existing content, such as tweets, blog posts or uploaded photos and videos without creating new tweets, blog posts, photos or videos per se (Duh et al., 2012). Unlike content marketing, it *doesn't* drive people through their decision making process about products and services (Gaasterland, 2011). Research on curation tools and practices is in its preliminary stages (Chen & Moeller, 2011; Duh, et al., 2012; Fincham, 2011; S. B. Liu, 2010).

In this context, Storify emerged in September 2010 as one of these media content curation platforms. According to Fincham (2011), Storify helps journalists give context to the stream of social media information. Herman (as cited in Fincham, 2011, p. 56), co-founder of Storify, has defined Storify as the means of creating 21st century wire posts, dynamic stories that can be embedded across the web. Storify includes several sources, while at the same time posting one's own story as the primary source of information. Storify allows users to choose tweets, Facebook content, Flicker photos, YouTube videos, Google searches, RSS feeds and other users' Storify stories, which are then gathered into a single story with contextualizing comments (see Figure 1). These stories can be published on other platforms, such as Twitter, Facebook or blogs, where readers can comment on the story. Currently, readers can also directly comment upon Storify narratives. Storify represents an additional tool in the vast world of alternative journalism, one that questions the traditional role of gatekeeper journalists (Stanoevska-Slabeva, Sacco, & Giardina, 2012). Storify has been used by media professionals and amateurs not only to tell stories about entertainment but also for news reporting on natural disasters (e.g., Hurricane Irene) and conflicts (e.g., Arab Spring).

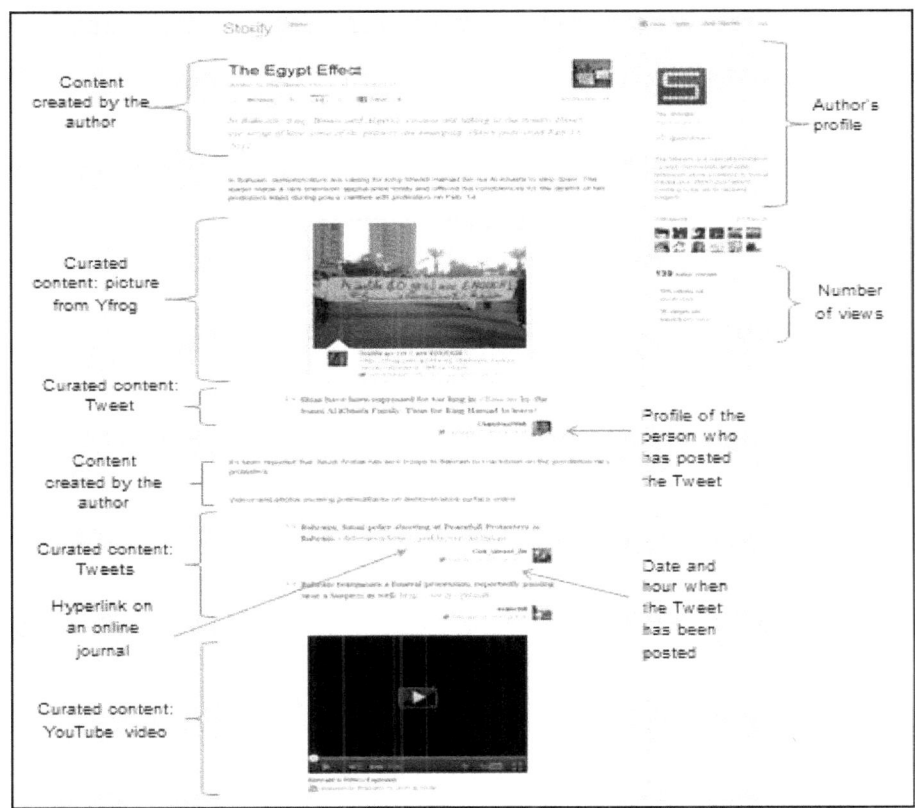

Figure 1: Example of curated media countent (source: Storify.com, August 2011)

We argue that media content curation platforms enable the same kind of "constant communicative presence" celebrated in the *War of the Worlds* radio drama (Hayes & Battles, 2011). By gathering content from different sources (i.e., traditional and social media) and reorganizing them into unique stories, Storify uses the technique of "dispatch" used in the *War of the Worlds* program to coordinate multiple communication media and send them to users (Scoble, 2010). Although Storify demonstrates continuities with broadcasting, it goes beyond dispatch to offer a platform for users to assemble diverse messages and to give context and insight into the meaning of information that is otherwise spread throughout social media.

This chapter explores the continuities and discontinuities between Storify and traditional forms of journalism. A content analysis of 100 Storify stories was performed to investigate the framing and sourcing employed. First, we asked whether the same frames found in traditional journalism were also present in Storify coverage of the Arab Spring. After investigating a range of news frames, we found that the *human interest* frame dominated Storify coverage. Second, we asked what kinds of sources Storify writers have drawn on most in covering revolutions in the Middle East. Our findings indicate that media organizations and citizens are the most-used sources.

Literature Review and Theoretical Background

Rosen (2005) contends that liberal access to television; the ubiquity of inexpensive digital cameras in mobile devices; and the instantaneous delivery of images via Twitter, Facebook, and other social networks, show a progressively visual culture. Specifically, war images seem to play a central role in what audiences discern about war (Sontag, 2003). Thus, it has become essential to analyze web-specific features, such as photos, multimedia and hyperlinks, to understand war coverage. Web-specific features have been explored mostly by using framing techniques. Indeed, Matthes (2009) claims that an understanding of the visual elements of framing is necessary to understand the framing process as a whole.

Performing a frame analysis helps to reveal how media organizations have chosen, ordered, underlined, reported and omitted certain aspects of an event using or discarding words and/or images and so on (Schwalbe, 2006). Tewksbury and Scheufele (2009) and Etman (2003) define framing as the practice by which journalists report some issues in the news with designated images and words to accentuate or support a certain interpretation. Visual images, multimedia and hyperlinks are some features of framing among several others, such as metaphors, exemplars and/or catch phrases (Gamson & Lasch, 1981; Hertog & McLeod, 2001). Based on Rodriguez and Dimitrova's (2011) study of framing typologies, this study identifies frames by numbering the items and distinct elements pictured in Storify stories. Frames result from distinguishing elements and by establishing or merging visual impressions into categories following principles of organization (Rodriguez & Dimitrova, 2011).

Goffman (1974) was the first to introduce the concept of framing, arguing that the context and organization of messages influence the public agenda about those messages. According to their coverage, visual, multimedia and hyperlink frames may influence the public's perception of war reporting. Fahmy, Kelly, and Yung Soo (2007) report that a large number of studies have been conducted on visual framing in media, focusing in particular on war and terrorism coverage. We explore some of those key findings below and use them to define the main variables of this investigation.

Photos

The power of the image has been investigated in many studies showing that governments try to influence public opinion by censoring images that could engender empathy for the enemy (Elliott & Lester, 2001). Moriarty and Show (as cited in Rodriguez & Dimitrova, 2011) have explored visual framing of Operation Desert Storm in three U.S. news magazines; they found that the most recurrent frame in the first Persian Gulf War was the ideological frame, combining war technology with science fiction imagery. They argue that this frame serves to restrict the audience's ability to discern the gravity of the conflict and the real cost of war.

Research on media coverage of the Gulf and Afghanistan Wars confirms that images do not picture "natural, spontaneous, or independent views of locations or occurrences" (Griffin, 2004, p. 399). Rather, Griffin (2004) finds that half of the images from the Iraq invasion employ frames that emphasize U.S. political and military power at the expense of covering the human and economic aspects of the conflict. In war coverage, "militainment" is likely to prevail, distorting combat news into fictional entertainment and frequently accentuating patriotic values (Andersen & Phillips, 2003, p. 219). Normally, people are not included in such coverage, but when they are, the portrayals are stereotypical or ethnocentric (M. Wall, 2006, p. 112). Correspondingly, King and Lester (as cited in S. Fahmy & Kim, 2008) show that images of the Iraq War rarely portray pictures of civilian casualties. Griffin (2004) challenges as myth the idea that news media picture human pain and show viewers the conditions of the oppressed to encourage social reform.

In contrast, Wojdynski's (2009) findings show that among online sources (e.g., photo galleries, audio slideshows, etc.) covering the Iraq War in 2007, civilian human interest frames were the most represented. Indeed, photos of the Abu Ghraib scandal have been one of the war's great media spectacles, engendering doubts regarding the U.S. invasion and occupation of Iraq (Kellner, 2008). With the advent of new technologies, then, people have used the power of the image to express themselves and to show their reality, encountering less censorship and reaching diverse audiences.

Multimedia

The space dedicated to multimedia and their preponderance in news has grown with the innovation and evolution of technologies and digital devices. Multimedia formats used by news outlets do not necessarily displace dominant news frames (Kelner, 2004; Dimitrova & Neznanski, 2006). However, with digital technologies and new media, new forms of reporting have emerged that challenge mainstream corporate media and government restrictions and, consequently, promote alternative media frames.

The cases of two Egyptian activists provide vivid examples of how digital media enabled new forms of reporting during the Arab Spring (Aouragh, 2011). Ramy Roof gathered camera phone content filmed during the shutdown of the Internet connection and posted it online once the Internet connection was reestablished. This content was then redistributed by media organizations (Aouragh, 2011). Wall and El Zahed (2011) have analyzed the role of YouTube during the Egyptian uprisings of 2011 as a form of participatory media. They have built a case study on videos posted by a young activist, Asmaa

Mafouz. The videos were initially viewed by Egyptians and then by people from Saudi Arabia. In contrast with past Egyptian political rhetoric, Mahfouz used simple words, deprived of overt ideology or political viewpoint, to call citizens to participate in protests. Moreover, Wall and El Zahed (2011) have claimed that these videos symbolize a sort of Egyptian citizens' guide to protest.

Hyperlinks

Hyperlink usage allows news organizations to gain space, time and distribution (Himelboim, 2010). Through hyperlinks, readers can have access to different sources of information and can better navigate through the volume of information provided on the Web (Connolly-Ahern, Williams, & Kaid, 2003). The online reporter has to link to relevant documents, sources and expert opinion to give more context to the story. Thus, hyperlinks can be a solution to achieving these goals. Furthermore, the power of hyperlinks seems to reside in their interactivity, connectivity (Peng, Tham, & Xiaoming, 1999), simplicity of learning (Eveland & Dunwoody, 2001) and ability to give control to readers (Althaus & Tewksbury, 2000).

Editorial norms, however, can restrict the way hyperlinks are included in online news. In his study, Himelboim (2010) demonstrates that news media prefer linking to traditional and/or recognized sources, such as other news media and/or governmental organizations rather than blogs or other Web sources (Himelboim, 2010). Using content analysis on online newspapers' hyperlinks, Connolly-Ahern et al. (2003) show that online newspapers use hyperlinks as a gate-keeping device.

Research Questions and Methodology

Data Gathering

This study investigates 100 Storify stories on the Middle East uprising, which include 220 photos, 165 multimedia, and 561 hyperlinks. These stories cover the period from April 25th 2011, when Storify opened to the public, to the end of August 2011, when the analysis was completed. A Google search was used to collect the sample because Storify lacked an internal search engine at the time of the study, and it was difficult to monitor the constant flow of updates on the Internet. The following keywords were used to build the dataset: *revolution, rebellion, freedom, flag, fight* and *civil war*, followed by the name of the specific country. The name of the cities or places where major events took place and the names of dictators were also used.

The sample is composed of stories written in English and covering Yemen (20), Syria (20), Bahrain (20), Libya (20) and Egypt (20). In our preliminary investigations, we observed that both Arab journalists and amateurs privileged the English language in their Storify stories about the Arab protests. Therefore, we decided to focus on how people report international events in English using content curation platforms to reach a broad audience. Restricting the language used within the curated stories was also helpful in creating a clearly focused and balanced sample. Moreover, only English speakers were available for coding.

Content Analysis

This study uses content analysis to identify which content and sources have been included or excluded in Storify news stories. Content analysis is the preferred method for analyzing visual and textual framing (S. Fahmy, 2007; Grabe & Bucy, 2008; Jackson, 2011; King & Lester, 2005; Sherer, 1989; Wanta & Chang, 2001). Past research has used content analysis to examine propaganda phenomena in wartime because it is difficult to get some information through surveys in times of crisis (Krippendorff, 2004). Content analysis distinguishes itself by its unobtrusive appraisal of communication, its ability to assess the effects of environmental variables and source characteristics on communication content, and its capacity to investigate the nature and effect of specific messages (Kolbe & Burnett, 1991). Content analysis limitations reside in reporting only specific elements in communication and returning categorical data (Kolbe & Burnett, 1991, p. 244).

Coding Process

Storify is a multimedia platform where curators can chose their sources and mix different Web-specific features as well as privilege or use only one specific channel. It was not uncommon to see stories that used only tweets, photos or videos alongside those that combined these sources. Following other framing analysts, this study coded photos, multimedia and hyperlinks as units of analysis (Dimitrova & Neznanski, 2006; Parry, 2008). The coder noted the number of photos, multimedia and hyperlinks present in each story. The hyperlink destinations were also identified (Connolly-Ahern, et al., 2003). Following Massey and Levy (1999), all digitized audios and videos were coded as multimedia features. With the statistical software R^1 and through crosstabs, relationships involving the coded variables were evaluated to make inferences about their meaning.

Frames

Scholarly studies by Xigen, Lindsay and Mogensen (2002), Semetko and Valkenburg (2000), Dimitrova, Kaid and Williams (2004) and Dimitrova and Neznanski (2006) identify recurring frames used by journalists when reporting on war. This study identifies several of these same frames in the photos, multimedia and hyperlinks of Storify stories:

- The *military conflict frame* represents conflicts between individuals, groups or institutions (Semetko & Valkenburg, 2000), and it is related to combat, troops, arsenals and the damage and destruction caused by the conflicts.
- The *human interest frame* evokes emotions in readers when presenting an event (Semetko & Valkenburg, 2000). It shows civilian, soldier, protester, prisoner and refugee and/or military lives as well as causalities, atrocities, suffering, protests and demonstrations.
- The *economic consequences frame* concerns the economic repercussions of an event on individuals, groups, institutions, regions or countries (Semetko & Valkenburg, 2000). In these countries, this frame typically relates to changes in oil prices and economic slowdowns.

- The *morality frame* denotes the presence of moral messages, religious tenets or social prescriptions when the event is reported (Semetko & Valkenburg, 2000). It comprises stories covering collective behaviors, voices or opinions, which demonstrate antiwar or anti-government attitudes, the critique of political and war strategies, diplomacy and national/international interest in the rebellions.
- The *responsibility frame* corresponds to the attribution of responsibilities to the government, an individual or a group for the causes or solutions of an event (Semetko & Valkenburg, 2000).
- The *diagnostic frame* is related to the reasons for which an event has happened (Dimitrova, et al., 2004).
- The *prognostic frame* deals with information about the further evolution of an event and the post revolutions, constructions, life and opportunities for citizens (Dimitrova, et al., 2004).

Thus, if at least one of these frames was present in a photo, multimedia, or hyperlink, the coder marked 1; otherwise, the coder marked 0. Binary coding was chosen for framing categories because Storify stories are composed of several different ones. Because it was difficult to estimate the most emphasized frame in each story, the sum of the percentages of each column of Table 1 is not 100%. Instead, it was possible to count how many sources or hyperlink destinations were present in each story, which yielded discrete variables.

Since everyone can disseminate information using social media and no editorial norms are imposed, we hypothesize that social media are more egalitarian media where people have more freedom to express themselves and can post all kinds of content. Complexity and diversity can be expressed freely and without intervention of some to censor or to control the content. Therefore, we expect that the *human interest* frame will be the most covered frame by photos and multimedia, which show the more human and truthful face of everyday wars, protesters and civilians conditions.

Table 1. Frames of Web-specific Features

Frames	Photos (%)	Multimedia (%)	Hyperlinks (%)
Human	89	85	68
Military	27	48	68
Diagnostic	13	14	24
Responsibility	–	17	18
Prognostic	–	2	7
Economic	–	–	4
Morality	–	2	3

— means that the frame was not present at all.

Generally, the role of hyperlinks consist of helping to obtain in-depth reporting (Kovarik, 2002) and to complete the missing information. We expected the *human interest* frame to be the most common frame covered by hyperlinks because of this in-depth reporting, followed by the *diagnostic* and the *responsibility* frames, which give an overall picture of the conflicts. Therefore, we propose the following research question: Are the same frames of traditional journalism present in Storify coverage of the Arab Spring? Why or why not? In addition, we hypothesize that the *human interest* frame will be the dominant frame.

Sources

Storify's stories include original contributions from traditional and social media. All original contributions involved in the curated stories are attributed to the original authors themselves. For example, it is possible to click on Twitter accounts when tweets, Twitpic or Yfrog are used in the stories to see the original author's profile. We assume that if the person claims a specific origin, his contribution was marked as true. This allows us to construct a category for *citizens*, trusting what they claim to be. The limitation is that even if we can verify journalists' nationality and occupation through their official media companies, this option is not always possible for ordinary citizens. For example, if a person claimed to be Syrian, we considered him or her to be Syrian because we had no means of verifying origin and status. We know people can use fake profiles in social media. During the Arab Spring, the story of the Gay Girl in Damascus,[2] which produced a lot of buzz, highlights the limits of identification via social media. However, we estimate that some fake profiles are easier to recognize than others.

Based on Xigen et al (2002), Semetko and Valkenburg (2000) and Dimitrova et al.'s (2004) studies of information sources used in articles reporting on the war, the following source categories were coded:

- *Media* represents all members of traditional and online media, such as media organizations, journalists, reporters, photographers and correspondents of the entire world.
- *Citizens* corresponds to eyewitnesses, civilians, victims, prisoners, protesters, local participants, soldiers and their families present in the country where the uprisings have taken place.
- *Non-Arab People* are people not involved physically in the rebellions and who do not live in Arab countries. This includes U.S., European, Asian, and Latin American citizens, experts and/or civic groups.
- *Arab People* refers to Arab people, expatriates and refugees who do not live in the country of the rebellions but come from an Arab country.
- *Unknown sources* are sources not identified or that could not be attributed to the other categories. Some profile information on original contributors was inaccessible, which disallowed their classification. This category also includes websites, such as Wikipedia, Google map and/or NGOs when the actual contributor is unknown.

The Middle East revolutions have been characterized by the proliferation of participatory and citizen journalism (Eltantawy, 2011). It is likely that eyewitnesses covered the conflict as well as everyday life conditions because they were free from norms and policies. This leads to the following research question: What kinds of original sources are most used to report the Middle East Revolution in Storify's stories? In this context, we hypothesize that the most used sources will be *media organizations* and *citizens*.

Reliability

Intercoder reliability is the method by which independent coders assess a message characteristic and reach the same conclusion. In content analysis, reliability is represented by a tacit agreement among coders about classifying the inspected variables. As suggested by Riffe and Freitag (1997), we randomly selected ten percent of the sample to measure intercoder reliability. Since only one researcher coded the entire sample, another colleague was trained for coding the shared ten percent.

Krippendorff's α was chosen as the reliability index because it allows constant reliability standards and can be used for several metrics, for any number of values per variable (α is independent of this number), for any kind of sample size, and for samples containing missing values (Krippendorff, 2004). Researchers can rely on variables with reliabilities above α equal to 0.8 (Krippendorff, 2004). Variables with α between 0.667 and 0.8 are considered reliable only for drawing tentative conclusions (Krippendorff, 2004). Krippendorff's α = 0.88 measuring intercoder reliability of frames attributes (Table 1), which means that 88% agreement can be expected by chance. Instead, for sources (Table 2), Krippendorff's α = 0.82. Hyperlinks' redirection reliability index = 0.856 (with α normal). According to values of indices, these findings are acceptable.

Table 2. Sources of Web-specific Features

Sources	Photos (%)	Multimedia (%)	Hyperlinks (%)
Media Professionals	36	50	33
Citizens	22	23	40
Arab People	6	10	4
Non-Arab People	4	10	8
Unknown	32	7	15
Sum	100	100	100

Results

We found that 55% of the stories were written by media professionals and the remaining 45% were written by amateurs. In addition, the most prevalent Web-specific features were hyperlinks. They range from 0 to 198 (median[3] = 1 and sd = 20.50). This high presence of hyperlinks can be justified by the fact that the components present salient but relatively low information (e.g., tweets have only maximum 140 characters), the authors thus add material and in-depth coverage using hyperlinks. These findings are in line with those of Dimitrova and Neznanski (2006), which show that hyperlinks turn into an established feature of online news. Next, multimedia range from 0 to 18 (median = 1 and sd = 2.63). Finally, photos seem less represented, with a range from 0 to 14 (median = 1 and sd = 3.01) per story.

Photos

As demonstrated in Table 1, the most common frame in media content curation images was the *human interest* frame. Indeed, 89% of the selected stories cover this frame. Next was the *military conflict* frame, represented in 27% of the sampled stories, and finally the *diagnostic* frame, denoted in only 13% of the sample. In this sample, the other frames are not represented. It is quite difficult to have a visual representation of the other frames. They have been taken into account because we expected to find them in the multimedia and hyperlink categories.

Examples of the *military conflict* frame are images that present city destruction, weapons, maps and/or soldiers.[4] People holding signs with words like "freedom," which attest the reasons for protests, constitute one sort of *diagnostic* frame,[5] whereas images of dead bodies, injured people or protesters have been the most common portrayals forming the *human interest* frame.[6] Some of them have been raw images, picturing martyred and tormented bodies or injured children, unleashing the wrath of spectators. As advocated by Andersen (1989), we maintain that the authority of images within stories is to illustrate the truth of conflicts and their awful consequences on the entire world population, provoking reactions from watchers. However, in traditional media, these sensitive images would have been censored or at least would have been deemed unusual.

The most used sources were the *media, unknown sources,* and *citizens*; 36% of the stories use *media professionals* as main sources of information, 32% use *unknown* sources and 22% use *citizens*. The other categories of sources are present but with less importance than the ones quoted above. Only 6% and 4%, respectively, of the stories have used *Arab people* and *non-Arab people* as information sources (Table 2). This could explain the two major frames. *Citizens* posted photos of their everyday life during the conflict, perhaps because it didn't matter to them if photos had been about the conflict or human suffering. Their goal was to announce to the world what was happening in their countries. They were calling for new resistance and support. In times of crisis and disaster, people often take photos to report and illustrate events, and to call for support (S. Liu, Palen, Sutton, Hughes, & Vieweg, 2008). Both amateurs and media professionals also re-posted photos found on social networks or online media as a means of discussing the conflict, showing their indignation about government policies, or sustaining and giving dignity to protesters, victims and their families.

Sources unrelated to media organizations and independent media can provide media education, critiques and information about how media organizations work. But as already revealed by blogs during international events (Campbell & Gibson, 2009; Drezner & Farrell, 2004), they also have the potential to show another face of conflicts, since most of the time journalists are embedded with the army or NGOs, banned from access to ongoing events, or given a restrictive view of events. Often, censorship of local media gives us a superficial and limited vision of what is happening and what continues to happen in these countries. It is clear in these cases that having a direct witness who spreads content on social networks can open our eyes to the truth of the conflict.

One can argue that the prevalence of the *human interest* frame resulted from the expression of curators selecting and curating their own list of sources. Previous studies on the Arab Spring and its coverage showed that both media professionals and amateur curators have particularly accentuated this frame, mostly for the same reasons associated with *media* and *Arab/non-Arab* sources. When curators come from the countries where the revolutions are taking place, they are often motivated by citizenship ties; therefore it is not surprising that they would privilege the *human interest* frame (Sacco, Giardina, & Stanoevska, 2012; Stanoevska-Slabeva, et al., 2012). In addition, by encouraging more people to tell stories from their own perspectives, Storify, and other content curation platforms promote narratives with a more human face. Centering on the *human interest* frame, these stories have the potential to sensitize readers to support victims by helping them stop war atrocities and innocent deaths.

The high percentage of *unknown* sources (32%) challenges the stories' credibility. In these cases, verification must be made by readers themselves or new tools have to be adapted to ensure accuracy, norms, policies and quality. With all the information available, it is difficult to monitor sources. Both the author of the story and the readers should become virtual reporters or detectives. Media content curation implies that source verification can be done by the author of the story or by the reader through cross-checking or other methods. But the process takes time and dedication. It seems that, on the one hand, social media and media content curation increase the risk of getting false information. On the other hand, social media offer the possibility of several points of view from different sources that were previously unavailable.

Findings suggest a prevalence of the *human interest* frame and *media* and *citizens* as principal sources of information. But, the high percentage of *unknown sources* makes categorization difficult, which creates bias in computation. Hence, a limitation of media content curation resides in the impossibility of always verify its sources, thus leaving it a fragile tool to be used with caution and discretion. The Storify curator bares all the responsibility in terms of accuracy and integrity of such content. Storify does not yet present an adequately efficient way of filtering sources, however, which may be due to its policies. Sources have to be checked by the curator or the reader. So, if not previously done by the curator, the reader has to verify sources (Bruns, 2003, 2008; Stanoevska-Slabeva, et al., 2012).

Multimedia

The most common frames in content curation multimedia coverage are the *human interest* frame and the *military conflict* frame. They have been coded in 85% and 48% of the selected stories. The *responsibility* frame follows, denoted in 17% of the sampled stories, and the *diagnostic* frame comes next, perceived in 14% of the sample. The other frame categories are almost absent. In essence, the *prognostic* and the *morality* frame have been detected in only 2% of the stories, and there were no representations of the *economic* frame in this specific sample (Table 1). Multimedia seem to privilege human aspects[7] and the evolution and actions of conflicts.[8]

The main sources used for multimedia are *media* (50%) and *citizens* (23%). The other categories are marginally represented. *Arab* and *non-Arab people* have been coded as sources of information in 10% of the stories and *unknown* sources only in 7% of the stories (Table 2). Most posted videos have been taken from online sites of media organizations or from YouTube pages. Parts of the videos have no sources, no name and/or no link through which the reader can assess the legitimacy of the coverage. But, the percentage of *unknown sources* (7%) is less than the one for photos (32%). In times of crisis, storytellers seem to rely on the *media* and *citizens* as sources of information and to privilege the *human interest* frame.

Hyperlinks

The *military conflict* frame (68%), the *human interest* frame (68%), the *diagnostic* frame (24%) and the *responsibility* frame (18%) have been the most covered frames by hyperlinks. The three other frames have been presented with smaller percentages. The *prognostic* frame was coded in only 7%, the *economic* frame in only 4% and the *morality* frame in only 3% of the selected stories (Table 1).

Frames most covered in photos and in multimedia are also the most covered in hyperlinks. Hyperlinks seem to complete and illustrate in-depth coverage of the main subject. Since tweets are not longer than 140 words, RSS feeds are cut, Facebook comments do not exceed a few sentences and, on average, videos range from 30 seconds to 10 min, to get a real overview of events, one must rely on hyperlinks. Moreover, as we will see later on, almost one fourth of the hyperlinks belong to online newspapers, where readers can access a more traditional information source.

The most used sources are *citizens* (40%), *media* (33%) and *unknown* (15%) sources. Other categories of sources are marginally represented. *Non-Arab people* are quoted in 8% of the selected stories, whereas *Arab people* are included in only 4% of the sampled stories

(Table 2). As previously noted, the *media* and *citizens* are the main sources. The majority of hyperlinks are given in tweets. Photos and multimedia also have hyperlinks, but they show the same photo or multimedia existing in the story, redirecting readers to the main platforms where photos or multimedia were initially posted. In most cases, professional authors quote other media sources, giving hyperlinks to their websites. *Citizens* often tweet hyperlinks on videos to show the atrocities of the conflict or their fight for freedom. They also rely on media sources like Al Jazeera, finding them more credible because they report information about people who are physically in the heart of the conflict as eyewitnesses and/or reporters.

Authors have aimed to give relevance and accuracy to their stories by adding supplementary information through hyperlinks. As stated by Deuze (1999), incorporating hyperlinks can give readers more options for personalization. Through hyperlinks, readers can access archived stories and read original source materials.

Table 3. Destination of Hyperlinks

Redirection	Hyperlinks (%)
Videos	50
Online Journals	29
Social Media	10
Blogs	5
Other categories	6
Sum	100

Hyperlink redirection has been used for videos[9] in 50% of the cases, principally YouTube videos, and the websites of online newspapers[10] in 29% of the cases (Table 3). In addition, 10% of hyperlinks connect to social media networks,[11] 6% to various websites,[12] including NGOs and the White House websites, and 5% to blogs[13] (Table 3). These findings contradict the ones of Connolly-Ahern et al. (2003), who suggest that hyperlinks have been designed more for videos than for photos and that the majority of hyperlinks are of textual content. In the past ten years, it seems, there has been a diversification in hyperlink use and an increase in links to visual content.

Summary of Results

Since the end of the Cold War and the spread of broadband and wireless networks, user-generated content has been growing (Stochetti, 2003). The borderline that separates professional journalists and their audiences seems to be blurring (Bruns, 2005; Jenkins, 2006). Through new technologies, user-generated content shows more real-time and in-depth reporting.

As previously discussed, media content curation Web-specific features strengthen the *human interest* frame and the *military conflict* frame with sources relying on media organizations, their staffs and *citizens*. Unlike traditional media, media content curation allows the audience to participate in both the creation and reception of news. Thus, some changes in frames and sources have been made because of the evolution of people's thoughts and because of how the news is produced and delivered. Since the advent of participatory and citizen journalism, there has been a shift from official sources (Bennett, 1990; Cook, 1994; Griffin, 2004; Herman & Chomsky, 1994) to an increasing number of available voices with frames involving more human and emotional aspects (Dimitrova & Neznanski, 2006; Kellner, 2008; Wojdynski, 2009). Media content curation does not drastically change news reporting, but it continues to spotlight users as sources of information, giving the news a more human face. The presence of several sources and media organizations in the same story might help readers to assess the truthfulness of an event. Since curation enables the collection of content from several platforms, it may help promote more diverse views about wartime events (Keith, et al., 2009).

Conclusion and Discussion

In the past, mainstream media have primarily relied on official sources for war reporting, often conforming to the interests of political elites and relegating public opinion to the margins. Unlike mainstream media, media content curation seems capable of exceeding both government and editorial policies. It provides alternative sources about conflicts, overcoming geographic restrictions in an attempt to ensure international information flow. Media content curation continues to contribute to building a media space where several cultures and opinions may be represented and where everyone can create news content. Audiences appear more willing to participate in news production and in news distribution. Moreover, sources provided by non-professional reporters are free of journalistic norms, so amateurs and *citizens* have the potential to report upon even the most sensitive topics. As discussed in our results, Storify both perpetuates and disrupts traditional news frames and sources.

Storify allows media users to navigate a complex system of interconnections between media organizations, communication technologies, and diverse users. Like the role of radio dispatch in the *War of the Worlds* broadcast (Hayes & Battles, 2011), Storify provides a means of collecting and distributing several kinds of media content. In this sense, Storify illustrates the continuities between early broadcasting and social media collection processes. However, Storify also goes beyond dispatch in a number of ways. It allows users to make sense out of the constant flow of information shared on social media, helping them identify relevant information and giving it context. Storify also facilitates interconnection between, and about, constantly moving groups of actors without the need for a centralized site of dispatch.

The main drawback of content curation platforms like Storify, in relation to traditional journalism, is the incorporation of information from unknown sources. The high percentage of unknown sources present can result from superficial coverage or from limitations on source verification. Triangulation of sources remains an essential activity; and these new tools have to be adapted to do it more automatically. Otherwise, as with the 1938 *War of the Worlds* broadcast (Heyer, 2003), fiction can be confused with reality.

Notes

[1] http://www.r-project.org/
[2] http://www.guardian.co.uk/world/2011/jun/13/gay-girl-damascus-tom-macmaster
[3] We present the median because it is more robust when extreme or outlier observations are detected.
[4] Example of the *military conflict* frame (6th image by Wordpress): http://storify.com/ajstream/bahrain

⁵ Example of the *diagnostic* frame (3rd image by The Guardian): http://storify.com/citizenside/syrie
⁶ Example of the *human interest* frame (1st image by Ajstream): http://storify.com/ajstream/bahrain
⁷ Example of the *human interest* frame (4th and 5th videos by freelattakia): http://storify.com/citizenside/syria-the-showdown
⁸ Example of the *military conflict* frame (1st and 3rd videos by UgaritNews and freelattakia): http://storify.com/citizenside/syria-the-showdown
⁹ Hyperlink (video by NoonArabia): http://storify.com/interzonerebels/yemen3
¹⁰ Hyperlink to the *Los Angeles Times* (second-to-last tweet by jimmurphySF): http://storify.com/citizenside/syria-the-showdown
¹¹ Hyperlink to social media (by monaeltahawy): http://storify.com/ajstream/dispatches-from-sanaa
¹² Hyperlink on other website (by vnessi): http://storify.com/burhanco/ali-ferzat-syrian-cartoonist-attacked
¹³ Hyperlink to a blog (1st tweet of scoobydoo007): http://storify.com/interzonerebels/tweets-and-news-from-taiz

References

Althaus, S. L. & Tewksbury, D. (2000). Patterns of Internet and traditional news media use in a networked community. *Political Communication, 17*(1), 21–45.

Andersen, R. (1989). Images of war: photojournalism, ideology, and Central America. *Latin American Perspectives, 16*(2), 96–114.

Andersen, R. & Phillips, P. (2003). From saving Private Lynch to the "Top Gun" president: The made-for-TV "reality war" on Iraq. *Censored 2004: The top 25 censored stories*, 219–223.

Aouragh, M. A. A. (2011). The Egyptian experience: Sense and nonsense of the Internet revolution. *International Journal of Communication, 5*, 1344–1358.

Baran, S. J. & Davis, D. K. (2011) *Mass communication theory: Foundations, ferment, and future*. Belmont, Calif.: Wadsworth.

Bennett, W. L. (1990). Toward a theory of press state relations in the United States. *Journal of Communication, 40*(2), 103–127.

Bruns, A. (2003). Gatewatching, not gatekeeping: Collaborative online news. *Media International Australia Incorporating Culture and Policy: Quarterly Journal of Media Research and Resources, 107*, 31–44.

Bruns, A. (2005). *Gatewatching: Collaborative online news production* (Vol. 26). New York: Peter Lang.

Bruns, A. (2008). *Blogs, Wikipedia, Second Life, and beyond: From production to produsage* (Vol. 45). New York: Peter Lang.

Campbell, V. & Gibson, R. (2009). News blogs, mainstream news and news agenda. In S. Tunney & G. Monahan (eds.), *Web Journalism: A New Form of Citizenship?*

Brighton: Sussex Academic, 1–20.

Cantril, H. (1940). *The invasion from Mars: A study in the psychology of panic.* Piscataway, N.J.: Transaction Pub.

Chen, H. & Moeller, R. A. (2011). An analysis of online news comments on children's racial perceptions in the US. *Proceedings of the American Society for Information Science and Technology, 48*(1), 1–4.

Connolly-Ahern, C., Williams, A. P. & Kaid, L. L. E. E. (2003). Hyperlinking as gatekeeping: Online newspaper coverage of the execution of an American terrorist. *Journalism Studies, 4*(3), 401–414.

Cook, T. E. (1994). Domesticating a crisis: Washington newsbeats and network news after the Iraqi invasion of Kuwait. In W. L. Bennett & D. L. Paletz (eds.), *Taken by storm: The media, public opinion, and US foreign policy in the Gulf War.* Chicago: University of Chicago Press, 105–130.

Deuze, M. (1999). Journalism and the Web. *International Communication Gazette, 61*(5), 373-390.

Dimitrova, D. V., Kaid, L. L. & Williams, A. P. (2004). The first hours of online coverage of Operation Iraqi Freedom. In R. D. Berenger (ed.), *Global media go to war: Role of news and entertainment media during the 2003 Iraq War.* Spokane, Wash.: Marquette Books, 255-265.

Dimitrova, D. V. & Neznanski, M. (2006). Online journalism and the war in cyberspace: A comparison between US and international newspapers. *Journal of Computer Mediated Communication, 12*(1), 248–263.

Downey, R., Johnson, E. & Brewer, B. (2012). *Through the lens: Visual framing of the Japan tsunami in US, British, and Chinese online media.* University of Missouri March 20, 2012. Paper presented at the ISOJ, Austin, Texas.

Drezner, D. & Farrell, H. (2004). *The power and politics of blogs.* Paper presented at the American Political Science Association, Chicago, Illinois.

Duh, K., Hirao, T., Kimura, A., Ishiguro, K., Iwata, T. & Yeung, C. M. A. (2012). *Creating stories: Social curation of Twitter messages.* Paper presented at the Sixth International AAAI Conference on Weblogs and Social Media, Dublin, Ireland.

Elliott, D. & Lester, P. M. (2001). Ethics of patriotism: When is it OK to break the law? *News Photographer, 56*(11), 10–12.

Eltantawy, N. W. & Wiest, J. B. (2011). Social media in the Egyptian revolution: Reconsidering resource mobilization theory. *International Journal of Communication, 5,* 1207–1224.

Eveland, W. P. & Dunwoody, S. (2001). User control and structural isomorphism or disorientation and cognitive load? *Communication Research, 28*(1), 48-78.

Fahmy, S. (2007). *Filling out the frame: Transnational visual coverage and news practitioners' attitudes towards the reporting of war and terrorism.* Saarbrücken, Germany: VDM.

Fahmy, S., Kelly, J. D, & Yung Soo, K. (2007). What Katrina revealed: A visual analysis of the hurricane coverage by news wires and U.S. newspapers. *Journalism & Mass Communication Quarterly, 84*(3), 546–561.

Fahmy, S. & Kim, D. (2008). Picturing the Iraq war. *International Communication Gazette, 70*(6), 443-462.

Fincham, K. (2011). Review: Story (2011). *Journal of Media Literacy Education, 3*(1), 56–60.

Gaasterland, M. (2011). What is content curation? And how it's useful to you and your network. Retrieved 24 August 2012, from http://www.michielgaasterland.com/content-marketing/what-is-content-curation-and-how-it's-useful-to-you-and-your-network.'

Gamson, W. A., & Lasch, K. E. (1981). *The political culture of social welfare policy*. Paper presented at the Pinhas Sapir International Conference on Development: Social Policy Evaluation: Health, Education, and Welfare, Tel Aviv University, Israel

Goffman, E. (1974). *Frame analysis*. Harvard University Press Cambridge, MA.

Grabe, M. & Bucy, E. (2008). The struggle for control: Visual framing, news coverage, and image handling of presidential candidates, 1992–2004. *International Communication Association*, 1–42.

Griffin, M. (2004). Picturing America's 'War on Terrorism' in Afghanistan and Iraq. *Journalism, 5*(4), 381-402.

Hayes, J. E. & Battles, K. (2011). Exchange and interconnection in US network radio: A reinterpretation of the 1938 War of the Worlds broadcast. *Radio Journal: International Studies in Broadcast & Audio Media, 9* (1), 51–62.

Herman, E. S. & Chomsky, N. (1994). *Manufacturing consent: The political economy of the mass media*: Random House.

Heyer, P. (2003). America under attack I: A reassessment of Orson Welles' 1938 War of the Worlds broadcast. *Canadian Journal of Communication, 28*(2), 149–166.

Himelboim, I. (2010). The international network structure of news media: An analysis of hyperlinks usage in news web sites. *Journal of Broadcasting & Electronic Media, 54*(3), 373–390.

Jackson, J. H. (2011). Envisioning disaster in the 1910 Paris flood. *Journal of Urban History 37*(2), 176–207.

Jarvis, J. (2008). In Mumbai, witnesses are writing the news Retrieved 24 August, 2012, from http://www.guardian.co.uk/media/2008/dec/01/mumbai-terror-digital-media

Jenkins, H. (2006). *Convergence culture: Where old and new media collide*. New York: NYU press.

Keith, S., Schwalbe, C. B. & Silcock, B. W. (2009). Visualizing cross-media coverage: Picturing war across platforms during the US-led invasion of Iraq. *Atlantic Journal of Communication, 17*(1), 1–18.

Kellner, D. (2008). War correspondents, the military, and propaganda: Some critical reflections. *International Journal of Communication, 2*, 297–330.

Kendrick, M. (1994). The never again narratives: Political promise and the videos of operation desert storm. *Cultural Critique*(28), 129–147.

King, C., & Lester, P. M. (2005). Photographic coverage during the Persian Gulf and Iraqi Wars in three US newspapers. *Journalism and Mass Communication Quarterly, 82*(3), 623.

Kolbe, R. H. & Burnett, M. S. (1991). Content-analysis research: An examination of applications with directives for improving research reliability and objectivity. *Journal of Consumer Research, 18*(2), 243–250.

Kovarik, B. (2002). *Web design for the mass media*. Allyn and Bacon.

Krippendorff, K. (2004). *Content analysis: An introduction to its methodology*. Sage Publications, Inc.

Liu, S., Palen, L., Sutton, J., Hughes, A. & Vieweg, S. (2008). In search of the bigger picture: The emergent role of on-line photo sharing in times of disaster. *Proceedings of ISCRAM, 8*.

Liu, S. B. (2010). Trends in distributed curatorial technology to manage data deluge in a networked world. *Upgrade: The European Journal for the Informatics Professional, 11*(4), 18–24.

Massey, B. L. & Levy, M. R. (1999). Interactivity, online journalism, and English-language Web newspapers in Asia. *Journalism and Mass Communication Quarterly, 76*(1), 138–151.

Matthes, J. (2009). What's in a frame? A content analysis of media framing studies in the world's leading communication journals, 1990-2005. *Journalism & Mass Communication Quarterly, 86*(2), 34 9–367.

Newman, N. (2011). Mainstream media and the distribution of news in the age of social discovery. *Reuters Institute for the Study of Journalism*

Parry, K. (2008). A visual framing analysis of British press photography during the 2006 Isreal-Lebanon conflict. *International Communication Association*, 1–35.

Peng, F. Y., Tham, N. I. & Xiaoming, H. (1999). Trends in online newspapers: A look at the US Web. *Newspaper Research Journal, 20*(2), 52–63.

Riffe, D. & Freitag, A. (1997). A content analysis of content analyses: Twenty-five years of journalism quarterly. *Journalism and Mass Communication Quarterly, 74*, 515–524.

Rodriguez, L. & Dimitrova, D. V. (2011). The levels of visual framing. *Journal of Visual Literacy, 30*(1), 48–65.

Rosen, C. (2005). The image culture. *The New Atlantis: A Journal of Technology & Society, 10*, 27–46.

Rosenbaum, S. (2011). Curation, community and the future of news. *Nieman reports: Links that bind us*.

Sacco, V., Giardina, M. & Stanoevska, K. (2012). *"Digital activism" on social media platforms: Story breaks the newswires*. Paper presented at the the International Media Conference - "Media Trends 2012", Webster University, Geneva, Switzerland.

Schwalbe, C. B. (2006). Remembering our shared past: Visually framing the Iraq war on US news websites. *Journal of Computer-Mediated Communication, 12*(1), 264–289.

Scoble, R. (2010). The seven needs of real time curators. Retrieved 28 June, 2012, from http://scobleizer.com/2010/03/27/the-seven-needs-of-real-time-curators/

Semetko, H. A. & Valkenburg, P. M. (2000). Framing European politics: A content analysis of press and television news. *Journal of Communication, 50*(2), 93–109.

Sherer, M. D. (1989). Vietnam war photos and public opinion. *Journalism Quarterly, 66*(2), 391–395, 530.

Sontag, S. (2003). *Regarding the pain of others*. PUF.

Stanoevska-Slabeva, K., Sacco, V. & Giardina, M. (2012). *Content curation: A new form* of gatewatching for social media? Paper presented at the 13th Internation Symposium on Online Journalism, Austin, Texas.

Stochetti, M. (2003). Wagging the dog or serving the cause? Assessing ICTs and intelligibility in transnational war coverage broadcasting. *Millennium-Journal of International Studies, 32*(3), 643–671.

Tewksbury, D. & Scheufele, D. A. (2009). News framing theory and research. In J. Bryant & M. B. Oliver (Eds.), *Media effects: Advances in theory and research* (pp. 17–33). New York: Routledge.

Wall, M. (2006). Blogging Gulf War II. *Journalism Studies, 7*(1), 111–126.

Wall, M. & El Zahed, S. (2011). "I'll be waiting for you guys": A YouTube call to action in the Egyptian revolution. *International Journal of Communication, 5,* 1333–1343.

Wanta, W. & Chang, K. (2001). Visual depictions of president Clinton in the international press after the release of the starr report. *News Photographer, 56*(7), 9–12.

Wojdynski, B. (2009). *The interactive newspaper: Online multimedia and the framing of the Iraq War*. Paper presented at the International Communication Association.

Xigen, L., Lindsay, L., & Mogensen, K. (2002). *Media in a crisis situation involving national interest: A content analysis of the TV networks coverage of the 9/11 incident during the first eight hours*. Paper presented at the Association for Education in Journalism and Mass Communication (AEJMC), Miami Beach, FL.

CHAPTER ELEVEN

Microblogging and Crises: Information Needs and Online Narratives During Two "Bombing" Events in Nairobi, Kenya

MELISSA TULLY

In this chapter, Tully investigates social media communication surrounding a deadly bomb explosion and an unrelated bomb scare that occurred in Nairobi, Kenya within three days of each other in 2010. The chapter reports that although these two bombing incidents had very different outcomes, the reaction on social media followed similar communication patterns as people reacted in similar ways. Tully identifies compelling similarities in public responses to both the Nairobi events and the *War of the Worlds* broadcast, including the effort to seek and share information on the part of the users and audiences, and the importance of environment in shaping the response to media crises.

Introduction

The global spread of Facebook and Twitter has made sharing information via social networking sites common practice. During crises and disasters when information is critical for decision-making and response, these social network posts intersect with official communications and mass media in a space where facts and rumors compete. It is within this convoluted space that individuals try to understand and make sense of unfolding crises and threats (Heverin & Zach, 2012; Mäkinen & Kuira, 2008). Known for giving people the ability to report and discuss breaking news, social media sites offer people the opportunity to share information, debate facts and rumors, and interpret events surrounding unfolding crises. A number of recent studies have examined the use of social media during and after crises and disasters to understand the features of this communication, and to assess source credibility, information sharing behaviors, and response (Heverin & Zach, 2010, 2012; Mendoza, Poblete, & Castillo, 2010; Palen, Vieweg, Liu, & Hughes, 2009; Perng et al., 2012; Thomson et al., 2012). The microblogging site, Twitter, has been at the center of a number of studies about social media and crises. Despite growing interest in this area and the development of the field of *crisis informatics* (Palen et al., 2009), little research has examined social media information flows and crisis "scares," such as bomb threats. This study examines a situation in which a deadly bomb explosion and an unrelated bomb scare occurred in the same city within three days of each other. This moment offers an opportunity to explore how people understand crises in relation to each other and the social, political and cultural context in which they live. Although these two bombing incidents had very different outcomes, the reaction on social media followed similar communication patterns as people perceived the events similarly.

On June 13, 2010 two explosions rocked a political rally in downtown Nairobi, Kenya at Uhuru Park. The explosions killed six and injured hundreds. Social media sites, Facebook and Twitter, lit up with questions, reports, and rumors surrounding the incident. Three days later, reports of explosives planted along a major Nairobi road began to surface. Police received information that two men buried an unknown object under a bridge leading to speculation that the object was a bomb. Again, the Kenyan social mediasphere filled with comments and questions about the report; however, this incident turned out to be only a scare. With a major Constitutional referendum approaching and the International Criminal Court (ICC) investigations of the 2007–2008 post-election violence (PEV) underway, potential political unrest was very much part of public consciousness during June 2010. At the same time, the Constitutional referendum, which was held on August 4, 2010, highlighted political divides in the country around key issues, such as land reform and religious freedoms. The post-election violence, its aftermath, and Kenya's political instability provide the backdrop for the two "bombing" incidents.

This chapter examines the communication behaviors, content, and narratives that emerged on social media sites around these events.[1] Using evidence from these two "bombing" incidents, I analyze the information flow and narrative development as the events unfolded and new facts and rumors became available to the public through citizen and mainstream media reports. This study is guided by a number of questions, including: how does the content disseminated via social networking sites change over the course of a crisis? What narratives emerge to help explain and make sense of actual and potential crisis events? And, how does the content disseminated via social networking sites differ between an actual crisis and a scare? The communication patterns following both incidents followed similar trajectories starting with predominantly information-related content—seeking, sharing, and negotiating—followed by increasing amounts of opinion and commentary. The Uhuru Park explosion, which killed six and injured many, was a larger incident with a distinct political angle. The narratives that emerged were distinct as the Mombasa Road bomb scare was contextualized through the recent experience with the Uhuru Park explosions and was resolved within a few hours. In many ways, the activities that Twitter users engaged in during both of these crises is markedly similar to the activities of radio listeners who sought out information and connection during the *War of the Worlds* broadcast—in the face of what some saw as a deadly attack on the United States.

Data Collection and Method

Using Google Realtime[2] and the Twitter search function, I collected tweets containing keywords and hashtags related to the two incidents. Twitter enables users to send short messages (140 characters) known as "tweets." The default Twitter profile is public meaning that other users can "follow" accounts without permission, and tweets are part of a public stream. A hashtag is used to mark topics in a tweet. It begins with the # symbol and can be used to follow topics and trends. Hashtags have been used in a number of crisis events. For example, #tsunami was used to mark tweets about the devastating 2011 tsunami in Japan; and #oslobomb and #osloexpl were used in tweets about the 2011 bomb in Oslo, Norway. For the Uhuru explosions, hashtags #Uhurublast and #Uhurubomb, and keywords "Uhuru" AND "bomb" were used to collect the publically available tweets. The use of search directives, AND/OR, help filter the search results to return relevant tweets. In total, 802 tweets about the crisis from June 13 to June 17, 2010 were included in the analysis. Unrelated tweets—e.g., references to finance minister Uhuru Kenyatta—were removed from the results. The Mombasa Road incident lasted one day as the police determined that the buried items were only communication cables; therefore, relevant tweets were collected for June 16 only. Using keywords, "bomb" AND "Nairobi" OR "Mombasa;" "explosive" AND "Nairobi" OR "Mombasa;" and "explosion" AND "Nairobi" OR "Mombasa," returned 95 relevant public tweets, which were included in the analysis. No consistent hashtag emerged for this incident.

I used textual analysis to look for evidence of information-related behaviors, patterns over time, and similarities and differences between the two incidents (Fairclough, 1995, 2003; Heverin & Zach, 2012; McKee, 2003). Textual analysis is a data-gathering and analysis process that allows researchers to examine how "human beings make sense of the world" (McKee, 2003, p. 1). Analyzing the text for themes, I interpret individual contributions to draw conclusions about the larger discourses that developed as a result of the information shared on Twitter. I analyzed original tweets and retweets to uncover the major themes and conversations that developed. Retweeting, a Twitter convention that involves sharing another user's tweet, with or without commentary, has been found to be a major part of microblogging during crises (Heverin & Zach, 2010; Mendoza et al., 2010; Starbird & Palen, 2010). Consistent with previous research, I included retweets to examine the sources and information that were redistributed and to compare retweets with original tweets (Starbird & Palen, 2010; Thomson et al., 2012). I also consider the timing of the tweets. With quickly developing crisis situations, it is important to take time into account to better understand the information flow and environment in which contributors were operating. Also, links to external sources that were included in tweets were considered in the analysis as they provide further evidence of the discourses that were developing across the web.

Uhuru Park Bombing

The Uhuru Park bombing occurred on the evening of June 13, 2010 during a "No" rally—a rally against the proposed constitutional changes. Throughout the months preceding the August 4, 2010 constitutional referendum, politicians and other public figures held events to show their support or opposition to the proposed constitution. Christian groups organized this particular rally. The attendees, who numbered in the thousands, were saying the closing prayer when the explosions occurred. Two explosions—one near the back of the crowd and one near the front—caused injury and commotion as the large crowd scattered. In total six people died and approximately 100 were wounded as a result of the explosions and ensuing stampede ("It was a scene from hell," 2010; Pflanz, 2010). The first explosion occurred around 6 p.m. local time and the second followed approximately 10 minutes later. Local news organizations were at the rally and captured footage of the explosions and subsequent chaos.

Communication Patterns

Information-related behaviors of seeking, sharing, and negotiating dominated the tweets about the Uhuru Park explosions. The earliest tweets contained predominantly information-seeking content about the number of injuries and deaths as little confirmed information was available. As more information became available and was shared on Twitter, people began debating the validity of the information and seeking more in-depth information beyond the injury and death numbers, including speculating over who was to blame for the explosions and the potential outcomes of the incident. After the initial hours, more commentary began to surface online. Three themes emerged: debating the cause of the explosions and who was to blame including promulgating conspiracy theories; contextualizing the tragedy by relating it to the 2007–2008 post-election violence; and promoting peace and unity among Kenyans.

Information-related Behaviors

Heverin and Zach (2012) identified three types of information-related behaviors in their analysis of post-crisis microblogging: information seeking, information sharing, and information negotiation. In their study of tweets about a Seattle, Washington-area police officer shooting, Heverin and Zach (2010) found that 79 percent of tweets contained information-related content with the vast majority containing information-sharing material. About half of the information-sharing tweets contained links to outside sources including news reports, photos and videos. These same behaviors were common in the tweets about the Uhuru Park explosions. The majority of the tweets within the first two hours involved asking for more information and sharing bits of information as they became available. It does not appear that any of the tweets are from people at the scene so very little firsthand information was shared on Twitter in the initial hour following the blasts. The mainstream media featured heavily in the tweets about the explosions, as contributors, information sources and objects of criticism.

The first tweet came from an individual user and referenced a news report from *Citizen TV*, a popular Kenyan television station: "Reports of explosion at Uhuru Park, Nairobi at NO Rally..Citizen TV."[3] Not long after the initial tweet, Oliver Mathenge, a journalist for the *Daily Nation*, Kenya's largest newspaper tweeted, "bomb explodes at Uhuru Park." A consistent stream of tweets continued throughout the evening and into the night. References to news reports, news outlets and journalists were consistent throughout the hours following the explosions with many relying on mainstream media confirmation of the information being shared. Many tweets simply asked if the reports were true while others inquired about the number of deaths and injuries:

- Someone please confirm this vybe about Uhuru Park Blast.... True?
- Bomb explosion....at Uhuru park....is this true? #Kenyansontwitter

- So, what's this news I hear about a BP oil bomb at Uhuru Park?
- bomb @ uhuru park 2day? any injured? dead? what a tragedy. is there a hashtag.

The last tweet mentions a hashtag. This tweeter was the first person to ask about a specific hashtag. In the case of the Uhuru Park explosions, debate over the hashtag arose among those tweeting about the event. Two main options, #UhuruBomb and #UhuruBlast, gained prominence.

#UhuruBomb was first suggested, but as more information became available and doubt began to arise as to whether the explosions were caused by a bomb or something else, #UhuruBlast emerged as the preferred option.[4] At one point in the discussion over what hashtag to use, someone commented, "I see why we Kenyans would blast each other ... we cant even agree on a #hashtag => #uhurublast #uhurubomb." His tweet provides interesting commentary on both the incident—blaming other Kenyans for the explosions—and conversation about the event, while also making light of a tragic situation. This type of commentary contributed to the blame theme discussed later. Eventually, Erik Hersman, a well-known blogger and Twitter user in the Kenyan community, who suggested the #UhuruBomb hashtag, tweeted: "Let's set it at #UhuruBlast then. Keep the news flowing from those who have confirmed info on the Nairobi bomb blast." Hersman's tweet was re-tweeted twice in the next 30 seconds. Hersman is one of the most followed tweeters in the Kenyan Twitter community. Although he is not Kenyan, he was raised in Kenya and currently lives in Nairobi. Hersman is the co-founder of the nonprofit technology company, Ushahidi. The Ushahidi platform has been used to crowdsource crisis information in a number of well-known global crises. Hersman is well known in the Kenyan and global technology and humanitarian communities. In short, he is a trusted figure. Hersman's social status makes his tweets more influential than others. Throughout the first night, Herman's tweets were retweeted regularly. The hashtag debate and eventual decision supports previous findings that show a small number of influential members of a network (hubs) have great influence over information flow within a network and are often retweeted sources (Starbird & Palen, 2010; Thomson et al., 2012). It also indicates that people were looking for a way to share information easily with a group of dedicated individuals—a community of interest. In the early stage of this crisis, the community consists of Kenyans or those interested in Kenya. No international mainstream media outlet posted about the incident until 10:30 p.m. local time, more than four hours after the initial explosion.

Retweets were common during the initial hours following the explosions. Retweets often contained information-seeking content or asked for verification. Retweeting is one way of filtering information and passing on content that is deemed relevant to the crisis while limiting unrelated or less useful information (Starbird & Palen, 2010). The act of retweeting helps spread tweets to a wider network and may indicate that the retweeter has some level of trust in the original tweet. The source influences if and how often the tweet is retweeted with trusted users such as mainstream media outlets and official sources receiving the most retweets (Heverin & Zach, 2010; Starbird & Palen, 2010; Starbird et al. 2010; Thomson et al., 2012). Information-seeking retweets often featured additional commentary, opinion or emotion:

- Dude. just caught the end of dat bulletin. any casualties? RT @OliverMathenge: *bomb* explodes at *uhuru* park
- RT *Bomb* explodes at *Uhuru* Park. Several injured. >> What?? Details??
- So sad that things are getting this ugly RT [Twitter users] Citizen say 74, KTN say 24, NTV say several injured in *uhuru* park blast
- RT [Twitter user] Being told someone threw a grenade in the crowd during the NO Campaign rally at Uhuru Park. I why? saddening

Retweets and @ replies, responding to an individual poster directly, contribute to developing a conversation and connections between people and posts. In their study about Twitter activity after the 2010 earthquake in Chile, Mendoza et al. (2010) argue:

> " ... re-tweet activity reflects how the social network helps in the propagation of the information. An active social network facilitates the quick dissemination of relevant tweets. ... when a user reads a tweet and re-tweets this to other users, it determines the importance of the original tweet.

As a collective phenomenon, how deep re-tweets cover the social graph indicates the relevance of the tweet for the community." (p. 5)

However, retweets were not always desired because they do little to add to the facts:

- according to my twit feed uhuru park. it occured at a "no' rally lakini [but] im waiting for confirmation not just retweets
- I'm concerned that most of what I'm seeing about #UhuruBlast is just retweeting MSM reports, rather than first hand info.

Tweets of posts containing relevant information—number of deaths, injuries, official response—were retweeted throughout the "critical period" following the explosions and contributed to the information-sharing behaviors of the Twitter community. The critical period of a crisis is when the crisis is unfolding after some "triggering event" and ends when the danger has been removed (Heverin & Zach, 2012; Stein, 2004). The critical period for the Uhuru Park explosions lasted through the night, as it was unclear why the attack occurred and who committed the crime. Although the perpetrators were never caught, the critical period ended when police found no further evidence of danger at the park. However, the Mombasa Road bomb scare reignited fear in Nairobians after the original threat had passed.

Consistent with other recent findings, tweets from journalists and news outlets were more widely distributed than tweets from non-news sources (Mendoza et al., 2010; Thomson et al., 2012). The Twitter account for KTN, a national television news station, was the first mainstream media outlet to tweet about the crisis. The KTN tweet, "Explosion reported at Uhuru Park this evening with several injured. More details to follow!" also directed people to a post on the KTN Facebook page. Tweets from reputable news outlets were often shared with and without additional commentary. These retweets highlight the importance of recognition and influence in the twittersphere—KTN and CNN are more trusted and recognizable than the average Twitter user. The CNN Breaking News tweet was posted almost three hours after the first tweet around 10:30 p.m. local time, but it spread more than any earlier tweets with at least 67 retweets of the original.

Others retweeted CNN's post with additional commentary, and retweeted it after someone else had retweeted. In total, reference to the CNN Breaking News tweet occurred 77 times. With the CNN tweet, the local crisis rose to an international news event. The retweets of CNN were by people in and outside of Kenya. To verify information, tweeters often quoted local mainstream news sources such as KTN, Citizen TV or the *Daily Nation*. However, tweets from international news sources, CNN and BBC with links to stories with more information, were retweeted more than any other.

Until the final death toll and injuries had been confirmed, a wide range of numbers circulated through the discussion with discrepancies floating around the twittersphere and the mainstream media:

- Nairobi PPO Kibuchi confirms 24 people hurt in two mystery explosions at Uhuru Park Church meeting as Ruto calls ... (Standard Group)
- via Citizen tv about 74 believed to be injured after suspected homemade bomb exploded in Uhuru park at end of "No" rally
- AT least 20 people rushed to hospital with serious injuries after unknown assailants hurl a petrol bomb after No rally at Uhuru Park
- Big difference in reports - @KTNKenya say 24 injured in *Uhuru* Park blasts , citizen tv say 74

The previous tweets were posted within 15 minutes of each other. Eventually news reports and videos from the scene and images of the victims at Kenyatta National Hospital began circulating and numbers became more accurate with final numbers indicating six dead and between 75 and 100 injured. Tweets with widely different reports of deaths and injuries continued to appear throughout the night despite mainstream media reports that confirmed the numbers. In addition, people continued to ask for firsthand accounts of the explosion and called on the mainstream media to provide more thorough information more quickly. As information began swirling, some tweeters suggested possible reasons for the explosions while others pushed back reminding people that little evidence was available for making such claims.

Blame and Conspiracy Theories

Within the first hour of the initial tweet, blame and conspiracy theories began to emerge with implicit and explicit claims about the cause of the explosions: "Explosion reported at Uhuru Park. Referendum debate gets nasty. More to this than meets the eye says my gut." Despite this example, this type of content was uncommon in the first hour, but became more prevalent as the night went on:

- Waiting to get more details but the #uhurublast continue to adds fuel to the PNU-secretly-sabotaging-Yes rumour
- On the real tho, that panzy #uhurublast attack is sad...but this is Kenya, there has to be high-level inciters! @notoimpunity
- Please! it could have been the NO team seeking sympathy vote! and it could be YES team to intimidate! #uhurublast
- This 'uhuru park blast' was stage-managed... no other explanation.
- the same pple who inserted th offensive clause in th draft r th same ones who bombed uhuru park #uhurublast. And no, it aint #muslims... #fb"

Similarly, Heverin and Zach (2010) found that the types of tweets changed over time with opinion-related tweets rising from 6.8 percent in the initial 12 hours following the first tweet to 21.8 percent during hours 26–48. The inability of the police and other official bodies to find the culprit continued to fuel the rumors and conspiracy theories with people promulgating a variety of perspectives including blaming the "No" camp, blaming the "Yes" camp, blaming Kenyan politicians and calling it an act of terrorism committed by Al Shaabab.

Contextualizing Through the Post-election Violence

The post-election period was a time when many Kenyans were disunited and overwhelmed by ethnic, class, and political loyalties. Despite pre-election practices that were in violation of the electoral process, there was still a sense of hope that democratic principles had taken hold and the election would indeed be "free and fair." However, it soon became clear that the election results were rigged. The announcement that incumbent President Mwai Kibaki had won incited violence as supporters of both politicians began to lash out.

The violence continued for two months and left more than 1,500 people dead and 500,000 internally displaced.

In addition to the wide-scale violence, the mainstream media was heavily restricted during the PEV. The government banned live broadcasts and warned that people could be arrested for distributing inflammatory material (Gettleman, 2007; Mäkinen & Kuira, 2008; Tully, 2011). Commentary on blogs and other social media criticized the mainstream media for its lack of in-depth coverage and narrow focus, while offering alternative narratives that provided more facts, rumors, analysis and opinion.

The post-election violence, including the mainstream and social media coverage, permeated the comments shared on Twitter in the hours following the Uhuru Park explosions. Within the first hour, tweets began referencing the PEV. Although the vast majority of tweets in the period following the explosion were information-related, opinion and commentary trickled through the conversation. For example, one person posted: "2007 was machetes,2010 grenades.Wat should i expect in 2012? nuclear heads? #uhurublast," which was retweeted numerous times. Criticism of the mainstream media was often contextualized with references to the post-election violence as well: "Seems like media hasn't learnt anything from '07, watch how much airtime hate-mongers will get during the news #uhurublast." The post-election violence provided a common experience for Kenyans to reference as a means for understanding and making sense of this crisis. A number of references to the PEV called on Kenyans to unite and not allow for a repeat of the violence while others claimed that the Uhuru Park bombers would never be brought to justice comparing them to post-election violence perpetrators.

Promoting Peace and Unity

The final theme, promoting peace and unity among Kenyans, developed as people shared their feelings and emotions about the explosions and asked fellow Kenyans to choose nonviolent paths. These tweets also often referenced the post-election violence or other political events to situate the comment:

- #uhurublast is a sad way to end an awesome day, let us not do the 2008 thing again. #kenyansontwitter and everywhere we're all family
- …Kenyan's we will never agree on anything politically without going for each others throats.I condemn political violence! #UhuruBlast
- Whether a new constitution, old constitution or no constitution at all, we all need to learn how to live with each other. #uhurublast

These types of tweets offer a way for those affected by the explosion and past violence to share messages that help them cope with the situation. Heverin and Zach (2012) describe this type of comment as indicative of the "talking cure"—when individuals express their thoughts and feelings without expecting a response. These types of tweets were not retweeted with the same frequency as information-related tweets, but they provide the author with an opportunity to express emotions and opinions relevant to the crisis.

Mombasa Road Bomb Scare

Three days after the Uhuru Park explosions, rumors of explosives planted along Mombasa Road, one of Nairobi's busiest streets, began to surface. On the morning of June 16, police received a call from a local security guard who reported seeing two men drive under a bridge and bury an object. The police and other security officers responded to the scene and closed one side of the road to investigate. After two hours, the police discovered that the items were not explosives or any kind of bomb, but rather harmless communications equipment.

Communication Patterns

Analyzing this rather small incident offers an opportunity to compare how content disseminated via social networking sites differs between an actual crisis and a scare. Information-related behaviors were the most dominant type of content disseminated in this case as well; however, information-sharing was more prevalent than information-seeking. As competing information entered the twittersphere, information-negotiation increased as people tried to make sense of the conflicting facts and rumors. In this case, the incident was contextualized through the Uhuru Park explosions and not the post-election violence and tweets focused on fears about insecurity in Nairobi.

Information-related Behaviors

The early tweets about the incident indicated that a bomb or some form of explosives had been found on Mombasa Road. Many of these tweets assert the explosives were found as fact. For example, someone tweeted, "explosives found somewhere in mombasa road... OMG wtf is wrong with #kenya?" and Citizen TV reported "A major scare as police discovered a bomb planted along Mombasa Road, near General Motors." *Daily Nation* reported similarly, "#Police unearth explosive device in Nairobi" with a link to news coverage. This tweet was re-tweeted by a number of users. Once it was confirmed by police that the mysterious device was communication equipment, *Daily Nation* updated their twitter status with "#Bomb scare in #Nairobi: #Police dug up area only to discover power cables!!" with the same link from their earlier tweet to a story that reports the incident as a scare. This post has a very different tone from their early tweets—it reads as much more lighthearted when just minutes earlier people were tweeting in fear and disgust. After the incident had been confirmed as a scare, *Citizen TV* ran a story tracing the timeline and discussing the incident.

Unlike the Uhuru Park explosions, individual tweeters and official sources more quickly shared information, which in this case turned out to be false, rather than seeking confirmation or verification. With the Uhuru Park explosions still fresh, the likelihood that a bomb was planted on a major road seemed plausible and was shared with little interrogation. When reports surfaced that the suspicious items were harmless, people began sharing this information; however, the false reports continued to circulate. Hours after the official report that the items were communication cables, false reports of a bomb were still being tweeted.

Contextualizing through Uhuru Park Explosions and Insecurity

With the Uhuru Park explosions only three days prior, it was a reference point for the Mombasa Road scare. With direct and indirect references to the Uhuru Park explosions, tweets offered context and social commentary about safety and security in Nairobi:

- RT @dailynation: BREAKING NEWS: A major scare as police discover a explosives planted along Mombasa Road, near General Motors. [NOT AGAIN]
- Police uncover #explosive along Mombasa Rd in #Nairobi. After Sunday's twin blast, we're on to something? // #uhurublast
- this nairobi is proving to be tooo unsafe, i need to pack my bags and go to warm area for a week or two, these bomb threats are not funny!!
- Explosives all over nairobi!!! Haiya wats going on in this hellhole

Although the majority of tweets related to this incident contained information-related content, some offered opinion and criticism that situated the incident in its larger social and political context. The threat of violence, only three days after a deadly explosion, created an environment in which people were fearful and felt that the city was insecure. This environment differed from earlier in the week because of the level of social anxiety about political violence and terrorism that resulted from the Uhuru Park explosions. This comparison shows that the environment in which a crisis occurs should be considered to more fully understand response and communication behaviors. With tensions high, it is not surprising that people were more willing to share unverified information as fact and to discuss their fears about potential violence and insecurity.

Conclusion

Similar to previous research, information-related behaviors—seeking, sharing and negotiating—were the most prominent patterns of communication following the two bombing incidents. However, although the second incident was a scare based on false information, the early tweets shared the information as fact. People experienced the scare as a potential crisis and therefore reacted as such. The tweets about the Mombasa Road incident featured greater information-sharing than seeking, while the Uhuru Park explosion tweets contained information-seeking content followed by information-sharing as more details became known.

The two Nairobi bomb events had very different outcomes and different online narratives emerged around the incidents. Despite the differences in the narratives, the communication patterns and behaviors were similar in both circumstances. Because of the uncertainty of both situations, people reacted in similar ways—seeking, sharing, and commenting on the crisis/scare as it developed. So, although the outcomes were different, for a period of time, individuals perceived the events to be similar. The Mombasa Road scare was understood in relation to and as part of a larger discussion about the Uhuru Park tragedy and insecurity in the city. But interestingly, the Mombasa Road incident, which had far less evidence, was taken as a given while the Uhuru Park explosions were questioned and debated online. Although individual motivations cannot be derived from tweets, it appears that people were more willing to accept the Mombasa bomb as fact because of the current social state. A bomb exploded three days earlier at a major public event, why couldn't it happen again on a major public road? The outcomes of the Uhuru Park explosions created an environment in which violent acts seemed more likely and plausible without substantial evidence.

Official (police, news, disaster management teams) and unofficial (concerned citizens, victims) sources interact on Twitter during crises creating an information stream that contains verified and unverified information as well as opinion, commentary and emotions (Heverin & Zach, 2010, 2012). In the case of Uhuru Park and Mombasa Road, unofficial sources dominated the conversation, although official sources were critical sources of information and updates. This interaction between official and unofficial sources and reports is not unique to Twitter or online social networking sites, but rather typical of communication behaviors during times of uncertainty. Hayes and Battles's (2011) reinterpretation of the *War of the Worlds* reaction shows that ordinary people interact with each other and officials to share, seek, confirm and disconfirm information to make sense of a confusing, possibly dangerous, situation. The similarities between the reactions during the *War of the Worlds* broadcast and reactions during the two bombing incidents in this study are stark. We see that individuals will use whatever communication channels are available to them to seek and share information. The findings from this study can be situated within a larger historical trajectory of crisis research, which examines how people use "new media"—radio during the *War of the Worlds* and Twitter during the Kenya bombs—to negotiate and navigate potentially life-threatening situations.

As Twitter continues to grow in global popularity and more people access the site from Internet-enabled phones, it is likely that crisis communication will continue to be affected by individuals sharing information, opinion, and commentary online as crises develop. In situations where facts are critical, responders and concerned communities will be tasked with sifting through the flood of information to uncover relevant and actionable information.

Notes

[1] Most Internet users in Kenya are young, educated, and located in urban areas such as Nairobi. Social networking sites are very popular among Kenyan Internet users. The majority of social networkers are between 18 and 35. According to a 2010 study by research firm TNS Research International, 85 percent of Kenyan Internet users visit social networking sites with Facebook ranking first and Twitter ranking third, slightly behind Hi5. At the time of this study, Twitter was gaining popularity among Nairobians, particularly those accessing the Internet from mobile devices.

[2] Google Realtime was a feature of Google Search from late 2009 until July 2011. Google shut down the service after an agreement with Twitter ended (Sullivan, 2011). I archived the search results from Google Realtime and saved them in an offline document.

[3] All tweets and comments appear as originally posted. Individual Twitter users' names have been removed unless they are public figures (e.g., journalists) or the identity is relevant.

[4] News outlets described the explosives as homemade grenades.

References

Fairclough, N. (2003). *Analysing discourse: Textual analysis for social research*. London, UK: Routledge.

Fairclough, N. (1995). *Critical discourse analysis: The critical study of language.* London, UK: Longman.

Gettleman, J. (2007, December 31). Disputed violence plunges Kenya into bloodshed. *New York Times.* Retrieved from http://www.nytimes.com/2007/12/31/world/africa/31kenya.html?pagewanted=all.

Hayes, J. E. & Battles, K. (2011). Exchange and interconnection in US network radio: A reinterpretation of the 1938 *War of the Worlds* broadcast. *Radio Journal: International Studies in Broadcast & Audio Media, 9*(1), 51–62.

Heverin, T. & Zach, L. (2010). Microblogging for crisis communication: Examination of the Twitter use in response to a 2009 violent crisis in the Seattle-Tacoma, Washington area. In S. French, B. Tomaszewski, & C. Zobel (Eds.), *Defining crisis management 3.0: Proceedings of the 7th International Conference on Information Systems for Crisis Response and Management* (pp. 1–5). Seattle, WA.

Heverin, T. & Zach, L. (2012). Use of microblogging for collective sense-making during violent crises: A study of three campus shootings. *Journal of the American Society for Information Science and Technology, 63*(1), 34–47.

"It was a scene from hell, I saw people dying." (2010, June 15). *The Standard.* Retrieved from http://www.standardmedia.co.ke/?id=2000011625&cid=4&articleID=2000011625

McKee, A. (2003). *Textual analysis: A beginner's guide.* London, UK: Sage.

Mendoza, M., Poblete, B. & Castillo, C. (2010). Twitter under crisis: Can we trust what we RT? *Proceedings from the 1st Workshop on Social Media Analytics* (pp. 1–9). Washington, DC. Retrieved from http://snap.stanford.edu/soma2010/papers/soma2010_11.pdf

Palen, L., Vieweg, S., Liu, S. B., & Hughes, A. L. (2009). Crisis in a networked world: Features of computer-mediated communication in the April 16, 2007, Virginia Tech event. *Social Science Computer Review, 27*(4), 467–480.

Perng, S-Y., Buscher, M., Halvorsrud, R., Wood, L., Stiso, M., Ramirez, L., & Al-Akkad, A. (2012). Peripheral response: Microblogging during the 22/7/2011 Norway attacks. In L. Rothkrantz, J. Ristvej, & Z. Franco (Eds.), *Proceedings of the International Conference on Information Systems for Crisis Response and Management* (pp. 1–11). Vancouver, Canada.

Pflanz, M. (2010, June 13). Explosion at Kenyan referendum rally kills five. *The Telegraph.* Retrieved from http://www.telegraph.co.uk/news/worldnews/africaandindianocean/kenya/7825446/Explosion-at-Kenyan-referendum-rally-kills-five.html

Starbird, K., & Palen, L. (2010). Pass it on? Retweeting in mass emergency. In S. French, B. Tomaszewski, & C. Zobel (Eds.), *Defining crisis management 3.0: Proceedings of the 7th International Conference on Information Systems for Crisis Response and Management* (pp. 1–10). Seattle, Washington.

Starbird, K., Palen, L., Hughes, A. L., & Vieweg, S. (2010). Chatter on the Red: What hazards threat reveals about the social life of microblogged information. *Proceedings of the 2010 Computer Supported Cooperative Work Conference* (pp. 241–

250). Savannah, Georgia.

Stein, M. (2004). The critical period of disasters: Insights from sense-making and psychoanalytic theory. *Human Relations, 57*(10), 1243–1261.

Sullivan, D. (2011, July 4). As deal with Twitter expires, Google Realtime Search goes offline. Search Engine Land. Retrieved from http://searchengineland.com/as-deal-with-twitter-expires-google-realtime-search-goes-offline-84175

Thomson, R., Ito N., Suda, H., Lin, F., Liu, Y., Hayasaka, R., ... Wang, Z. (2012). Trusting tweets: The Fukushima disaster and information source credibility on Twitter. In L. Rothkrantz, J. Ristvej, & Z. Franco (Eds.), *Proceedings of the International Conference on Information Systems for Crisis Response and Management* (pp. 1–11). Vancouver, Canada.

TNS Research International (2010, March 5). Digital Kenya: A study to understand the on-line life of Kenyans' key findings. Retrieved from http://www.ict.go.ke/.

Tully, M. (2011). "Ushahidi" and the Kenyan blogosphere: Alternative online media in the 2007 post-election crisis in Kenya. In B. Musa & J. K. Domatob (Eds.), *Communication, Culture, and Human Rights in Africa* (pp. 153–171). Lanham, MD: University Press of America.

CHAPTER TWELVE

Risk, Crisis, and Mobilization in the Twitter Use of US Senatorial Candidates in 2010

ADAM RUGG

In this chapter, Rugg argues that, in much the same way that the *War of the Worlds* broadcast was simplified into a metaphor for the emergent power of broadcasting, social media have been simplified into a metaphor for spontaneous, democratic, two-way interaction. He explores the growing use of Internet-based social networking sites in US political campaigns and investigates the extent to which 2010 US senatorial campaigns used Twitter to mobilize users and initiate two-way communication or interactivity. The chapter argues that politicians often viewed the risks associated with unfiltered, multidirectional communication as outweighing the benefits. In the case of the senatorial campaign, the chapter explores the specific aim of Twitter output vis-à-vis other communication platforms such as television, websites, and newspapers.

Introduction

Three months prior to the 2010 British general election, Conservative party leader David Cameron made news when the *Daily Mail* revealed the details of an internal email from the politician to the party explaining a new policy. Every Tory candidate across the country would have to submit all messages intended for posting on Twitter, Facebook, blogs, and other social media platforms to be vetted by the party before the messages could be posted. While a Tory spokesman tried to downplay the actual impact of the edict, claiming that vetting would only be required of messages discussing policy, many reacted negatively to the decision. The *Daily Mail* (Groves, 2010) labeled Cameron the "Tory Twitter Police" in its headline for the story and Rod Liddle (2010), in a disparaging editorial in the *Sunday Times of London,* snidely declared that the new policy "undermines the only commendable thing about Twitter—its immediacy and spontaneity" (p. 19).

While the policy looked counterproductive as first glance, as it would seem to stymie much of the value inherent in a platform like Twitter, it perfectly illustrates how Twitter, despite being capable of creating a conversational space for candidates and citizens as well as a place for quick mobilization of users or ideas, can succumb to the same controls as other media. However, especially in regards to politics, Twitter is too often presented in the media (and by some academics) as having reorganized the relationship between people and communication technologies and practices. In the same way the *War of the Worlds* event came to be simplistically understood as the realization of the power of broadcasting to dominate and influence the public to an unprecedented degree, the 2008 election of Barack Obama is often seen as the realization of social media's power to promote a more participatory form of communication, citizenship, and campaigning. Unfortunately, these narratives are often based on abstracted and extrapolated potential rather than sustained evidence. This study, then, seeks to move past these extrapolated narratives to understand whether Twitter use in an American election cycle actually leveraged the unique conversational and mobilization potential of Twitter or instead relied on existing communicative techniques used in other communication channels.

Twitter has considerable potential as a means of political communication. In addition to the conversational space for an explicit dialogue between a politician and citizens, it also offers an opportunity for a unique communicative space outside of press releases and official statements where candidates and their campaigns may directly and immediately convey thoughts, opinions, and personal details to citizens that otherwise may not work their way through traditional communication channels. Additionally, the immediacy of conversation on Twitter, and its quick dissemination of messages, make it a potentially valuable tool in crisis management and mobilization. In exploring these potentialities, this chapter attempts not only to understand the extent that conversational interactivity actually takes place on Twitter, but also to gauge the extent to which politicians actually use Twitter to create an environment conducive to conversational interactivity. Specifically, this chapter asks whether politicians have embraced the unique conversational qualities of Twitter, or simply used it to extend existing one-way communication practices and mimic other media platforms. Unfortunately, at least in relation to the 2010 American senatorial campaigns, this study finds that the unique communicative potentials of Twitter went largely unrealized.

A Twitter Primer

Launched in 2006, Twitter, commonly misunderstood as a medium, is a social networking service founded on the idea of "microblogging." Users use Twitter to post text-based messages fewer than 140 characters in length, called "tweets." Other users can then "follow" that user and receive his or her tweets. Once a user logs into Twitter from a phone or the website, she or he can access and view his or her "timeline," which is a reverse-chronologically ordered feed of tweets from everyone that user follows (from friends to sports stars to politicians). While Twitter does offer the ability for private accounts, the vast majority of users make their tweets public, open to be seen and commented on by anyone. In addition to posting and reading tweets, a unique aspect of Twitter is the ability to publicly address a tweet to another user by using an "@" symbol in front of another user's username. While being able to message another user is not a novel concept in social networking services, the public nature of Twitter and the ease of accessing and using the service enables interactions and conversations to take place between users who do not personally know one another, such as a celebrity and his or her fans.

While Twitter can be accessed and used from its website, it is its accessibility from mobile devices that has come to define the service and drive its popularity. Twitter can easily be used from any smartphone using a Twitter client or from any feature phone (commonly called "dumb phones") that can send out SMS (i.e., text messages). Posting to Twitter is as simple and quick as sending off a text message, resulting in a culture of immediacy on the service, where topics are often events happening in the present moment (the fullest realization of this culture of immediacy can be seen in the popular practice of "live-tweeting," where users extensively document events they are currently attending/viewing). Therefore, it is easy to see why in a communicative environment increasingly concerned with timeliness, Twitter has emerged as a major platform for the instantaneous dissemination of breaking news, reaction, speculation, opinion, and debate in the globalized media environment. The ability to post quickly from a number of devices (most importantly the mobile phone), and the ease with which users can share others posts to their own followers, creates an environment where information can spread from a single, isolated source to millions of users in mere minutes.

Twitter's rapid message distribution has much to offer in the realm of political campaigns, where a 24/7 news cycle, brought about by the Internet and proliferation of cable news outlets, has expedited the news gathering and dissemination process. As Gurevitch, Coleman, and Blumler (2009) have effectively detailed, these developments have created a new model of political campaign coverage:

> Now that viewers have far more options, there is an increased premium on the production of arresting content. Top political broadcasters are projected as stars. Some journalists respond by simplifying political complexities to expand their audience. They have tried to engage viewers in making and commenting upon political narratives, as well as injecting a more compelling dramaturgical flavor to coverage. Politics is often projected as an arena of gamesmanship, failure, scandal, and gaffes rather than the deliberative discussion of issues. (p. 172)

The "horse race" mentality of mainstream news coverage had perhaps its fullest realization in the 2008 presidential election, especially during the primary battle between Barack Obama and Hillary Clinton. As Castells (2009) argued, the mainstream news channels, already committed to a merger of information and entertainment, jumped on the bevy of ready-made narratives (the black man against the white woman, the rebel against the establishment, etc.) to produce a "six-month political show, the likes of which the world has rarely seen" (p. 398).

This "horse race" mentality can be amplified with social media, especially something as immediate as Twitter. Indeed, modern campaigning has had to react to a new state of aggressive, obsessive, narrative journalism, practically becoming a perpetual crisis management machine. As Politico's Roger Simon, quoted in Enda (2011), said, "the candidates are more afraid of us because of the echo chamber effect that the electronic media feed into. Everything is written, tweeted, retweeted, goes on TV, in print, blogged. The smallest slip can destroy a candidacy" (para. 27).

Despite the accelerated news cycle and echo chamber that social media have played a part in creating, social media have also had a hand in mobilizing new voters, initiating and extending grassroots efforts, and becoming key cogs in campaign strategies. It is this history that Twitter proponents draw from in proclaiming the service's ability to bring about positive change in the electoral process.

Political Campaigns and Social Media

The Internet has increased in importance for federal electoral campaigns in every election since its first use in 1992, when the Clinton-Gore campaign posted press releases and speeches onto Internet bulletin boards (Klotz, 2004). In the early era of Internet campaigning (1992–1999, according to Klotz, 2004), most candidates' use of the Internet was limited almost exclusively to the dissemination of one-way information. The websites merely presented information available elsewhere, such as official biographies, positions, and press releases, and were effectively an electronic brochure or pamphlet (Tedesco, 2004). Even then, it is worth noting, some dark horse candidates were experimenting with the possibilities of the Internet, such as former Tennessee governor Lamar Alexander, who held chat sessions with voters during his presidential run in 1996 (Davis, 1999).

It was not until 2004 that the majority of campaigns began to move beyond digital reproductions of existing campaign literature and utilize the unique properties of the Internet in their websites. They primarily did this through the embrace of social media, often referred to as Web 2.0. Social media are often understood as the "*read-write* web" where passive viewing, similar to that of television watching, is replaced with a more active, participatory engagement with content. This interaction varies from something as significant as content contributions on the part of the audience, as is the case of wikis or forums, to something as small as the tailoring of a site's display for individual users (Sweetser, 2008).

In 2004, blogs were the social media tool of choice for most campaigns. In fact, many campaign sites either incorporated blogs into the main site page or constructed the entirety of the campaign site around a blog (Trammel, 2007). In the Democratic primary season, for example, six of the ten candidates vying for the nomination featured blogs on their campaign website (Trammel, 2006). However, blogs were not typically used for their interactive properties. Following the lead of previously notable online campaigns, such as those of Arizona Senator John McCain and Minnesota governor Jesse Ventura, many of the 2004 online campaigns were tightly controlled and managed (Hindman, 2009). In practice, campaign blogs were primarily used for political statements and attacks on opponents (Trammel 2006).

Howard Dean's 2004 Campaign

Howard Dean's 2004 campaign for the Democratic nomination is uniquely regarded as a "qualitative leap" forward in Internet campaigning and the modern antecedent to Barack Obama's 2008 presidential campaign (Hoff, 2009). In contrast to the other campaign sites that were message-driven, Dean's site was user-driven. According to Pollard, Chesebro, and Studinski (2009), Dean recognized the interactivity of the web, allowed his supporters to provide feedback, and utilized them to shape his platform and policies. Further, Pollard et al regard Dean's website itself as a social network (notable, considering the social networking boom did not crystallize for a few more years). Additionally, Monica Ancu (2010) noted that the "genuine interactivity" of Dean's site led to "skyrocketing success" (p. 578). Even Mathew Hindman (2009), who took a critical view of the potential of the Internet to improve democratic interaction in his book "The Myth of Digital Democracy," acknowledged that Howard Dean did something "smart, brave, and unprecedented . . . he created a genuinely interactive campaign" (p. 24).

However, not all scholars view Dean as an Internet revolutionary. Stromer-Galley and Baker (2006), in a case study of Dean's campaign site, declared that many of the revolutionary aspects of Dean's campaign were overstated. While they credited his website with cultivating interactivity *between users* they argued that his site offered up a "façade of interactivity" between users and the campaign and that Dean's blog facilitated "parasocial interaction" similar to that of consumers' constructed "interactions" with celebrities through mass media (Stromer-Galley & Baker, 2006, p. 117). Scholars and the press alike have levied similar critiques at more recent political campaigns (Rich, 2010; Sweetser, 2010).

Barack Obama and the 2008 Election

By the time the 2008 electoral season came around, social media's importance as an online campaigning tool was firmly cemented and comprehensive social media strategies were employed for every presidential campaign. In addition to blogs and other social media tools that operated from within the main campaign site, 2008 represented the first presidential election to embrace the use of social media that was hosted *outside* the campaign's website. Primarily, these sites were social networking sites, or SNSs.

SNSs are sites that allows users to "(1) construct a public or semipublic profile within a bounded system, (2) articulate a list of other users with whom they share a connection, and (3) view and traverse their list of connections and those made by others within the system" (Boyd & Ellison, 2007, para. 4). By 2008, the main SNSs used for political campaigning were Facebook, YouTube, and Twitter.

Similar to the reactions to Howard Dean's campaign, the press frequently regarded Barack Obama's campaign for the Democratic nomination and his subsequent campaign for the presidency as something unique, unprecedented, and a sea change in the organization and mobilization of voters. The campaign has also been heralded as a model for future electoral campaigns, being called the "the first truly 21st century campaign" by the *Telegraph* (Colville, 2008). *Bloomberg* (Goldman & Tackett, 2008), as well, declared that Obama "leveraged technology as never before, rewriting the template for campaigns in the digital age."

Many have even identified Barack Obama's use of social media as the deciding factor in the election. Arianna Huffington, head of the liberal-leaning Huffington Post website, stated, "If not for the Internet, Barack Obama would not be President or even the Democratic nominee." Dave Kopel (2008) of the *Rocky Mountain News* offered a similar take just before the presidential election when he noted that Obama would not have had performed so well in the caucuses if "he had not done social networking so vastly better than his competitors. "Even as recently as October 2010, Frank Rich for *The New York Times* acknowledged the narrative that Obama's victory was due to the "miracle of social networking."

Twitter was not quite popular enough in 2008 to be highlighted as influential in Obama's victory or that of any other election winner. Despite this, however, Twitter is routinely grouped with other Internet technologies and social media services that have had significant impact in previous elections. As Arceneaux and Weiss have noted (2011), between 2006 and 2009, Twitter was frequently portrayed in the mainstream as the bringer of expanded participatory democracy. Further, Twitter was frequently depicted in mainstream media coverage as opening up political information and interaction to more people and disrupting the ways in which the election process was run. Academics have been known to trumpet Twitter (and social media in general) in broad, vague terms as well. In discussing social media, Jason Gilmore (2011) stated that Twitter and Facebook have taken the "direct connection between candidates to a new level" and that, "ultimately, digital media tools ... can convert the sometimes two-dimensional traditional media campaigns into dynamic and interactive experiences for voters" (p. 619). Ultimately, the simplified narratives border on positively deterministic understandings of technology that in many ways mirror the negatively deterministic narratives that surrounded the emergence of broadcasting in the wake of the *War of the Worlds*.

Interactivity as a Theoretical Concept

Inherent in all this talk of social networking is the promise of the Internet to modify traditional relationships between producers and consumers. This potential is routinely expressed through the idea of "interactivity. " Indeed, "interactivity" or "participation" forms the foundation of "web 2.0," "participatory culture," "convergence culture," or any of the other labels given to the increased economical and technical ability of consumers to produce and distribute media content and information (Jenkins, 2006).

While routinely spoken of in celebratory terms that border on technological determinism, participatory culture is not a static result of technological advances that create predictable patterns of interactions. Its emergence has led to a renegotiation of roles between producers and consumers that can result in genuine two-way communi-communication and cooperation or can result in a modified sphere that nonetheless maintains traditional power structures (Andrejevic, 2008). Further, the stark chasm found between the praise of Dean by numerous scholars and the critical approach exhibited by Stromer-Galley and Baker's (2006) analysis reflects the very real difficulties in understanding and appraising what actual interactivity looks like on any given online platform.

Much of this has to due with inconsistent use of the word "interactive." As Rob Cover (2006) noted, a cemented definition of interactivity has never been agreed upon and the wildly divergent interpretations of the word have caused it to lose all "significatory value" (p. 141). Thus, when writing about interactivity, it is imperative to provide a specific description of *what type* of interactivity is being explored. Using the ambiguous term "interactivity" results in situations like the disagreement over the extent of interactivity in Dean's 2004 web campaign where he is lauded by some for the infrastructure that connected users with each other (one form of interactivity) while being criticized by others for his campaign's lack of direct communication with those users (another form of interactivity).

Sally McMillan (2002) provided a useful multi-dimensional model that provides nuance in defining four separate areas of interactivity: Allocution, Consultation, Registration, and Conversational. For the purposes of this study, McMillan's conversational interactivity framework is used. McMillan sees this mode of interactivity occurring when "individuals interact directly with each other bypassing central controls or intermediaries. Individuals choose their communication partners as well as the time, place, and topic of communication" (p. 273).

As a Twitter stream is composed entirely of messages directed at specific people or groups of followers, this study conceptualizes each campaign's Twitter feed as a "voice" for conversation. It then seeks to understand and detail how often that voice directly interacts with other Twitter users.

The Risk of Conversational Interactivity on Twitter

Currently, as the scholarship surrounding Dean's campaign in 2004 shows, there is much disagreement on the extent that the Internet and social networking have changed the relationship between the campaign and the citizenry. While almost all federal campaigns have adopted social media tools for their online campaigns, the mere presence of campaigns on these platforms does not necessarily result in an increased conversational interactivity with the citizenry.

One possible reason for a conservative approach to social media tools is the risk involved in having an unfiltered and un-vetted communication platform for candidates. With Twitter apps available on many mobile phones, a short message broadcast to anyone who cares to see it is never more than a few keystrokes away from a Twitter user at any given moment. The ease and immediacy of sending out a Twitter message, as well as the inability to completely delete it from public view once it is sent out, has resulted in a steady stream of Twitter "gaffes" that have led to embarrassing and damaging moments for many celebrities, athletes, politicians, and other public figures (Banerjee, 2010; Burt, 2010; Evans, 2010; Irvine, 2009; Jackson, 2010a & 2010b; Wheeler, 2010). In addition, the ease at which it is possible to mistakenly post a public message intended to be private (the letter "d" at the beginning of the post is all the separates a private message from a public one) has led to many embarrassing scandals, most notably for New York Congressman Anthony Weiner, who mistakenly tweeted a picture of his penis, meant as a private communication, to all of his users.

So despite the obvious benefits of Twitter in connecting candidates to other Twitter users, there is also much risk involved in exposing candidates and campaigns to a less structured communicative environment. Since campaigns are inherently risk-averse organizations, they will generally apply cautious behavior toward environments where risk is perceived to outweigh possible benefits (Schneider & Foot, 2004). One place where this is the common perception is in a new media environment where there is the possibility of a loss of control due to the introduction of unknown and unfettered human variables into the campaign message. Instead of cultivating a discourse around issues, campaigns aim to construct a consistent image and message for the candidate that appeals to enough people to win the election. Thus, message discipline is an integral part of this strategy, requiring candidates to lead instead of discuss (Stromer-Galley, 2000).

Methodology

This study looks at the messages delivered across the social media platform Twitter by Republican and Democratic candidates in ten senatorial races in the 2010 American election season. The ten most competitive races were chosen under the assumption that a close race would encourage more activity on Twitter between both candidates than a race that was barely contested. To determine the ten most competitive races of the election season every poll in the month prior to the election date for each individual race was compiled from the *New York Times*. The polls were then averaged for each race and the ten races with the closest average poll numbers between the Democratic and Republican candidates were selected for the study.

The methods of this study build off the work of Robert J. Klotz's (2009) study of citizen interactivity in 2008 U.S. Senatorial candidates' YouTube channels. In his study, Klotz used each video uploaded by the campaign as a "message." These "messages" became his unit of analysis. This study extends the concept of message into "tweets" posted on Twitter. A single tweet is this study's unit of analysis.

To perform the study, each campaign's Twitter feed was accessed one day after the election. All Twitter messages posted in the month running up to, but not including, Election Day, were archived. Fifty messages from each feed, evenly distributed across the entire sample period, were selected for analysis. To do this, tweets were selected at consistent intervals, starting with the first tweet archived. The interval used for each candidate's Twitter stream was determined by dividing the total number of tweets archived by fifty. After collection, each individual tweet was analyzed and coded according to the following criteria.

The messages were first recorded as "nonresponsive content" or "responsive content." Messages were considered "nonresponsive content" if the message was addressed to a general audience. "Nonresponsive content" was further categorized as "original content" or "repurposed content." Messages were considered "repurposed" if the message's primary purpose was to point the user toward content somewhere else (e.g., the campaign's blog, a newspaper article, a YouTube video, etc.).

If the message was "nonresponsive," the content of the message was then recorded as "Media on Candidate," "Media by Candidate," "Media on Opponent," "Personal," and "Mobilization." "Media on Candidate" refers to posts that linked to media outside the campaign's own media infrastructure that concern the candidate. "Media by Candidate" refers to posts that linked to media produced by the campaign, such as ads, blog posts, and position papers. "Media on Opponent" refers to posts that linked to external media concerning the candidate's opponent or opposing party. "Personal" refers to any message that was of a personal nature, such as commenting on a local sports team, the candidate's travels, or other non-political issues. Single pictures posted were also considered "personal." Finally, "Notification" refers to posts that notified users of an impending event, such as a campaign fundraiser, "Get Out the Vote" operation, or television appearance.

Messages were coded as "responsive" if they were directed toward a specific audience, whether individual or group. "Responsive content" was further broken down into "grateful" or "discussive." Messages were coded as "grateful" if they only contained acceptance of praise. Retweets, the display of another user's tweet on a candidate's feed with no modifications, were considered "grateful." Messages were coded as "discussive" if they engaged the individual or group, whether this was through answering questions, asking questions, responding to criticism, clarifying information, or engaging in any other response that was representative of a continuing dialogue.

The author collected all of the data. Before the collection, a pilot study was performed on 5% of the total data to identify problems or confusion with the coding process. Following the pilot study, the coding sheet was finalized and an intercoder reliability test was carried out. The author and a second coder both coded the same randomly chosen, 10% subsample of data. Using Holsti's formula, intercoder reliability came out to 88%.

Twitter as a Campaign Dumping Ground

The use of Twitter by 2010 American senatorial candidates was nearly universal. Every candidate selected for the study had a current

Twitter account set up for the campaign. However, instead of capitalizing on the unique potential of the platform to create conversational interaction between the campaigns and citizens on Twitter, most campaigns primarily used Twitter in conservative ways that mimicked other communication channels or were subservient to them.

Table 1. Breakdown of Messages (N = 1,000)

	Twitter responsive content	Twitter non-responsive content
All candidates (% of whole)	16.1	83.9
Scott McAdams (D—AK)	2 (4%)	48 (96%)
Joe Miller (R—AK)	1 (2)	49 (98)
Barbara Boxer (D—CA)	4 (8)	46 (92)
Carly Fiorina (R—CA)	19 (38)	31 (62)
Michael Bennet (D—CO)	0 (0)	50 (100)
Ken Buck (R—CO)	24 (48)	26 (52)
Alexi Giannoulias (D—IL)	6 (12)	44 (88)
Mark Kirk (R—IL)	5 (10)	45 (90)
Harry Reid (D—NV)	11 (22)	39 (78)
Sharon Angle (R—NV)	5 (10)	45 (90)
Joe Sestak (D—PA)	5 (10)	45 (90)
Pat Toomey (R—PA)	7 (14)	43 (86)
Patty Murray (D—WA)	20 (40)	30 (60)
Dino Rossi (R—WA)	19 (38)	31 (62)
Russ Feingold (D—WI)	4 (8)	46 (92)
Ron Johnson (R—WI)	21 (42)	29 (58)
Jack Conway (D—KY)	3 (6)	47 (94)
Rand Paul (R—KY)	2 (4)	48 (96)
Richard Blumenthal (D—CT)	0 (0)	50 (100)
Linda McMahon (R—CT)	3 (6)	47 (94)

The first research question was: to what extent are the competitive Senate races in 2010 using Twitter to conversationally interact with their audience? Analysis of the messages posted by the campaigns on Twitter indicates a severe lack of actual conversational interactivity, as defined by specifically engaging with individuals or specific groups. As Table 1 shows, of all the Twitter messages posted by the campaigns, only 16.1% were coded as "responsive." Of these, 93% were "grateful" messages and only 6.84% were "discussive." Many of the grateful messages were simply some form of "thanks" addressed to a specific Twitter user. Wisconsin Republican Ron Johnson's tweet offers an example:

> Thanks! RT @Dailytakes: Just voted for Ron Johnson, Scott Walker and Leah Vukmir!

The conservative nature of this interaction is not surprising in a political environment that stresses discipline and message control, especially where new media are concerned. Saying "thank you" to supporters and/or echoing their sentiments is by far the safest way to interact with the public while minimizing any risks from off-the-cuff statements.

It should be noted here that these "grateful" interactions are not inherently wasted interactions, however. There may not be a two-way dialogue that stems from these interactions, but they still represent a personalized connection between the campaign and specific individuals. These interactions, with no ends other than recognition, ultimately represent a utilization, albeit a very conservative one, of social media platforms to directly and personally communicate with voters in novel and unique ways.

It is also worth noting that this conservative approach to interaction on Twitter may be the product of the election season. While a candidate may be more averse to conversational interactivity during the intense scrutiny of an election campaign, they may loosen the reins once they obtain or retain office and encounter a period of job security. In this case, the limited interaction cultivated by a candidate during the campaign may lay the groundwork for more robust interaction later.

As Table 2 shows, the discussive messages, just 1% of all the messages collected, ranged from answering questions to clarifying positions. No campaign used Twitter to debate or argue with other candidates or users. A tweet from Washington Democrat Patty Murray is a good example of the type of discussive tweets sent out: "@LilMissSocial there are two separate events, the rally is def free and open."

Table 2. Breakdown of Responsive Messages (N=1,000)

	Grateful Messages (Twitter)	Discussive Messages (Twitter)
All candidates (% of whole)	15%	1%
Scott McAdams (D—AK)	1 (2%)	1 (2)
Joe Miller (R—AK)	0 (0)	1 (2)
Barbara Boxer (D—CA)	4 (8)	0 (0)
Carly Fiorina (R—CA)	17 (34)	2 (4)
Michael Bennet (R—CO)	0 (0)	0 (0)
Ken Buck (R—CO)	24 (48)	0 (0)
Alexi Giannoulias (D—IL)	6 (12)	0 (0)
Mark Kirk (R—IL)	5 (10)	0 (0)
Harry Reid (D—NV)	11 (22)	0 (0)
Sharon Angle (R—NV)	5 (10)	0 (0)
Joe Sestak (D—PA)	5 (10)	0 (0)
Pat Toomey (R—PA)	7 (14)	0 (0)
Patty Murray (D—WA)	18 (36)	2 (4)
Dino Rossi (R—WA)	16 (32)	3 (6)
Russ Feingold (D—WI)	4 (8)	0 (0)
Ron Johnson (R—WI)	19 (38)	2 (4)
Jack Conway (D—KY)	3 (6)	0 (0)
Rand Paul (R—KY)	2 (4)	0 (0)
Richard Blumenthal (D—CT)	0 (0)	0 (0)
Linda McMahon (R—CT)	3 (6)	0 (0)

With 83.9% of the content posted to Twitter of the nonresponsive variety, then what were the campaigns primarily posting on Twitter? For the most part: links to other content. As Table 3 shows, of the 831 messages coded as "nonresponsive," 534 of them, or 64.25%, were coded as "repurposed" content. Only 297 of the "nonresponsive" messages, or 35.7% were coded as "original."

Breaking down all "nonresponsive" messages, the content of the messages was spread out among the five categories. As Table 4 shows, the three categories with the highest percentages were all link driven: "media on candidate" (241 messages), "media about the candidate" (196), and "media about opponent" (151). Following those were "personal" (131) and "notification" (103). The abundance of these links serves to turn Twitter into a subservient communication platform that feeds users into the campaign's controlled media arena. Indeed, many of these posts were serving the same purposes as press releases normally would: pointing users toward campaign ads, position papers, positive press, positive poll numbers, and negative press about the opponent or opposing party.

Table 3. Breakdown of Nonresponsive Messages (N=1.000)

	Original Twitter Content	Repurposed Twitter Content
All candidates (% of whole)	29.7%	53.4%
Scott McAdams (D—AK)	40 (80%)	8 (16%)
Joe Miller (R—AK)	18 (36)	30 (60)
Barbara Boxer (D—CA)	0 (0)	46 (92)
Carly Fiorina (R—CA)	16 (32)	15 (30)
Ken Buck (R—CO)	3 (6)	47 (94)
Michael Bennet (D—CO)	0 (0)	26 (52)
Alexi Giannoulias (D—IL)	14 (28)	30 (60)
Mark Kirk (R—IL)	16 (32)	29 (58)
Harry Reid (D—NV)	2 (4)	35 (70)
Sharon Angle (R—NV)	12 (24)	30 (60)
Joe Sestak (D—PA)	13 (26)	32 (64)
Pat Toomey (R—PA)	10 (20)	33 (66)
Patty Murray (D—WA)	22 (44)	9 (18)
Dino Rossi (R—WA)	15 (30)	16 (32)
Russ Feingold (D—WI)	22 (44)	24 (48)
Ron Johnson (R—WI)	16 (32)	11 (22)
Jack Conway (D—KY)	18 (36)	29 (58)
Rand Paul (R—KY)	13 (26)	35 (70)
Richard Blumenthal (D—CT)	8 (16)	37 (74)
Linda McMahon (R—CT)	39 (78)	12 (24)

Table 4. Content of Messages (N=1,000)

	Link to Media on Candidate	Link to Media by Candidate	Link to Media on Opponent	Personal	Mobilization
All candidates (% of whole)	19.6%	24.1%	15.1%	13.1%	10.3%
Scott McAdams (D—AK)	14 (28%)	6 (12%)	7 (14%)	11 (22%)	12 (24%)
Joe Miller (R—AK)	16 (32)	8 (16)	13 (26)	1 (2)	12 (24)
Barbara Boxer (D—CA)	8 (16)	8 (16)	6 (12)	5 (10)	3 (6)
Carly Fiorina (R—CA)	26 (52)	0 (0)	9 (18)	0 (0)	6 (12)
Ken Buck (R—CO)	5 (10)	35 (70)	2 (4)	2 (4)	5 (10)
Michael Bennet (D—CO)	13 (26)	6 (12)	6 (12)	0 (0)	1 (2)
Alexi Giannoulias (D—IL)	8 (16)	12 (24)	8 (16)	0 (0)	4 (8)
Mark Kirk (R—IL)	13 (26)	17 (34)	8 (16)	2 (4)	5 (10)
Harry Reid (D—NV)	4 (8)	20 (40)	12 (24)	3 (6)	0 (0)
Sharon Angle (R—NV)	14 (28)	11 (22)	7 (14)	12 (24)	1 (2)
Joe Sestak (D—PA)	9 (18)	10 (20)	11 (22)	5 (10)	10 (20)
Pat Toomey (R—PA)	11 (22)	15 (30)	14 (28)	2 (4)	0 (0)
Patty Murray (D—WA)	13 (26)	4 (8)	0 (0)	10 (20)	4 (8)
Dino Rossi (R—WA)	6 (12)	10 (20)	12 (24)	2 (4)	1 (2)
Russ Feingold	9 (18)	8 (16)	11 (22)	12 (24)	5 (10)

(D—WI)					
Ron Johnson (R—WI)	6 (12)	3 (6)	1 (2)	15 (30)	4 (8)
Jack Conway (D—KY)	4 (8)	17 (34)	7 (14)	11 (22)	8 (16)
Rand Paul (R—KY)	7 (14)	26 (52)	2 (4)	3 (6)	10 (20)
Richard Blumenthal (D—CT)	8 (16)	18 (36)	11 (22)	8 (16)	5 (10)
Linda McMahon (R—CT)	2 (4)	7 (14)	4 (8)	27 (54)	7 (14)

Real or Calculated Expression?

"Personal" tweets encompassed a range of messages. Most of the personal tweets were positive messages concerning some aspect of the state (the weather, the beauty of the countryside, local fairs or merchants, etc.) or statements about the candidate's travel. Many personal messages concerned the prospects of local sports team, such as Connecticut Republican Linda McMahon's tweet: "http://twitpic.com/2tzc4m UCONN Tailgate!! Beat Vanderbilt. Happy Homecoming to the Huskies and Coach Edsall! #LINDA2010 #UCONN #CTSEN."

Unsurprisingly, the personal posts are almost certainly political in effect (by connecting voters to the candidate as a person), or in design (by crafting an image of a personable candidate). The personal messages routinely praised the intrinsic values of the candidate's state and almost never addressed topics or issues that did not include the state in some way. Further, the personal messages that operated as a travel log frequently mentioned the drive and determination of the candidate as well as positive qualities of the places visited and the people met.

It is difficult to not be cynical about the sincerity of these "personal" expressions. As argued earlier, Twitter has routinely been seen as a site of enormous risk for public figures, especially those who run their own accounts. Thus, as Gurevitch, Coleman, and Blumler (2009) argue, new media services do not liberate political communication from the grasp of political communication strategists, but rather force them to work harder to effectively use new media within a coordinated, disciplined messaging operation. Additionally, as social media services such as Twitter become increasingly required by those in office, the expectation for them to competently adhere to the interpersonal conventions and norms of the service will increase, reinforcing current trends in political marketing. As Gurevitch et al. (2009) state, "In an age when politicians do not benefit from seeming to be politicians, affected unprofessionalism may well hold the key to successful communication" (p 176). Indeed, the primary effect of the new media ecology, then, may not be to liberate the candidate from the messaging machine, but instead to make him or her ever more dependent on it as they struggle to adapt to shifting, ever-expanding modes of media representation.

Despite this, however, Twitter still represents a unique space for candidates to be represented outside of the traditional media structure. With no mediating barrier between a campaign's Twitter account and its followers, new forms of representation may emerge. Additionally, candidates who feel misrepresented or underrepresented may find new resources for presenting themselves to the public in the unmediated sphere of Twitter.

Mobilization: When Time Is of the Essence

Of posted tweets, 10.3% were mobilizing in nature. The presence of these messages shows that campaigns were tentatively leveraging the immediacy of Twitter to get out time-sensitive messages to their followers. However, these messages were less concerned with quickly responding to misinformation than they were with alerting the campaign's followers to spectatorship opportunities. Typically these messages notified users of impending television and radio interviews by the candidate, fundraisers, meet and greets, and debates. A tweet from Alaskan Democrat Scott McAdams typifies the type of notifying messages sent out: "So much energy and #McMentum! GOTV Rally tonight at 6! 4th and Denali at Carpenters Hall. Hope to see you there! #AK#AKSenMon."

However, in the few days before election day, the mobilizing messages became less about collecting audiences for events and more about providing resources for voters. In the immediate lead-up to election day, almost every campaign studied provided notifications and information about polling stations, polling problems, and polling problem hotlines. Colorado Democrat Michael Bennet's tweet provides an example: "Do you know where you're voting tomorrow? Find polling places and mail ballot drop off locations: http://b4c.co/Vote-- RT to share."

Given the history of voting problems in America, either through inadequate infrastructure and management or deliberate attempts to depress voter turnout, Twitter's potential to aid citizens in voting is notable. Indeed, campaigns devoted a great deal of energy to establishing their Twitter accounts as two-way communication services designed to both disseminate voting information and receive reports of voting problems. While these messages were ultimately a small share of tweets overall, they provide examples of how campaigns, and citizens in general, might use Twitter to improve the overall political process.

Going forward, it will be crucial to see if the content posted on social media platforms by campaigns trends toward the type of messages most tailored to those platforms, namely responsive messages toward voters, personal information and media about the candidate, and timely notifications of important information. Currently, the study shows a minor presence of these messages in varying degrees of frequency across many of the campaigns studied. Overshadowing those messages, however, is content that either duplicates or is in service to existing content hosted elsewhere.

What *War of the Worlds* Can Teach As about Twitter

To better understand Twitter, or any communication platform or medium, one has to move beyond interpretive frameworks solely based on the "potential" of the medium. The *War of the Worlds* broadcast has come to be understood as a seminal moment demonstrating the power of radio. Unfortunately, however, that power is often misunderstood as the ultimate fulfillment of radio's potential to enable authoritative control over mass audiences and inspire uncritical acceptance on the part of listeners. While the broadcast represents a fascinating moment of audience response to mass-disseminated communication content, listeners may have responded for a variety of reasons not tied to radio's potential for one-way, instrumental and persuasive communication. As Hayes and Battles (2011) argue, listeners responded to the broadcast based on a range of complex social relationships, including their relationship with radio as an institution. Although radio may have had the potential to produce a singular, authoritative voice, it actually existed within a larger social context in which it was but one participant; a very powerful participant, yes, but a participant nonetheless.

The main reason for the misunderstanding of Twitter comes from a focus on what its structure can *potentially enable* rather than how it is actually *used*. In the same way that the structure of radio potentially enabled authoritative manipulations of mass audiences (despite much deviation in its actual use), Twitter potentially enables a purely interpersonal, interactive communication experience. Its low barrier of entry (access is possible via any SMS-capable phone or Internet-capable device), the equality of users (at least in relation to use of the service) and the ability to message, and receive messages from, anyone on the service suggests a new kind of participatory communication. In a political context, Twitter has the potential to create a communicative public sphere where the only currency is the power of ones words.

However, in much the same way that the *War of the Worlds* event was simplified into a metaphor for the emergent power of broadcasting, Twitter, and social media in general, have been simplified into a metaphor for spontaneous, democratic, two-way interaction. Both of these simplifications stem from simply focusing on the *potential form* of the communicative structure, rather than the actual mechanics of its use.

This study reveals that, at least in the 2010 U.S. Senatorial elections, Twitter was not being used to initiate much of any two-way communication, or was only used to mobilize users in limited ways. Most importantly, this study shows that the bulk of Twitter output by the campaigns was integrated into existing communication strategies and, for the most part, was subservient to more familiar platforms such as television, websites, and newspapers.

This is not to say that Twitter is not capable of achieving two-way communication between previously distanced parties or in being a primary tool in political mobilization. Recent history has seen Twitter users play a substantial role in interacting with mainstream news coverage, such as during the Mumbai bomb blasts in 2008 and the emergency water landing of a US Airways flight in 2009 (Murthy, 2009). Further, as Howard and Hussain (2011) detail, the political mobilization potential of Twitter was explicitly on display during the series of "Arab Spring" uprisings in the Middle East during the end of 2010. In many of these uprisings, Twitter was a valuable tool used by dissidents to coordinate political and social action as well as to build and maintain ad hoc networks under threat of government repression. As the authors conclude, however, the labeling of the uprisings as "Twitter Revolutions" is wrong and misplaced, as the revolutions were not found in Twitter itself, but in the political dissidents that used it. Further, as Christenen (2011) states, simplistic celebratory narratives about social media in repressive countries ignores the ways in which many authoritarian governments use the Internet and social networking services to "simplify surveillance, disinformation, and repression." Indeed, though it is quite easy to trumpet the positive change that Twitter and other digital services can enable, it is still vitally important to heed James Carey's (2005) words on the failure of academic prognosticators to critically interpret the early days of the Internet:

> It was a widespread notion in the 1990s that internet technology was a force in globalization, creating borderless worlds and borderless communities, borderless organizations and borderless politics. There is truth in that generalization. But what is equally true, is that as one set of borders, one set of social structures is taken down, another set of borders is erected. (p. 453)

While Twitter does offer potential for a broad reorganization of political communication and participation in respect to US elections, it also must interact with existing structures of political communication and representation. Further, while Twitter may offer more fulfilling forms of political communication and interaction to some, it is vitally important to understand it within the larger structures of power and inequality. Only by actively tracking and critically analyzing the way Twitter is used, and placing it within a broader cultural and social environment, can we hope to accurately understand its impact on political and civic communication.

References

Ancu, M. & Cozma, R. (2009). MySpace politics: Uses and gratifications of befriending candidates. *Journal of Broadcasting & Electronic Media*, 53(4), 567–583.

Andrejevic, M. (2008). Watching television without pity: The productivity of online fans. *Television & New Media*, 9(1), 24–46.

Arceneaux, N., & Weiss, A.S. (2010). Seems stupid until you try it: Press coverage of Twitter, 2006–9. *New Media & Society, 12*(8), 1262–1279.

Banerjee, S. (2010, April 20). Who's the bigger twit? *Daily News and Analysis.* Retrieved from http://www.dnaindia.com/entertainment/report_who-s-the-bigger-twit_1373489

Boyd, D., & Ellison, N. B. (2007). Social network sites: Definition, history, and scholarship. *Journal of Computer-Mediated Communication, 13*(1). Retrieved from http://jcmc.indiana.edu/vol13/issue1/boyd.ellison.html

Burt, M. (2010, July 29) Your call: Should athletes re-think the way they use Twitter? *TSN.* Retrieved from http://www.tsn.ca/nhl/story/?id=328896

Carey, J. (2005). Historical pragmatism and the internet. *New Media & Society, 7*(4), 443–455.

Castells, M. (2009). *Communication power.* Oxford, UK: Oxford University Press.

Christensen, C. (2011). Twitter revolutions? Addressing social media and dissent. *The Communication Review, 14*(3), 155–157.

Colvile, R. (2008, November 8). Barack Obama's grassroots campaign was unprecedented. *The Telegraph.* Retrieved from http://www.telegraph.co.uk/comment/personal-view/3563300/Barack-Obamas-grassroots-campaign-was-unprecedented.html

Cover, R. (2006). Audience inter/active: Interactive media, narrative control and reconceiving audience history. *New Media and Society, 8*(1), 139–158.

Davis, R. (1999). *The web of politics: The Internet's impact on the American political system.* Oxford, UK: Oxford University Press.

Enda, J. (2011). Campaign coverage in the time of Twitter. *American Journalism Review,* Oct/Nov 2011.

Foot, K. A., & Schneider, S. M. (2002). Online action in campaign 2000: An exploratory analysis of the U. S. political web sphere. *Journal of Broadcasting & Electronic Media, 46*(2), 223–244.

Gilmore, J. (2011). Ditching the pack: Digital media in the 2010 Brazilian congressional campaigns. *New Media & Society 14*(4), 617–633.

Goldman, J., & Tackett, M. (2008, November 4). Obama sealed win by taking biggest risks, making fewest errors. *Bloomberg.* Retrieved from http://www.bloomberg.com/apps/news?pid=newsarchive&sid=acCoBJXeBvU8

Groves, J. (2010, February 5). The Tory Twitter police: Election hopefuls told their online comments must be approved first. *Mail Online.* Retrieved from http://www.dailymail.co.uk/news/article-1248898/The-Tory-Twitter-police-Election-hopefuls-told-online-comments-approved-first.html

Gurevitch, M., Coleman, S. & Blumler, J.G. (2009). Political communication: Old and new media relationships. *The ANNALS of the American Academy of Political and Social Science, 625,* 164–181.

Hayes, J., & Battles, K. (2011). Exchange and interconnection in US network radio: A reinterpretation of the 1938 *War of the Worlds* broadcast. *The Radio Journal—International Studies in Broadcast and Audio Media, 9*(1), 51–62.

Hindman, M. S. (2009). *The myth of digital democracy.* Princeton, NJ: Princeton University Press.

Hoff, J. (2008). Can the Internet swing the vote? Results from a study of the 2007 Danish parliamentary election. *Institute of Technology Assessment*. Retrieved from http://epub. oeaw. ac. at/ita/ita-manuscript/ita_08_02. pdf

Howard, J., & Hussain, M. (2011). The role of digital media. *Journal of Democracy*, 22(3), 35–48.

Irvine, M. (2009, November 29). For stars, high-tech gaffes hard to hide. *The Herald Sun*. Retrieved from http://www. heraldsun. com/view/full_story/4935535/article-For-stars--high-tech-gaffes-hard-to-hide?

Jackson, S. (2010, March 22). Risks aplenty in media's new fad: Twitt-a-lism. *The Australian*. Retrieved from http://www. theaustralian. com. au/business/media/risks-aplenty-in-medias-new-fad-twitt-a-lism/story-e6frg996–1225843478126

Jackson, S. (2010, May 10). Axing highlights the risks and rewards of Twitter. *The Australian*. Retrieved from http://www. theaustralian. com. au/business/media/axing-highlights-the-risks-and-rewards-of-twitter/story-e6frg996–1225864249998

Jenkins, H. (2006). *Convergence culture: Where old and new media collide*. New York, NY: New York University Press.

Klotz, R. J. (2004). *The politics of Internet communication*. New York, NY: Rowman & Littlefield.

Klotz, R. J. (2009). The sidetracked 2008 YouTube senate campaign. Presented at the *2009 Journal of Information Technology and Politics Annual Conference*.

Kopel, D. (2008, August 27). KOPEL: Text and twitter your way to victory. *Rocky Mountain News*. Retrieved from http://www. rockymountainnews. com/news/2008/aug/27/20080827_kopel/

Liddle, R. (2010, February 7). David Cameron has ordered conservatives ... *The Sunday Times*, p. 19.

McMillan, S. (2002). A four-part model of cyber-interactivity: Some cyber-places are more interactive than others. *New Media & Society, 4(2),* 271–91.

Murthy, D. (2011). Twitter: Microphone for the masses? *Media, Culture & Society*, 33(5), 779–789.

Pollard, T. D., Chesebro, J. W., & Studinski, D. (2009). The role of the Internet in presidential campaigns. *Communication Studies*, 60(5), 574–588.

Rich, F. (2010, October 9). Facebook politicians are not your friends. *New York Times*. Retrieved from http://www. nytimes. com/2010/10/10/opinion/10rich. html

Schneider, S. M., & Foot, K. A. (2006). Web campaigning by U. S. presidential primary candidates in 2000 and 2004. In A. P. Williams and J. C. Tedesco (Eds.), *The Internet election: Perspectives on the web in the 2004 campaign* (pp. 21–36). Lanham, MD: Rowman & Littlefield.

Stromer-Galley, J. (2000). On-line interaction and why candidates avoid it. *Journal of Communication*, 50(4), 111–132.

Stromer-Galley, J., & Baker, A. B. (2006). Joy and sorrow of interactivity on the campaign trail: Blogs in the primary campaign of Howard Dean. In A. P. Williams and J. C. Tedesco (Eds.), *The Internet election: Perspectives on the web in the 2004 campaign* (pp . 111–131). Lanham, MD: Rowman & Littlefield.

Sweetser, Kaye D., and Lariscy, R. W. (2008). Candidates make good friends: An analysis of candidates' uses of Facebook. *International Journal of Strategic Communication*, 2(3), 175–198.

Tedesco, J. C. (2004). Changing the channel: Use of the Internet for communicating about politics. In L. L. Kaid (Ed.), *Handbook of political communication research* (pp. 507–532). Mahwah, NJ: Lawrence Erlbaum Associates, Inc.

Trammell, K. D., Williams, A. P., Postelnicu, M., & Landreville, K. D. (2006). Evolution of online campaigning: Increasing interactivity in candidate web sites and blogs through text and technical features. *Mass Communication and Society*, 9(1), 21–44.

Wheeler, B. (2010, February 10). Twitter etc and the election: Is it worth the risk? *BBC News*. Retrieved from http://news. bbc. co. uk/2/hi/uk_news/politics/-8459624.stm

Williams, A. P., Trammell, K. D., Postelnicu, M. &, Landreville, K. D., & Martin, J. D. (2005). Blogging and hyperlinking: Use of the web to enhance viability during the 2004 US campaign. *Journalism Studies*, 6, 177–186.

Contributors

Kathleen Battles is an associate professor of communication and journalism at Oakland University, USA. Her research focuses on the cultural history of broadcasting in the United States and contemporary media representations of sexuality. Her book, *Calling All Cars: Radio Dragnets and the Technology of Policing* (2010, Univ. of Minnesota Press), examines the intersection of police reform and radio crime dramas during the Great Depression. Her current project is an introduction to the relationship between sexual identities and the media. She has published articles in *Critical Studies in Media Communication*, *Journal of Homosexuality*, and *The Radio Journal*.

Saba Bebawi is a lecturer of journalism at Swinburne University, Australia. Her research interests include international news networks, media and globalization, alternative media, and investigative journalism. Currently her projects include the *Interaction between Mainstream Journalists and Alternative Media Practitioners during the Arab Spring Protests* and *Reaping and Sowing the News from an Arab Spring: The Politicized Interaction between Traditional and Alternative Journalistic Practitioners* both in conjunction with Diana Bossio. She has published in *Global Media Journal Australia* and the *Journal of International Communication*.

Diana Bossio is a lecturer of media, communications, and journalism at Swinburne University, Australia, where she teaches courses in media and journalism. Her research interests include media representation, journalism practice and education, as well as the relationship between government communication and journalism practice. Currently her projects include *The Interaction between Mainstream Journalists and Alternative Media Practitioners during the Arab Spring Protests* and *Reaping and Sowing the News from an Arab Spring: The Politicized Interaction between Traditional and Alternative*

Journalistic Practitioners, both in conjunction with Saba Bebawi. She has published in the *International Journal of the Humanities* and *Continuum: Journal of Media and Cultural Studies*.

Marco Giardina is a research program manager at Sensiel Research and a research scientist at the Academy of Journalism and Media, University of Neuchâtel, Switzerland. His research interests include media curation, media economics, media management, emerging and future media channels, journalism and new media innovation. He has authored and co-authored several papers, scientific reports, and patent applications in the domain of emerging technologies.

Dana Gravesen is a Ph.D. candidate in communication studies at the University of Iowa, USA, where he has assisted in teaching persuasive speaking and writing, television criticism and history, and general media studies courses. His current research interests include nationalism and identity with regard to Dominican-American media, U.S. broadcast history, and critical cultural media theory.

Joy Elizabeth Hayes is an associate professor of communication studies at the University of Iowa, USA. Her research focuses on the cultural history of broadcasting in the United States and Mexico. Her current research on Mexico explores the history and impact of community radio at the local, national and transnational levels. Her recent work on U.S. radio examines the performance of white, middle-class family life in the serial *One Man's Family*. Along with her book, *Radio Nation: Communication, Popular Culture and Nationalism in Mexico, 1920-1950* (2000, Univ. of Arizona Press), she has published articles in *The Radio Journal, The Journal of Radio and Audio Media, Diálogos*, and *Cinema Journal*.

Wendy Hilton-Morrow is an associate professor of communication studies at Augustana College, USA, where she teaches media studies courses. Her research includes work on broadcast news conventions and local broadcast news coverage of national events and crises. Her current project is an introduction to the relationship between sexual identities and the media. She has published in *Critical Studies in Media Communication* and the *Journal of Homosexuality*.

Kate Lacey is Senior Lecturer in Media and Cultural Studies at the University of Sussex, UK, where she teaches media history and theory. She has published widely on broadcasting and is author of *Feminine Frequencies: Gender, German Radio and the Public Sphere 1923 to 1945* (1996, University of Michigan Press) and *Listening Publics: The Politics and Experience of Listening in the Media Age* (2013, Polity). She was a founding member of the Radio Studies Network, serves on the editorial board of *The Radio Journal: International Studies in Broadcast and Audio Media* and sits on the UK Radio Archives Advisory Committee.

Jefferson Pooley is an associate professor of media and communication at Muhlenberg College, USA, where he teaches courses in media history and social theory. His research examines the history of communication, the consumer and the self. His current work is a short book on communications theorist James W. Carey. He has published in conjunction with David W. Park, *The History of Media and Communication Research: Contested Memories* (2008, Peter Lang) and a book chapter titled "The Consuming Self: From Flappers to Facebook," in *Blowing up the Brand: Critical Perspectives on Promotional Culture* (2010, Peter Lang).

Adam Rugg is a Ph.D. student in communication studies at the University of Iowa, USA. He studies the intersection of media studies and sports studies. He is very interested in the ways in which the NFL's emergence into the global marketplace upends notions of place, race, and identity.

Vittoria Sacco is a Ph.D. candidate at the Academy of Journalism and Media, University of Neuchâtel, Switzerland. She has a first degree in economic sciences with major in management and a master's degree in science in statistics. She teaches regression model exercises to students in economics, and she holds a seminar on quantitative information and statistics in the media for the master's in journalism. Her research interests focus on social media, 'new' media technologies and the changes in journalistic values in times of crisis.

Michael J. Socolow is an associate professor of communication and journalism at the University of Maine, USA, where he teaches courses in mass communication and broadcast journalism. His research includes historical studies of propaganda, broadcast journalism, and mass communication. He has published in *Journalism: Theory, Practice & Criticism*, *American Journalism*, and *Journalism & Mass Communication Quarterly*.

Keith Somerville is a Senior research fellow at the Institute of Commonwealth Studies, University of London, and teaches at the centre for Journalism and in the School of Politics and International Relations at the University of Kent, UK, where he lectures about African affairs, journalism, and global media. For 28 years he worked as a senior editor and program maker with the BBC World Service. His research interests include media coverage of conflict, radio and other media propaganda, media coverage of Africa and contemporary African politics. He is currently writing a history of contemporary Africa for Wiley-Blackwell. He recently published *Radio Propaganda and the Broadcasting of Hate: Historical Development and Definitions* (2012, Palgrave). He writes regularly for the Royal African Society's *African Arguments,* and has published in *British Journalism Review* and *Journal of Eastern African Studies*.

Katarina Stanoevska-Slabeva is Associate Professor and Vice President of the Institute for Media and Communications Management at the University of St. Gallen, Switzerland. She also holds the Chair of Journalism and New Media at the Academy of Journalism and Media, University of Neuchâtel, Switzerland. Her research interests focus on social media, social media curation and crowdsourcing. Her research has received funding from the European Commission and the Swiss National Foundation, and she has published more than 150 publications, including three edited books, several proceedings, and 15 articles in scientific journals.

Zack Stiegler is an assistant professor of Communications Media at Indiana University of Pennsylvania, USA, where he teaches courses in broadcasting, media history and theory, communication law and policy, and alternative media. His research includes work in media history, communication law and policy, and critical studies of popular culture. He recently edited *Regulating the Web: Network Neutrality and the Fate of the Open Internet* (Lexington Books, 2013).

Brandon Szuminsky is a doctoral candidate of Communications Media and Instructional Technology at Indiana University of Pennsylvania, USA. He is also a Lecturer of Communication at Waynesburg University and a columnist for the *Herald-Standard* in Uniontown, Pennsylvania.

Melissa Tully is an assistant professor of journalism and mass communication at the University of Iowa, USA, where she teaches digital communication, multimedia and philanthropy communication. Her research interests include international communication, media in developing countries, digital media technologies, and nonprofit communication. She has published in *Journalism: Theory, Practice, and Criticism, Television and New Media, Newspaper Research Journal,* and *Africa Today.*

Neil Washbourne is a Senior Lecturer of Media Studies at Leeds Metropolitan University, UK, where he teaches courses on media and politics. His research focuses on the complex and crisis-ridden relationship between contemporary media and politics in the contemporary world, as well as the historical emergence of celebrity practices from the nineteenth century onwards. Among other books and book chapters, his most recent publication is *Mediating Politics: Newspapers, Radio, Television and Internet* (Open University Press, 2010). He has published in *International Studies of Management and Organisation.*

Index

A

Al Jazeera, 127, 191, 196, 198-200, 202, 204, 228
Arab Spring, 13, 182, 189-191, 194, 196-197, 199, 203-206, 211, 213-214, 216, 221, 225
audience, 1, 3-14, 19, 21-24, 26, 28-32, 37, 57, 59, 61-62, 67, 69, 71, 76-78, 88, 92-99, 113, 118, 126-131, 133-141, 145-148, 151-152, 155, 165-177, 179-182, 190-191, 195, 197, 201, 206, 214-216, 218, 229-230, 237, 260-262, 267-269, 275-276

    listener, 2, 7-11, 13, 19-32, 36-37, 39-40, 42, 52, 58-64, 67, 69, 71-78, 84-91, 96-97, 99-100, 109,111, 113-114, 116-119, 125, 129-130, 133, 137-139, 141, 145, 147-156, 158-161, 171-172, 199, 239

    user, 1-4, 11-15, 145, 149, 159,165-166, 174-182, 192-193, 197, 202, 211-214, 229-230, 237, 239-240, 242-253, 257-263, 265-270, 272-275, 277

    viewer, 2, 10, 93, 172-173, 199-200, 216, 260

B

BBC, 10, 71-79, 92, 94-97, 191, 196, 198, 200, 204-205, 246

    World Service, 125-131, 140

body, 11, 143-144, 155-160

    disembodied, 10, 61

    embodiment, 10, 143, 153-158, 160

    genre, 10, 154-156, 160-161

    grotesque, 154-155, 161

bomb scare. see scare, bomb

Broadcasting from the Barricades, 57-58, 71-79

C

CBS, 20-22, 27-28, 30, 32, 35-36, 38, 40, 46, 52, 72, 87, 90, 94, 109, 111-112, 126, 147, 150-151, 156, 173

    D-Day Invasion coverage, 10, 109-123

CNN, 127, 152, 173, 181, 183, 191, 196, 198, 200, 204, 245-246

campaigns. see political campaigns

Cantril, Hadley, 7, 21, 23, 29, 31, 35-39, 41-52, 79, 88, 92, 94, 96-100

censorship, 60-67, 75, 202, 215-216, 220, 225

checking up. see critical abilities, checking up

citizen, citizenship, 2, 7, 26, 86, 88, 116, 169, 179, 182, 217, 220-222, 226, 239, 252, 258, 266-269

    journalism. see journalism, citizen

constant communicative presence, 19, 23-28, 32, 126, 130, 213

critical abilities, faculties, 6-7, 20-22, 36, 40, 52, 83, 165, 181-182, 276

    checking up, 29, 37, 40-41, 47-48, 52, 170, 175, 181, 226

curation, social media, 3, 13, 199-200, 211-213, 218-219, 221, 224-227, 229-230. see also Storify

D

D-Day Invasion coverage. see CBS, D-Day Invasion coverage
Der Minister ist ermordet! see *Minister's Been Murdered!, The*
disc jockey, 11, 171
    shock, 11, 143-144, 146-147, 150-161
disembodied. see body
dispatch, 23-27, 132, 145, 151-153, 159, 212-214, 230-231

E

Ebermayer, Erich, 58, 64-66, 70, 78
exchange and interconnection, model of, 7, 14, 19, 21-24, 26, 30-32, 141, 144, 153, 160
embodiment. see body

F

Facebook, 12, 152, 176, 182, 196, 198-199, 202, 212-214, 227, 237-238, 245, 253, 258, 263-264
Flesch, Hans, 61-64, 69-71,

G

Gaudet, Hazel, 21, 31, 35-37, 39-40, 43-44, 50-51
Great Depression, 4-5, 21, 60, 62, 67

H

Herzog, Herta, 21, 31, 35-37, 39-43, 45, 47, 48, 50-53
hoax, 6, 11, 20, 91-92, 100, 165-183
Howard Stern Show, 145, 150-153, 155-157, 159, 161. see also Stern, Howard

I

Invasion From Mars: A Study in the Psychology of Panic, IFM, 7, 19, 21-22, 28, 35-44

J

Journalism, 166, 180, 189-191, 193, 196, 200, 202-204, 212-215, 219-220, 225, 253, 260-261
    citizen, alternative, 12, 189-206, 212-214, 216-217, 221-231, 239, 252
    news, breaking, rolling coverage, 2, 23-24, 42, 58, 64, 69, 71-73, 76, 86-87, 114, 117, 127-140, 170-172, 178, 198, 202, 212, 238, 245-246, 251, 260
    newspaper, 4, 11, 13, 73-76, 192, 197, 202
        British, 8, 74-75, 83-92, 94-96, 99-100
        German, 57-59, 62-64, 66-70, 78
        U.S., 20, 111, 114-115, 120, 122, 168-170, 263
    radio, 10, 12, 63, 97, 112-114, 120-122, 125-132, 136-141, 192, 198, 205
    social media, 177, 192-206, 214, 218, 221-228, 230, 242, 244-245, 253
    television, 173, 198-200, 204, 242, 244, 246, 250

K

Knox, Father Ronald, 71, 73-74, 100

L

Lazarsfeld, Paul, 7, 35-39, 41-53
listener. see audience, listener

M

Mathenge, Oliver, 242, 244

media audience. see audience

media hoax. see hoax

Minister's Been Murdered!, The, 57-58, 61, 65-71, 76, 79

mobile phone. see telephone, mobile

Murrow, Edward R., 112, 118-120, 126

"The Murrow Boys", 112

Mutual Broadcasting System, 22, 87

N

NBC, 20, 78, 87, 111, 121, 123, 172

networks, networking, 3, 12-14, 19, 22, 28-30, 38, 79, 145, 159, 174-175, 179, 190, 193-195, 201, 203, 214, 225, 228, 229, 237, 239, 243-244, 249, 252-253, 257, 259, 262-266, 278

radio, 19-20, 22-28, 30-31, 60, 78, 87, 109-118, 120-123, 125, 127-128, 145, 156

television, 152, 199

news, newspaper. see journalism

P

panic, 3, 5, 7-8, 20-21, 28-31, 35-37, 40-41, 47, 52, 60, 74-77, 79, 83-92, 94-100, 126, 167, 173, 175, 192. see also, scare

political campaigns,

Constitutional Referendum, Kenya, 238, 241-242, 244-246

U.S., 257-278

press. see journalism, newspaper

Princeton Radio Research Project, 21, 36-38, 41-47, 49-52

propaganda, 7, 41, 46, 64, 70-71, 111, 119, 141, 218

public, 8, 10-11, 26, 62-63, 69, 76-77, 84, 98, 100, 110, 116, 120-121, 143-145, 148-149, 168-169, 171-172, 179, 181, 183, 189, 204, 217, 238-241, 252-253, 258-259, 263, 266, 270, 274, 277

broadcasting, 59-60, 72, 78

interest, 6, 21, 109-110, 112, 114, 121, 153

listening, 59, 62, 69-70, 78, 113

opinion, 36, 38, 50, 52, 113, 215, 230

response, 13, 21, 23, 57, 59, 76, 83, 237

sphere, 27, 77, 110, 191

R

radio. see audience, listener; journalism, radio; networks, radio; scare, radio

Radio Research Project. see Princeton Radio Research Project

rally. see political campaigns

Rockefeller Foundation, 36-38, 41-47, 49-50

S

scare, 166, 238-239, 251-252

bomb, 13, 237-238, 249-252

radio, wireless, 8, 21, 57-59, 62-63, 66, 71-76, 78, 85

war, 21, 85, 88

September 11, 2001, 9/11. see Terrorist Attacks of September 11, 2001

shock jock. see disc jockey, shock

social media. see, Facebook, Storify, Twitter, YouTube

curation. see, curation

journalism. see, journalism, social media

social networks. see networks

Stanton, Frank, 35-38, 40-42, 48, 50-52

Stern, Howard, 11, 143-147, 150-153, 156-160. see also, *Howard Stern Show*

Storify, 13, 211-215, 217-231

T

telephone, 24-26, 30, 35-36, 52, 73-74, 76,

129, 151-152, 156-157, 170, 195, 205
caller, 11, 30, 152-153, 156-157, 160
mobile, 144-146, 150-153, 161, 198, 200-201, 216, 253, 259-260, 266, 277
switchboard, 30, 114
television. see audience, viewer; journalism, television; networks, television
Terrorist Attacks of September 11, 2011, 11, 130, 143-145, 150-153, 157-161
Trout, Bob, 109, 114, 117-118
trust, 6, 8, 14, 62, 76, 98, 111, 113, 120-121, 134, 141, 165, 171-173, 180-181, 192, 205, 221, 243-245
Twitter, 1-2, 12-14, 152, 174, 176-179, 182-183, 195-199, 202-203, 205, 212-214, 219, 221, 224, 227-228, 231, 237-253, 257-261, 263-278

U

user. see audience, user
user-generated content (UGC). see audience, user

V

viewer. see audience, viewer

W

War of the Worlds, 1-15, 19-32, 35-37, 39-42, 44, 51-52, 57-59, 61, 72, 74-79, 83-84, 90-94, 96-100, 109, 111, 114, 116, 121, 125-126, 131-141, 143, 145, 159-160, 165, 170, 172-173, 178, 189-192, 205-206, 211, 213-214, 230-231, 237, 239, 252-253, 257-258, 264, 276-277
Welles, Orson, 20-21, 24, 30, 39-41, 43-44, 47,74, 89-100, 109, 121, 133, 141, 170
Wells, H.G., 20, 85-91, 94, 125, 133
White, Paul, 112-115, 117-119, 122
wireless. see radio

Y

YouTube, 12, 152, 179, 196, 198-200, 212, 216, 227-228, 263, 267-268

SERIES EDITOR: DAVID COPELAND

Realizing the important role that the media have played in American history, this series provides a venue for a diverse range of works that deal with the mass media and its relationship to society. This new series is aimed at both scholars and students. New book proposals are welcomed.

For additional information about this series or for the submission of manuscripts, please contact:

>Mary Savigar, Acquisitions Editor
>Peter Lang Publishing, Inc.
>29 Broadway, 18th floor
>New York, New York 10006
>Mary.Savigar@plang.com

To order other books in this series, please contact our Customer Service Department:

>(800) 770-LANG (within the U.S.)
>(212) 647-7706 (outside the U.S.)
>(212) 647-7707 FAX

Or browse by series:

>WWW.PETERLANG.COM